Praise for *Five Stars: Putting Online Reviews to Work for Your Business*

This comprehensive book shows savvy business owners and marketers the techniques for getting the absolute most from online reviews. Apply these winning strategies and proven processes to gain visibility and customers.
—ANDREW SHOTLAND, localseoguide.com

Five Stars *spills the secrets for getting, managing, and leveraging customer reviews to influence stronger reputations, higher pricing, and positive purchase decisions. Smart marketers will open it again and again as they implement the invaluable advice. It's a goldmine!*
—BARBARA FINDLAY SCHENCK, Author of *Branding For Dummies* and *Small Business Marketing Kit For Dummies*

Your online reputation is in the hands of your customers. Make great use of this book in understanding how that might work best for you.
—CHRIS BROGAN, Publisher of *Owner* magazine and Coauthor of *Trust Agents*

As more people rely heavily on online reviews to make decisions about everything from where they're going to eat dinner to who they'll choose to sell their homes, business owners and professionals can no longer afford to ignore what customers are saying about them online. While the thought of monitoring and managing so many sites is daunting, this guide provides a handy road map to turning your customers' opinions into an effective marketing tool. This book is a worthwhile investment for any business, whether it has an online presence or not.
—GWEN MORAN, Award-Winning Small Business Expert and Author

Five Stars

Putting Online Reviews to Work for Your Business

Five Stars

Putting Online Reviews to Work for Your Business

Gradiva Couzin

Jennifer Grappone

SYBEX®

A Wiley Brand

Senior Acquisitions Editor: WILLEM KNIBBE
Development Editor: DICK MARGULIS
Technical Editor: PHIL ROZEK
Production Editor: DASSI ZEIDEL
Copy Editor: LIZ WELCH
Editorial Manager: PETE GAUGHAN
Production Manager: TIM TATE
Vice President and Executive Group Publisher: RICHARD SWADLEY
Associate Publisher: CHRIS WEBB
Book Designer: FRANZ BAUMHACKL
Compositor: MAUREEN FORYS, HAPPENSTANCE TYPE-O-RAMA
Proofreader: REBECCA RIDER
Indexer: JACK LEWIS
Project Coordinator, Cover: KATHERINE CROCKER
Cover Designer: RYAN SNEED
Cover Image: ©ISTOCKPHOTO.COM/ASISEEIT

Dear Reader,

Thank you for choosing *Five Stars: Putting Online Reviews to Work for Your Business.* This book is part of a family of premium-quality Sybex books, all of which are written by outstanding authors who combine practical experience with a gift for teaching.

Sybex was founded in 1976. More than 30 years later, we're still committed to producing consistently exceptional books. With each of our titles, we're working hard to set a new standard for the industry. From the paper we print on, to the authors we work with, our goal is to bring you the best books available.

I hope you see all that reflected in these pages. I'd be very interested to hear your comments and get your feedback on how we're doing. Feel free to let me know what you think about this or any other Sybex book by sending me an email at contactus@sybex .com. If you think you've found a technical error in this book, please visit http://sybex .custhelp.com. Customer feedback is critical to our efforts at Sybex.

Best regards,

Chris Webb
Associate Publisher
Sybex, an Imprint of Wiley

For Ferdal and Puffulfluf, my vilde chayas. May the wild rumpus never end! With all my love. —gc

To my dear friend Kelly Ryer, who is an inexhaustible source of beautiful music, clever life hacks, and great ideas. —jg

Acknowledgments

Stories from real-world businesses shaped this book. We are grateful for the generosity of business owners and marketers who shared their triumphs and tribulations with us: Shane McWeeny, Adam Sperling, Kathy Setzer, Armando Cosio, Eddy Polon, Russ Palmer, Michael Mandis, Searah Deysach, Sharon Couzin, Alex Smith, Patti Ernst, Steven Lawrence, Eden Marchant, and many others who shall remain anonymous but whose input is equally treasured by us.

Thanks to the academics and professionals in the online reviews, reputation management, and social commerce industries who offered us a wealth of insider knowledge and tips—Matt McGee, Mike Blumenthal, Greg Meyer, Kit Yarrow, Bing Liu, and representatives from the reviewscape—Morgan Remmers and Katrina Hafford of Yelp, Cheryl Reed and Lesley Thompson of Angie's List, Alison Croyle and Barbara Messing of TripAdvisor, Rick Berry of Demandforce, Richard Anson of Reevoo, Neville Letzerich of Bazaarvoice, Michelle Wohl of Revinate, Michaella Kissack of BrandsEye, Elaine Olshanetsky of ResellerRatings, Mike Waite of Market Metrix, Chris Campbell of ReviewTrackers, Ali Alami of Judy's Book, Jon Hall of Grade.us, and Brent Franson of Reputation.com. There is nobody more helpful than the kind soul who proffers an introduction, connecting a question with an answer. Many thanks to Alex Robinson, Sharon Farb, Anthony Severo, Phil Rozek, and Rafael Baptista for their assistance.

Two lawyers contributed their expertise on legal aspects of the online reviews space. We are indebted to Katherine Fibiger and Kenton Hutcherson for generously sharing their time with us.

We are grateful to our clients at Gravity Search Marketing, who privilege us with daily opportunities to collaborate, learn, and grow. To the Gravity team,

Andrew Berg, Abbie McConnell, and Sue Separk, we extend our humble gratitude, appreciation, and respect. Thank you for sharing your hard work and talent with us!

An abundance of gratitude and rave reviews are owed to our editors at Wiley: Willem Knibbe, whose off-the-charts charm and flexibility made this project possible; Pete Gaughan, who supervised the project and fielded a bevy of difficult questions; Dick Margulis, who helped us shape a whirlwind into sensible text; our hard-working technical editor Phil Rozek; our brilliant and gracious copy editor, Elizabeth Welch; our unflappable production editor and schedule-keeper, Dassi Zeidel; our compositors at Happenstance Type-O-Rama; and the other talented members of the production team.

Surely we were born under lucky stars to have been blessed with such amazing friends and family. Janet Sahni provided invaluable research support to keep our ducks nicely aligned. Kelly Ryer, Joanne Toll, Gloria Felix, Judy Reilly, and Kris Curry offered advice, insights, laughs, and libations throughout the project. Odilon Couzin, Yuen Chan, Rich Frankel, Merry Selk, and Eve Greenfield extended helpful emails and late-night Skype visits. Thanks to our beloved husbands, Lowell Robinson and Todd Grappone, who have given us love beyond measure and supplied us with the things every author needs to be successful: time, leeway, encouragement, and candy. And to our precious children, Jonah, Zehara, Bennett, and Enzo, who spent far too much time fending for themselves while their mothers were buried in research and writing, we can hardly find the words to thank you, so we'll say this: You're more breathtaking than a triple backflip on the trampoline, more treasured than a black belt, more awe-inspiring than Godzilla, and more amazing than a game-winning touchdown. We love you.

About the Authors

Gradiva Couzin and Jennifer Grappone are online marketing consultants and partners at Gravity Search Marketing, a full-service SEO, paid search, and social media marketing firm. Gradiva and Jennifer have spent over a decade improving the online presence of a wide variety of companies in entertainment, software, local services, nonprofit, and retail. They work with clients to develop and implement thoughtful, results-oriented strategies for SEO, social media, and paid search. Equally adept with B2B and B2C, the human element and technical details, and local and international targeting, together they deliver a well-rounded, left-brain/right-brain approach to their clients' digital strategies. Jennifer and Gradiva have been working together in various settings since 1999, and coauthored the book *Search Engine Optimization: An Hour a Day* (Wiley, 2011).

Gradiva Couzin, San Francisco Gradiva has been working in search marketing for over 15 years. Her work is focused on her clients' success, with service, transparency, and integrity as her professional touchstones. With a history as a civil engineer and experience in website and database development, Gradiva enjoys the analytical side of SEO and social media and loves to facilitate communication between techie and non-techie types. Gradiva works closely with client teams to ensure that SEO best practices are integrated into all web development processes. She lives in the San Francisco Bay Area with her husband and two school-age children.

Jennifer Grappone, Los Angeles Jennifer works with clients to develop and implement SEO and social media strategies. She is familiar with the marketing goals and challenges of a wide range of industries and enjoys weaving together customized action plans that are both practical and effective and helping businesses navigate a constantly changing online marketing environment. Jennifer advocates a holistic approach, one that combines elements of good writing, search-friendly site design, usability, and compelling content. Jennifer lives with her family in Los Angeles and sings with the Pasadena Master Chorale.

Learn more about Gradiva, Jennifer, and Gravity Search Marketing at www.yourseoplan.com.

Contents

Introduction

"I don't know what to do about our online reviews!"

You live in a time when online reviews are prominent and powerful, and you may have even written a few reviews yourself, but if you're like many business stakeholders, you're confused or overwhelmed by online reviews. Some businesses prefer to hide their heads in the sand, and others take an uneducated stab at dealing with reviews and find themselves facing negative consequences.

One friend of ours, a restaurant owner, told us that he used to read his reviews every night, feeling thrilled at the positive ones and furious at the negative ones. He never shared negative feedback with his head chef—"That would only upset her!"—but he did post angry anonymous responses and eventually got banned from the review site.

Another friend, a boutique owner, told us that she doesn't look at her online reviews. She's been running her business for 30 years, and it's difficult to shift gears now: "I can't change them, so why bother looking?"

And we've lost count of the number of marketing managers who tell us they don't want to add product reviews to their online stores because they are afraid they'll all be negative.

Lots of businesses make up their own rules about review responses and management, or choose to ignore their reviews altogether. But there's a better way.

Managing your reviews does not have to be a white-knuckle ride or a stumble in the dark. There are effective strategies and proven processes that you can apply to your work with online reviews, and there is a large and growing body of research that illuminates the way toward best practices and improved outcomes.

Smart businesses—some of which may be your competitors—are already doing this right. They're maximizing their visibility and customer acquisition via reviews, using review feedback wisely, responding to reviews with candor and humility (and with future customers in mind), and avoiding unethical practices. This set of activities, which we call *online reviews management*, is a relatively young area of online marketing, and the businesses that are doing it well have mostly improvised their way to the best practices.

We've talked with a lot of businesses in the course of writing this book and as part of our daily consulting work, and we've encountered a lot of unproductive misconceptions about online reviews. Perhaps you've bought into some of them yourself:

Myth "Only angry customers write online reviews."

Fact Most online reviews are positive. On Yelp, 79% of all reviews are 3-star or above. Other review sites show similar statistics.

Myth "Online reviews don't affect my business."

Fact Reviews are highly influential. Studies show that consumers trust online reviews as much as personal recommendations, and adding online product reviews to an e-commerce site can lift sales.

Myth "One negative review could bury my business."

Fact Studies show that most people take the time to read review text and process review content through the filter of their unique circumstances. Rather than blindly following the star count or accepting every negative comment, they apply their own judgment to determine whether a review is applicable to them. Negative comments are actually desirable in some ways. They add credibility to your body of reviews and offer helpful insights that can help you manage customer expectations and drive the right customers your way.

Myth "It's pointless to respond to reviews."

Fact Most review sites offer a way for businesses to respond to reviews, and several experts we've spoken with suggested that businesses should reply to some or all of their online reviews—both positive and negative. It's not uncommon for a reviewer to change a negative review after a situation is resolved to their satisfaction.

Myth "All of our negative reviews are fake or from crazy people."

Fact Any business that has multiple negative reviews, especially if the reviews share common complaints, should consider the possibility that these are legitimate complaints from customers. Denial is a powerful force and could be detrimental to your business.

Now that you've been relieved of bad ideas that could be holding you back, read on to find the information, tools, and techniques you need to put your online reviews to work for your business!

What's Inside

This book combines how-to instructions, advice from experts, insider tips from review venue representatives, and insights into consumer behavior that you can use to improve your own online reputation, achieve greater customer satisfaction, and leverage your reviews for customer acquisition.

We'll also tell you stories of real businesses so that you can learn from their good ideas and avoid the mistakes they made. Here are some of the true stories in this book:

- A service professional who wasted time and money trying to fix a bad review that nobody saw

- A hotel that has it all figured out on TripAdvisor

- A small business owner who attributes $100,000 in yearly revenue to leads that have been generated through reviews

- A restaurant manager who developed a simple, repeatable process for learning from her reviews

Here's what you'll find in the chapters ahead:

Chapter 1: You Are Here: Understanding Your Opportunity Whether your business is a brick-and-mortar, e-commerce retailer, brand, destination, or nonprofit, your approach to online reviews management will require tailoring to match your business type. Get a handle on where and how your online reviews are created and consumed.

Chapter 2: The Online Reviews Landscape The online reviews space is complex, with numerous review sites and platforms, often feeding into one another. Find your path through the thicket with this chapter's demystifying explanation of the various types of review venues.

Chapter 3: Understanding Reviewers and Reviews Learn the customer experiences that are most likely to trigger a review and what factors make a review influential.

Chapter 4: Monitoring and Learning from Your Reviews Find your reviews and figure out which review venues are most important for your business. Then take action to develop a sustainable plan for monitoring reviews and incorporating review feedback into your business.

Chapter 5: How to Get More Reviews There are numerous ways for a business to encourage new online reviews. Peruse a bounty of effective techniques to find workable ideas for your business and avoid common pitfalls that could get you into hot water.

Chapter 6: Review Venues: Need-to-Know Tips for Your Action Plan Insider details and how-to tips for six high-priority review venues: Yelp, Google+ Local, TripAdvisor, Angie's List, ResellerRatings, and Bazaarvoice.

Chapter 7: Navigating Negative Reviews Many businesses suffer from negative review anxiety. This chapter holds your hand as you prevent negative reviews when you can, and calmly and strategically cope with the ones you can't prevent.

Chapter 8: Showing Off and Being Found Help your reviews help you: Maximize the visibility of your positive online reviews, and use basic search engine optimization (SEO) techniques to help your online reviews benefit you in Google.

Chapter 9: Maintaining Your Momentum Translate the knowledge you've gained about online reviews into a sustainable plan for your business.

Conventions Used in This Book

This icon indicates a task assignment. Get your gears turning with practical step-by-step exercises to help you make progress in your own reviews management efforts.

Ethical concerns abound in online reviews. You'll see this icon to alert you to be cautious about techniques that have the potential to veer into unethical territory, or when we describe examples of businesses that have unfortunately already crossed over to the dark side.

Hang onto your wallet! This icon indicates that we're talking about your precious greenbacks. Sometimes we're steering you in a cheap or free direction; other times we're letting you know when a technique tends to be pricey.

We know you can handle the truth, even when it hurts. This icon indicates a difficult or inconvenient fact that may be hard to hear but is well worth knowing.

You Are Here: Understanding Your Opportunity

1

A boost in your online reputation. A stream of new customers. What's holding your business back from fully realizing the benefits of online reviews? Do you need more reviews? Or do you need reviews that more accurately reflect the excellence of your business's offerings? This book is not just about chasing a higher star rating. It's about using reviews wisely as a marketing tool and respecting and responding to the customer voice—in all its honesty, complexity, insight, and nuance—in every aspect of your business.

In this chapter:
Online reviews: an important marketing channel
Know where you fit in and how to focus

In this book, you'll learn about establishing practical protocols to attract more reviews, monitor the customer voice, and identify the most important review venues for your business. You'll immerse yourself in the technology and psychology of online reviews, learning what makes reviewers tick. You'll learn how to respond to commentary that puts your online reputation at risk and how to flaunt your positive reviews to the best possible benefit of your business.

You're reading this book, so we're betting you have a good idea of what's at stake for your business. In case you work with someone who needs convincing, here are some must-see stats to illustrate the importance of online reviews:

- On average, a consumer will look at over 10 information sources before making a purchase. (Bazaarvoice, 2012)

- 79% of consumers trust online reviews as much as personal recommendations. (BrightLocal, 2013)

- Over half of young people aged 18 to 34 say they trust online reviews *more than* the opinions of friends and family. (Bazaarvoice, 2012)

And here's the kicker: As the years go by, the influence of online reviews just keeps growing.

Many business owners lose sleep over bad reviews like this one:

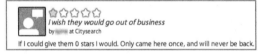

It's not an exaggeration: Your bottom line—even your business survival—is on the line. But you don't need to live in fear of being put out of business by bad online reviews. Strategies in this book will help you minimize the likelihood of getting bad reviews and be responsive, attentive, and hands-on in your handling of the few bad reviews that you just couldn't prevent.

Online Reviews: An Important Marketing Channel

When business owners we know describe their feelings about online reviews and the people who write them, we rarely hear "love" featuring prominently. One common attitude is apathy. Some business owners don't think about reviews much. They know they're accruing them but assume all is well unless they learn otherwise through the grapevine. Another common attitude is one of suspicion, or even fear. We suspect that some business owners have blown out their birthday candles with a secret wish for Yelp to suffer a permanent 500 Internal Server error. Still another stance is "I'll deal with it when I have time." Some business owners are aware that online reviews can attract new customers, but they regard online reviews as one of the many forms of marketing that they are too busy to think about. Whatever your attitude, we're here to tell you that your success in a modern marketplace depends on embracing reviews as a top-priority online marketing effort and fostering a review-friendly approach to your customer interactions.

Why learn to love online reviews? For one, they can attract a lot of customers. From digital natives to senior shoppers, consumers are seeking online reviews for help with nearly every spending decision: which camera to buy, what museum to visit, where to get their teeth cleaned, and where to give birth to their next baby. Business-to-business (B2B) decision-makers are also scouring the Web for wisdom about the software, equipment, and services they need. They have money in their pockets and want plentiful, legitimate, credible, and informative reviews to help them find the right way to spend it.

The usefulness of online reviews extends beyond consumer decisions to personal ones: Choosing which recipe to cook is now a social process, and college students have been rating their professors online for years. Even houses of worship are finding that the path to new members is paved with online reviews. Figure 1.1 shows a review of a local church.

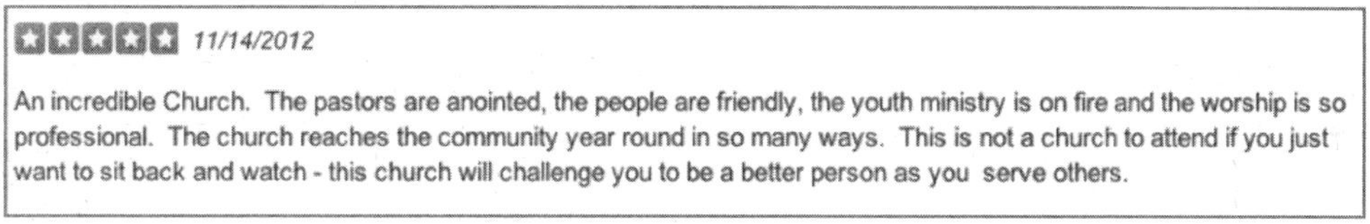

⭐⭐⭐⭐⭐ *11/14/2012*

An incredible Church. The pastors are anointed, the people are friendly, the youth ministry is on fire and the worship is so professional. The church reaches the community year round in so many ways. This is not a church to attend if you just want to sit back and watch - this church will challenge you to be a better person as you serve others.

Figure 1.1 One of the many glowing reviews on Yelp for a Kentucky church

People are tapping into the wealth of Internet-based word-of-mouth to find great businesses and make informed product decisions, and they are not going to stop. Here are some of the other benefits they've reaped:

- Lower costs for the same product. The Internet has made comparison-shopping a snap.

- Product information that offers a variety of perspectives, not just those of the provider, manufacturer, or retailer.

- An opportunity to sound off (a.k.a, complain, vent, and grumble) about problems they've experienced with products or services.

And how do business owners benefit? You have access to the kinds of free business enhancement ideas that were never available to you before the first review star lit up the Internet.

To get the best results from your online review management program, you'll need to embrace the reality of what consumers want and need and be both practical and creative as you identify the opportunities available to you and your business.

Gauging the Dollar Value of a Review

Taming and managing your online reviews takes some effort. You'll be working to encourage positive reviews for your business, product, or service. You'll be monitoring reviews, improving communication channels, responding and reacting wisely, and using the latest tools to show off reviews on your site and on the Web. And you have every right to wonder: What does all this translate to, on a strictly cash basis? Seriously, what do George, Andrew, Ulysses, and Ben have to say about all this? Here are some ways a business might start to gauge the dollar value of its online reviews:

What would an unscrupulous business pay for a good review? In 2012, the *New York Times* reported that VIP Deals, a maker of leather cases for the Kindle Fire, was refunding customers the price of the product in exchange for an Amazon review. Cost of the reviews: $10 each. Whether or not this ploy worked is another story.

How much more will customers pay for a product or service with good reviews? 2007 research at New York University's Stern School of Business found that purchasers spent an average of $5.86 more on Amazon.com for the same product when its reviews included the words "wonderful experience." On the flipside, they paid $7.46 less for products with reviews including the deadly words: "never received." In a similar vein, 2012 research by Cornell's Center for Hospitality Research found "if a hotel increases its review scores by 1 point on a 5-point scale … the hotel can increase its price by 11.2 percent and still maintain the same occupancy or market share."

How many customers can you lose from a negative review? A 2009 survey in the UK by Convergys Corporation estimated that a negative tweet could cause a business to lose 30 customers. And lawsuits over bad reviews have claimed $80,000 (dentist), $400,000 (dentist), and $750,000 (contractor) in damages. Granted, none of those plaintiffs has won, so take those numbers with a ledger-sized grain of salt.

As they say, YMMV (your mileage may vary). How to calculate the value of your online reviews will depend on the type of business. Here's a hypothetical example:

A local restaurant has been monitoring its reviews on Yelp and notices some 1- and 2-star reviews after they were short-staffed over a holiday weekend. The owners know that about half of their business is from loyal repeat customers, and in good times, roughly a tenth are new customers who come in after looking at Yelp. Since the bad reviews appeared on Yelp, the wait staff has asked all customers how they heard about the restaurant and observed no Yelp-sourced visits. The upshot: If this restaurant's average daily income is $2,500, then these negative reviews could be costing them $250/day in revenue. If it takes five positive, genuine reviews to push those negative ones out of top listings, then each of those reviews is worth about $50/day, at least in the short term. This does not factor in the potential lifetime value of a lost customer, which increases the effect even further.

Continues

Know Where You Fit In and How to Focus

Whether you're pouring beers or foundations, there is a place on the Web for people to review you. Your approach to finding these reviews, and managing this piece of your online reputation, will need to be tailored to your type of business. Let's take a look at what people are reviewing and where they are leaving their feedback, and we'll get you started thinking about how far your sphere of influence extends.

Your business may fall into more than one category. For example, a bakery that designs custom wedding cakes deals with concerns that affect both brick-and-mortar and service providers. If you sell products both in a storefront and online, be sure read both the "Brick and Mortar" and "E-commerce Retailers" sections that follow. We know a company that makes 3D printers, sells them both online and in a storefront, and offers custom 3D printing services. By our count, that company has four reading assignments: brick and mortar, e-commerce, brand, and service.

Brick and Mortar

Brick-and-mortar businesses such as restaurants, cafes, and shops fuel the online review engine. For example, as of late 2012, 44% of Yelp's 30-plus million reviews were written for businesses in the shopping and restaurants category. Whether you're a new business looking to build up a reputation or an established company trying to move the needle from negative to positive, online reviews management is no small part of your business strategy.

What They Review

What *don't* they review? Whatever a customer can see or experience is fair game for online reviews: staff, products, food, prices, facility, location, parking, even the other clientele. Many of these attributes can be catalogued and rated separately, and these bits of sentiment come together to tell the overall story of your online reputation—ideally, a large and credible narrative in which the finest aspects of your business shine through. But the sheer volume of fodder your business provides for reviews may also leave you feeling vulnerable. Your excellent gourmet meal loses stars because the customer two tables down had an annoying laugh? Your top-notch merchandise gets dinged because a customer got a parking ticket while shopping? You probably find this nitpicking distressing, but the good news is that people who read your reviews don't expect to encounter an unending expanse of compliments. Studies show they won't avoid you in droves due to the quirks of an individual biased review.

Where They Review You

Review sites like Yelp, location-aware social media venues like Foursquare or the Facebook check-in feature, or search/review hybrid Google+ Local (which you often see when you search for a local business in Google Maps) can all be places where your customers leave their feedback. You may have created your own listing, but you don't control the content of the reviews or the filters and processes that govern their visibility. Figure 1.2 shows Google Maps search results with review excerpts.

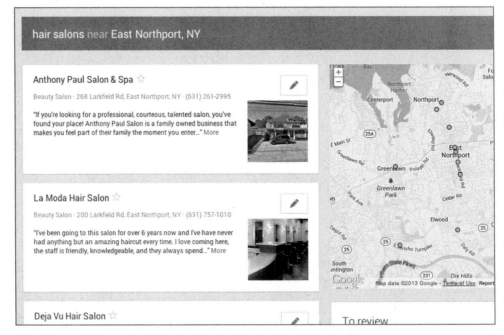

Figure 1.2 Google Maps search results showing hair salon reviews from Google+ Local

Review sites make it easy for customers to post feedback for brick-and-mortar establishments, with a wealth of prepopulated categories such as food, décor, ambiance, and dozens of other options that reviewers can rate with just a few clicks and minimal thinking.

Your customers are using mobile devices at a significant and growing rate, and many of your reviews and comments may be read or submitted while your customers are physically at your location. According to a 2012 Google study, 78% of US consumers use their mobile device while in brick-and-mortar stores. Sure, many of them are texting with pals, but others are checking in on Facebook or Foursquare (that is, telling the world that they patronize your business), or popping off a quick compliment or complaint to the Twittersphere. Some are reading tips and reviews while they peruse your menu or merchandise. And, like it or not, some of them are comparison shopping online—pitting your prices against those of your competitors.

Your Unique Advantages and Disadvantages

You may be wondering why you should bother trying to influence a review landscape when you have so little control over the whims of your reviewers and the review venues. But you do have several factors that can work in your favor, not the least of which is volume. Customers are more likely to be in the habit of writing reviews for brick-and-mortar businesses like yours than they are for, say, a mortgage broker or an orthopedic surgeon. With the help of this book, your strategy will include various methods to encourage those of your customers who are review-savvy, socially connected, and smartphone-enabled to become your loyal advocates.

Another advantage you have is face time. Your customers have the opportunity to see you and your staff as real people, not an impersonal Buy Now button. This gives you and your staff multiple opportunities to work toward improving your online reputation by swiftly remedying problems and exhibiting a "customer comes first" attitude. Other types of businesses have these opportunities, too, but you have the advantage of being on display—often to multiple customers simultaneously—when you're being excellent. And of course you already know this face time is a double-edged sword, because your customers see you on bad days, too.

You also have the opportunity to gain some online cred with check-ins. These quick location announcements that customers make on sites like Facebook or Foursquare—for example, "Knocking back a slice—at Brownstone Pizzeria"—are not formal reviews with stars attached, but if you think of them as shorthand endorsements, they'll fit nicely alongside reviews in your online reputation management strategy.

As you read on, we'll help you identify the places where your customers connect, and we'll give you strategies for facilitating check-ins, preempting negativity, and encouraging the creation of authentic positive reviews from happy customers. We'll also help you understand how to navigate the features and editorial processes of the online review services that matter to you.

E-commerce Retailers

You sell your own products, or those of others, online. That means your customers take a chance sending you their precious bucks, days or weeks before a purchase makes it into their hands. Clearly, customer trust is paramount, and online reviews can be a major avenue to that trust.

What They Review

Two words: customer service. Did the item arrive on time? How was it packaged? Did returns go okay? What about the accent of the call center rep? We won't deny that product reviews will inevitably discuss product quality, price, and value, but don't doubt it:

There is no product fabulous enough to overcome a poor customer experience.

Customer service issues can run your online reviews off the rails. In 2011, Bazaarvoice looked at 5 million consumer comments and concluded, "Product quality and interactions with brand representatives are inseparable in the minds of many consumers." The same Bazaarvoice study noted reviews that mention customer service had a 91% lower average rating than those that did not.

Many e-commerce sites sell products that can also be purchased via thousands of other sites on the Web. If that describes you, your customer service *is* your product, and online reviews are the perfect differentiator.

Where They Review You

Reviews that are applicable to e-commerce sites fall into two categories: product reviews and merchant reviews. Your product reviews take place on your own site's product pages, assuming you've set up a reviews platform. Your business as a whole may be reviewed on third-party platforms such as ResellerRatings.com and Shopper Approved. If you sell products on Amazon.com, both your products and your business can be reviewed there. If you list products on a comparison shopping site like Shopping.com or NexTag, customers have an opportunity to post reviews of their purchasing experience with you.

Your Unique Advantages and Disadvantages

Smile—you're online! Because your transactions take place online, your customers are already tapping on keyboards or swiping on smartphones when they order from you, which means that writing an online review should be within their abilities. Inevitably, you have your customers' email addresses and you've probably already sent them some emails, such as an order confirmation and shipping status. This will make your job pursuing online reviews easier, because you have a good way to contact your

HARD TRUTH

customers; you can even integrate review requests into transactional emails. As a second fun advantage of being an online merchant, if you have product reviews on your site, then your sales venue and at least some of your online reviews can both reside in the same place: on your own website. That means you don't have to do a lot of extra work to put reviews in front of your customers. They can see them naturally while shopping and use them to make their purchasing decisions.

Manufacturers, Brands, Software

You may sell your own products online or at stores. But for many companies in this category, the dominant portion of your revenue comes from other retailers selling what you create. The fact that your reviews are scattered around the Web doesn't mean you can't maintain a grip on them.

What They Review

Just like the product reviews discussed under "E-Commerce Retailers," your reviews will feature product quality, price, and value, with a heaping helping of customer service in the mix. How quiet was the dishwasher, and how many service calls has it required? Were the shoes true to size? Is software support available at a fair price?

Where They Review You

The majority of your reviews will show up on the sites that sell your products—including your own site, other retailers, and shopping comparison sites. Additionally, customer reviews can be posted on consumer help sites that feature both expert and customer opinions, such as CNET.com and Consumer Reports; complaint sites like PissedConsumer.com; or other product review sites such as SheSpeaks.com or Viewpoints.com that are not associated with a specific vendor.

Commentary about makers and brands also easily finds its way into Twitter and Facebook posts. In August 2012, the Burson-Marsteller Global Social Media Check-Up found Fortune 100 companies were mentioned on Twitter over 10 million times in a month. These social media conversations mirror face-to-face ones your customers are having every day, as seen in Figure 1.3.

Figure 1.3 Social media conversations mirror face-to-face ones your customers have every day.

Your Unique Advantages and Disadvantages

Some news articles include speculation that online reviews will mean the death of brands, because brands can no longer present their image in a carefully controlled way to reinforce customer perceptions and loyalty. The truth is, the old-school brand that offers no added value is not well-suited to our modern transparent marketplace. Take a deep breath and accept the inevitable: Your secrets are not safe, your status is not secure, and your message is not under your control. Brands are no longer in a position to dictate the discourse, but you can participate in it wisely.

A big challenge to brands and manufacturers is that your product reviews usually reside on retailer sites, not on your own. Your reviews will be distributed around the Web, sometimes to hundreds or thousands of websites. This will make it difficult for you to keep track of, understand, and respond to them. Furthering the challenge, a major component of reviews is the retailer's customer service—something you have little to no control over.

Some brands have the resources to throw their weight around and exert a bit of control over how their products are sold. For example, Oakland, California–based coffee roaster Blue Bottle Coffee Company requires coffeehouses that carry their coffee to follow strict guidelines, attend special trainings, and submit to inspections. It's no small effort, but it helps keep their reputation stellar and the lines for their coffee going around the block.

Chains and Franchises

If you're selling the same cell phone or foot-long sandwich as the store down the road, you might wonder how much online reviews matter. A 2011 study conducted by the Harvard Business School suggests that, at least for restaurants on Yelp, different influences are at play for chains than for independents.

The study found that a 1-star increase in the overall Yelp rating led to a 5% to 9% increase in revenue for independent restaurants, but it noted that this same revenue increase did not apply to chain restaurants. Why the difference? Perhaps the reviews are less influential because there is less room for persuasion in the customer's mindset. Chains strive to provide consistency from one location to the next—you drink one blue raspberry slush drink, you've drunk 'em all—which eliminates the guesswork and the need for customers to seek reviews. With Starbucks as ubiquitous as it is, this reviewer seems almost resentful about writing a review:

A Google User reviewed a month ago
Food **Very good**   Decor **Very good**   Service **Very good**
It's a freakin' Starbucks! It sells overpriced coffee and you are serviced by local kids from Occidental college. There's nothing wrong with it. I go there all the time. The service is pretty much like any other Starbucks, the drinks are fine, if you're okay paying $3-4 for coffee. Seriously, people....

Continues

Chains and Franchises *(Continued)*

With the prominence of reviews in Google's search results, people will stumble across reviews for local chains and franchises even if they are only trying to find the address. We recommend that individual chain and franchise locations put work into online review management. This is partially an administrative task—for example, making sure listings are claimed appropriately for individual locations and no incorrect or duplicate listings are floating around—but there is also an element of reputation management. Consider the following:

Reviewers may not distinguish between your location and your parent company. One review for a Sprint store (technically a dealership, not a franchise or chain) posted a low-star review for an individual location because of an interaction with the parent company: "Even my phone call earlier was transferred to an offshore agent who barely understood what I said and took FOREVER to answer my questions."

Reviewers speak up when chains fall short of expectations. A customer at a chain or franchise is expecting consistency with other locations. Since you can't significantly change the recipe or the price, it's difficult for your product or service to exceed customer expectations. But it can be easy to fall short, causing a pile of negative reviews to stack up before you know it.

Reviewers name names. Typically, reviews of chains and franchises focus on customer service. Because a location may have few distinguishing features, these reviews can get personal, with individual employees being cited for amazing or abhorrent service.

With online reviews expanding in scope and reach, chains and franchises may find themselves a bit squeezed. Online reviews have an equalizing function, reducing some of the advantages held by chains. As the volume of online reviews increases, more information than ever is available about independent businesses, making it less risky for customers to try out an unfamiliar independent shop and providing less incentive to stick with the safe choice of a chain. The same Harvard study we described earlier finds that "there is a shift in revenue share toward independent restaurants and away from chains as Yelp penetrates a market."

Brands also have the help of tools and services that allow them to track reviews around the Web, but these can be pricey. Social commerce companies such as Bazaarvoice (www.bazaarvoice.com) and Reevoo (www.reevoo.com) offer dashboards to track product reviews from multiple vendors. With this knowledge in hand, brands can identify and work to improve retailers with poor reviews—or cut them off, if necessary.

Tilt your ear carefully toward the chatter and you'll find that product and software reviews are a useful blend of free user testing, market research, and focus groups. Bless those verbose venters: Their complaints and wishes could put you on the path toward your next product enhancement—or maybe even inspire your next great product.

Destinations and Activities

Destinations and activities include hotels, museums, attractions, and theaters. It's natural that your potential customers and patrons seek out online reviews—after all, when a person is planning a trip to a distant and unfamiliar location, opportunities for gathering traditional face-to-face advice are limited.

What They Review

According to a 2012 study commissioned by TripAdvisor, 74% of their reviewers say that they write reviews "to share a good experience with other travelers." Unfortunately, it's not just the good stuff that will find its way into your online reviews! Visitors will review every aspect of their experience: Was it a good value, clean, enjoyable, convenient? How was the view from the orchestra seats? Were the lines for the special exhibition excruciatingly long? A 2012 survey by UK accommodations site LateRooms.com identified some hot topics for hotel reviews: Those describing a hotel as "dirty" or "noisy" gave travelers serious second thoughts about booking a room.

If you're wondering which aspects of their experience reviewers will focus on, you can get a hint by looking at preselected categories on review sites. Figure 1.4 shows Travelocity's list for hotels, and Figure 1.5 shows the prefab selections for rating attractions from TripAdvisor.

Where They Review You

TripAdvisor is the dominant travel review site, featuring not only hotels but also attractions and vacation rentals. Online travel agencies (OTAs) such as Orbitz and Expedia are also an important venue for travel-related reviews. 2011 research by travel market research company PhoCusWright found that two out of three online hotel reviews were posted on OTAs.

General-purpose review sites like Yelp and Google+ Local are another important venue, particularly for non-hotel destinations such as museums and theme parks. And location-aware social media channels deserve your attention as well. Using apps like Foursquare, anyone who is physically present at your location can check in to leave tips and mini-reviews visible to their friends and other users. These comments are often automatically posted to Twitter and Facebook as well, which amplifies their reach.

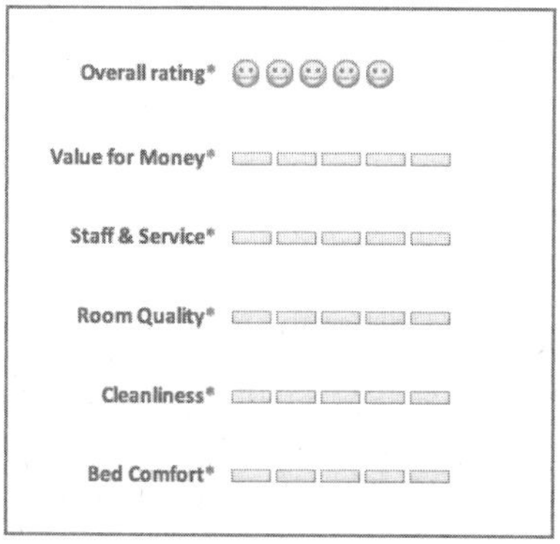
Overall rating*
Value for Money*
Staff & Service*
Room Quality*
Cleanliness*
Bed Comfort*

Figure 1.4 Travelocity's hotel review categories

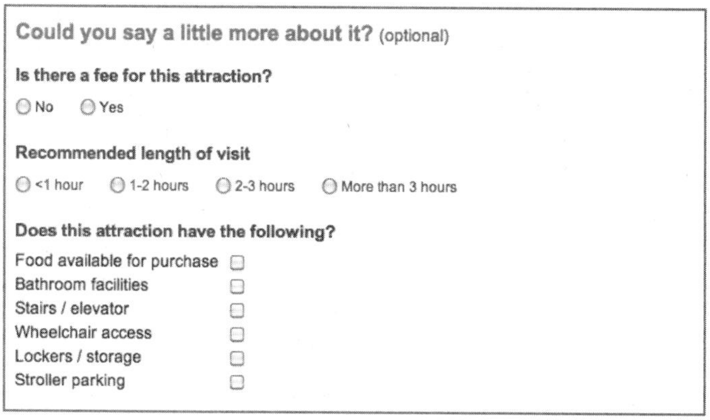
Could you say a little more about it? (optional)
Is there a fee for this attraction?
No Yes
Recommended length of visit
<1 hour 1-2 hours 2-3 hours More than 3 hours
Does this attraction have the following?
Food available for purchase
Bathroom facilities
Stairs / elevator
Wheelchair access
Lockers / storage
Stroller parking

Figure 1.5 TripAdvisor's museum review categories

Your Unique Advantages and Disadvantages

One nice thing about managing online reviews for destinations and activities is that you won't have to fight against the current just to get people to review your business. Although lots of people still find it odd and awkward to post a review of a lawyer or dentist, posting reviews of hotels and attractions is a well-established practice. Your ability to manage your online reviews—and your online reputation as a whole—is helped along by an established hospitality and tourism industry, complete with university departments doing research that you'll find helpful, as well as entrepreneurs building review monitoring tools they'd love you to purchase.

Some statistics for hotels and travel bear out the importance of online reviews for this industry:

- More than one-third of travelers would not book a hotel room without reading reviews first, according to 2012 survey by LateRooms.com.

- Travelers can be heavy researchers. A Cornell School of Hotel Administration study in 2011 showed travelers who booked at an OTA averaged 12 different visits to the website and looked at 7.5 pages per visit.

- A Forrester study commissioned by TripAdvisor found 75% of travelers surveyed said their vacation was better because they had used reviews.

Use of online reviews is less widespread among other destinations and travel services, such as airlines, cruises, and car rentals.

This book will walk you through claiming and improving your listings on review sites, guidelines for figuring out which niche sites you need to care about, available tools for monitoring reviews, and best practices for replying to reviews online, all of which are important efforts for hotels, attractions, and other destinations.

Service Providers

Service providers include lawyers, doctors, home contractors, real estate agents, hairdressers, and wedding planners, to name a few. You put your specialized skills to work for your clients, often at a price point that puts pressure on you to prove your value. To your customers, you have the upper hand in the relationship: Whether it's a favorable verdict, a dream wedding, an accurate diagnosis, or a flattering haircut, your work has a big impact on your clients' lives. The combination of power, price, and perceived value can make for high-drama customer experiences, and some dissatisfied clients may try to use online reviews as revenge for an unhappy experience. It's no coincidence that the bulk of high-profile litigation around online reviews involves service professionals.

What They Review

There's no way to sugarcoat this: it's you! For many service providers, your name is your business, and you're flying solo in the hot seat. Your approach, skills, personality and appearance, and of course, the service that you provide and its outcome are all subject to reviews. If you have staff or a facility, these can spark feedback, too.

Where They Review You

Your online reviews landscape is a bit of a turf war, with niche sites competing against broad ones. A service provider's reviews may be spread thin across the Web, with some on Yelp, others on general-purpose directories or map services like yellowpages.com and Google+ Local, and others on specialized sites, for example, Avvo.com for lawyers, Healthgrades.com for doctors, Zillow for real estate agents, and Angie's List and Kudzu for home services.

Your Unique Advantages and Disadvantages

You may be doing everything right for your customers but still find it a challenge to get new reviews. Some of the more popular review venues are not well matched to your service offerings. For example, while the Yelp review interface can include lots of helpful prefabricated survey questions that ask restaurant reviewers to describe everything from attire to noise level, service-oriented business reviewers are often presented with just one or two survey questions, limited to such bland topics as "Quality" and "Accepts Credit Cards." And though niche sites like Healthgrades may provide opportunities to review specific factors that are well suited to your business, as seen in Figure 1.6, there's no guarantee your customers have even heard of those sites. Plus, many service providers interact with customers off the wifi grid, so you may not know whether your clients are comfortable with the technology required to hop online and sing your praises.

To add to these challenges, service professionals like you are limited in the number of clients with whom they can interact. Whereas restaurants or stores can serve hundreds of customers a day, a roofing job could take weeks, a single legal case might play out over months, and a single engineering project may last years. Without a large volume of reviews, the few you have will carry a lot of weight whether or not they are accurate.

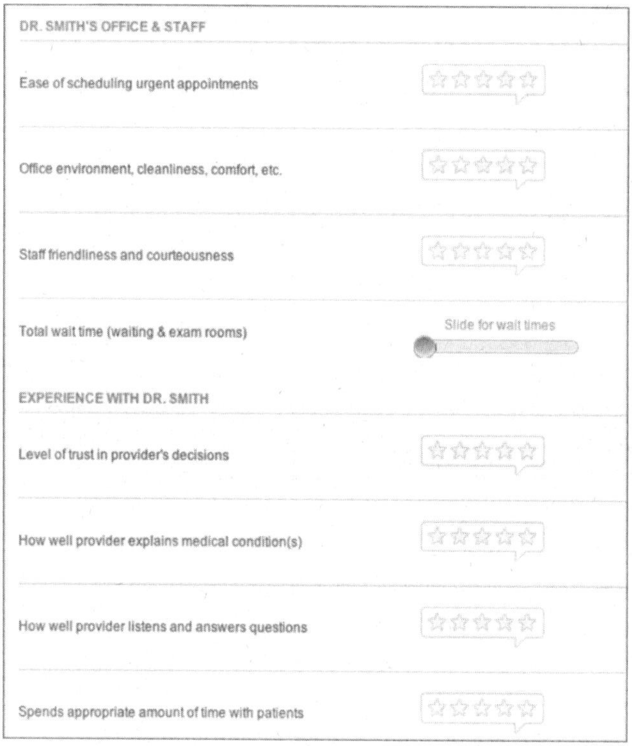

Figure 1.6 Healthgrades offers detailed features for reviewing medical providers.

You may be extremely well trained in your craft, but you were probably not trained in online marketing, nor are you prepared for the kind of exposure that can seriously affect your reputation. Your reviewers may make your fees public when you would prefer to keep them private, or they may publish photos of your handiwork. You may have specialized expertise that your customers just don't understand, and they may unintentionally misrepresent you in ways that make you cringe, even when they post positive reviews.

It can be hard for service providers to find appropriate channels to join the conversation or to defend against unfair criticism. Professionals such as doctors, lawyers, therapists, and members of the clergy work within strict confidentiality guidelines, but reviewers are not bound by the same rules. These confidentiality restrictions can be especially frustrating when they prevent you from responding to negative reviews!

We won't blame you if you're feeling that online sentiment is biased against you. The truth is that hiring you may be an expensive, stressful, or possibly life-altering decision for your potential customers. Adding to this issue, potential customers may be especially skeptical about the reviews they read for service providers. Particularly in the locksmith, carpet cleaning, plumbing, and roadside assistance industries, we've come across anecdotal reports of business owners posting fake reviews and customers being unpleasantly surprised by experiences not consistent with those reviews. Review sites work to allay customers' fears of getting cheated or worse. Angie's List, with 65,000 new reviews posted each month in over 500 service categories, serves up articles like "Worst Cleveland Contractors of 2012" and "Tips on how not to get ripped off!" Recognizing consumer anxiety is an important part of your job as you approach your online reviews management.

In the following chapters, we'll help you identify methods to show off your expertise in the venues where exposure matters, find and fix the sources of incorrect listing data, and use your existing relationships to generate the reviews you deserve.

Where Reviews Intersect with Online Reputation Management and Customer Acquisition

Just as it's not possible for your customers to separate your product from your customer service, we find that we can't talk about your online reviews without tying them to your online reputation management and customer acquisition strategies. We know you'll forgive us for straying into this broader territory occasionally, because it's always better for you to understand the big picture.

Online Reputation Management

Some companies pay teams of specialists to comb through Twitter sentiment, Facebook comments, press mentions, forum conversations, search engine listings, and more, just to better understand their own online reputation. The goal in online reputation management is to understand public sentiment, take an active role in shaping what folks encounter when they stumble across your name, and influence the conversation, either by communicating directly with those who are doing the talking or by laying out new business initiatives that will encourage favorable sentiment.

Continues

Where Reviews Intersect with Online Reputation Management and Customer Acquisition *(Continued)*

Online review management *is* online reputation management—it just happens to be focused on one slice of the reputation pie. Here's how your approach to online reviews intersects with reputation management strategy:

- Monitoring your reviews helps you understand why people love your business and what triggers the griping. This helps you improve your business, and it helps you know what topics to communicate about during customer encounters.

- Understanding the various review venues helps you determine which parts of your business are on display to whom, and it also helps you understand where to focus your efforts should you need to do damage control.

- Influencing the conversation helps you improve online sentiment around your business. If you join the conversation thoughtfully, prospective customers may get a glimpse of your responsiveness, current offerings, and exciting promotions, rather than being overrun with evidence that your company went through a rough patch last February. Opportunities to encourage good reviews and address bad ones pop up during customer transactions, on your website, and on social media, not just on review sites.

The online reviews management tactics you'll find in this book will go a long way toward improving your online reputation as a whole.

Customer Acquisition Strategy

A solid customer acquisition strategy involves identifying cost-effective methods for gaining and keeping new customers. When a company tries new advertising, spruces up its website, launches new promotions, or hires a sign shaker in a bunny suit, the strategy is set in motion. It becomes a truly useful strategy only when the business closes the loop by measuring what worked and what didn't.

It's critically important to incorporate review cultivation into every aspect of your business, because getting new reviews can help you attract more customers. But don't forget to monitor your reviews to help you gauge the effectiveness of all of your customer acquisition strategies.

Online reviews often mirror the ups and downs of online or offline acquisition experiments. Did you get a spike in subpar reviews after you publicized a coupon that was difficult to honor? Did you get a wave of "meh" after press coverage brought in customers who had the wrong expectations? Do you notice a big difference in the tenor of reviews you get from longtime vs. first-time customers?

It's the thoughtful and creative types like you who will get the most out of your online reviews by integrating them into all of your business initiatives.

Charities, Nonprofits, Civic and Community Organizations

You need new people: You want their posteriors in your pews, their kids in your class-rooms, and their dollars in your discretionary funds—but first you have to win over their hearts and minds. For your target audience, the decision to join, enroll, or donate is extremely personal and the criteria subjective, but studies show that word of mouth and a person's social network have an impact, and that's why online reviews can affect your bottom line.

What They Review

For organizations that serve their patrons in person, such as churches, synagogues, animal shelters, and libraries, your reviewers comment on typical brick-and-mortar qualities like your facility, parking, and staff. You also get wildly subjective experience-based reviews: Longtime churchgoers may award 5 stars based on several years of membership, whereas a church shopper may dole out high marks based on a single warm welcome. A bad fit between one teacher and one child can prompt a negative review for the school as a whole, or the love of one great puppy can start an owner wagging about an animal shelter on Yelp.

Schools and charities have another layer of scrutiny tacked on: organizational performance metrics and institutional data. Publicly available data about the organizational efficiency of charities or the academic achievement and teacher ratios of schools is aggregated and published by some watchdog websites, and this data is molded into specialized (and some argue, misguided) rating systems that are studied with interest by the people you're trying to attract. Whether or not you're a fan of these ratings, do keep an eye on them, because your target audience may be checking them. In a 2010 study by Hope Consulting on how people choose to give to charities, the organization's effectiveness was cited by 90% of respondents, compared to 34% of respondents who cited endorsements by trustworthy individuals.

Where They Review You

Organizations with a brick-and-mortar presence such as animal shelters, schools, libraries, and houses of worship get their hugs and slugs in general-purpose review venues like Yelp, Google+ Local, and regional favorites like Judy's Book and Berkeley Parents' Network. Specialized venues, such as Charity Navigator (www.charity navigator.org) and the Better Business Bureau's Wise Giving Alliance (www.bbb.org/us/charity) report on all types of charities, including those without a walk-in option.

GreatSchools (www.greatschools.org) is an example of a site that plays to the public's desire to base decisions on both official data and personal opinions (see Figure 1.7). This site mixes academic and demographic data with crowdsourced reviews and social sharing buttons, and solicits insider information with its "Are you the principal?" link.

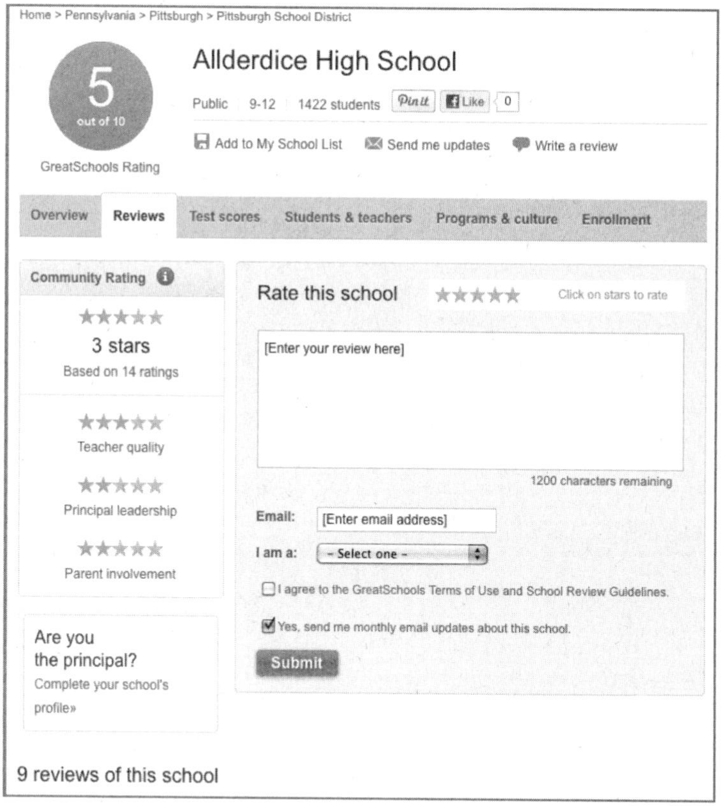

Allderdice High School

Public 9-12 1422 students *Pin it* ⬛ Like 0

💾 Add to My School List ✉️ Send me updates 💬 Write a review

5 out of 10

GreatSchools Rating

| Overview | **Reviews** | Test scores | Students & teachers | Programs & culture | Enrollment |

Community Rating ⓘ

★★★★★
3 stars
Based on 14 ratings

★★★★★
Teacher quality

★★★★★
Principal leadership

★★★★★
Parent involvement

Are you the principal?
Complete your school's profile»

Rate this school ★★★★★ Click on stars to rate

[Enter your review here]

1200 characters remaining

Email: [Enter email address]

I am a: – Select one –

☐ I agree to the GreatSchools Terms of Use and School Review Guidelines.

☑ Yes, send me monthly email updates about this school.

Submit

9 reviews of this school

Figure 1.7 GreatSchools.org mixes data and personal opinions.

Your Unique Advantages and Disadvantages

Studies show that donors tend to stay loyal to a charity once they choose it, and many organizations enjoy long-term or repeat patronage. So you may already have a treasure trove of potential 5-star reviews in reserve. On the flip side, many of your most loyal advocates are probably not thinking about online advocacy at all. It may seem like a stretch for a longtime congregant, regular donor, or permanent PTA parent to spontaneously pop over to Yelp, Charity Navigator, or GreatSchools and leave a review. Another barrier: Posting an online review invariably means some self-exposure for your reviewers. Not everyone wants to reveal their participation in churches or organizations, or details about their kids' school experience. Because your organization is likely to have fewer reviews than a big restaurant or a popular book, those that you do receive can hold an inordinate amount of sway over readers' opinions. After all, an organization with only five reviews can't afford to have two duds in the mix.

Profile completeness is another challenge for you. Since your potential patrons may be looking for both data and social context on niche sites, general-purpose review sites, and your own website, you'll need to be proactive in monitoring your many listings and keeping them updated.

With a better understanding of where your business fits in, you're ready to start navigating this complex terrain. Fasten your seatbelt, because in Chapter 2, "The Online Reviews Landscape," we'll take you for a tour of this exciting terrain.

The Online Reviews Landscape

*If you scratch the surface beyond the famil-
iar Yelp reviews and Amazon stars, the online
review landscape is large and complex. Whether
you're a local business owner, a brand manager,
a marketer, or a service professional, chances
are you didn't study this stuff in school. We
won't blame you if you feel lost! Read on to find
your way.*

In this chapter:
Types of online reviews
Types of review sites, platforms, and services
Fake reviews

In this chapter, you'll get your basic training on the various types of online reviews, where and how they are posted, and in what venues they are seen.

As we walk you through this landscape, we'll point out the ugly side too: fake online reviews. We'll explain why they exist, how many of them there are, and what the review sites and services are doing to fight them.

Types of Online Reviews

The expression *online review* can mean different things to different people. We define it as any online expression of a customer's, client's, patient's, or patron's opinion. Yup, that means everything that just about anyone you interact with says about you online counts.

To get a handle on a complicated system, it helps to parse it out into manageable pieces. Here are some basic types of online reviews:

Product Reviews Product reviews are customer-generated descriptions associated with a specific item. If you ever shop online, you've seen zillions of these on e-commerce retailer sites such as Amazon. Product reviews usually include a number of stars, along with a text description, and can also include customer videos and uploaded images. In some cases the review interface will present "pros" and "cons" or other similar elements, as seen in Figure 2.1.

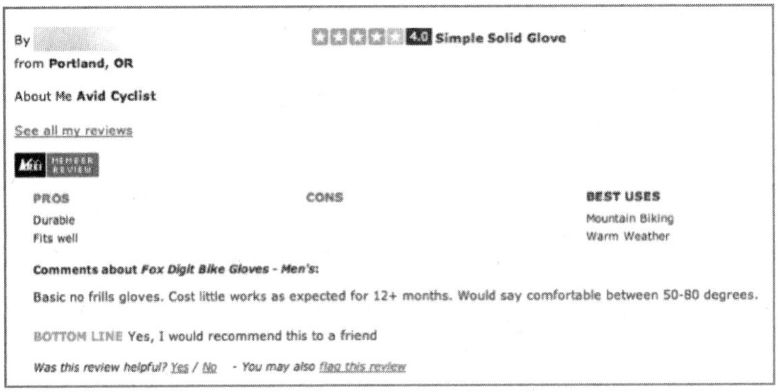

By ▮▮▮▮ from **Portland, OR**

About Me **Avid Cyclist**

See all my reviews

★★★★★ **4.0** Simple Solid Glove

REI MEMBER REVIEW

PROS	CONS	BEST USES
Durable		Mountain Biking
Fits well		Warm Weather

Comments about *Fox Digit Bike Gloves - Men's*:

Basic no frills gloves. Cost little works as expected for 12+ months. Would say comfortable between 50-80 degrees.

BOTTOM LINE Yes, I would recommend this to a friend

Was this review helpful? Yes / No   - You may also flag this review

Figure 2.1 Product review on REI.com

Company Reviews (Also Called Seller Ratings or Merchant Reviews) These are reviews that provide feedback about a business, organization, service provider, or brand as a whole. Company reviews include local business reviews on sites like Yelp, TripAdvisor, OpenTable, and Google+ Local, as well as reviews for brick-and-mortars, brands, service providers, or e-commerce sites on platforms such as ResellerRatings, Demandforce, Genbook, and Shopper Approved. Although these reviews are not about a specific product, they can be triggered by a specific purchase or experience with the company. Company reviews for e-commerce retailers may also be called seller ratings or merchant reviews. An example of a company review on ResellerRatings is shown in Figure 2.2.

Figure 2.2 Company review (also called seller rating or merchant review) of USB Memory Direct

Social Media Commentary Online word of mouth naturally finds its way into social media posts and streams. Customer comments about products, businesses, and brands can be expressed in Twitter, Facebook, and Pinterest, to name a few. Users can post their opinions, photos, and videos in real time, while shopping, eating, waiting in line, or winning the prize for Most Obnoxious Audience Member in a Movie Theater. Consumers in buyer-research mode can put out a call for opinions and recommendations and reap helpful responses from friends in their social circles. Figure 2.3 shows how a photo can be an integral element in a social media comment.

Figure 2.3 Brand comment on Twitter, including photo

Customer Q&A Question and answer sites such as Yahoo! Answers have been offering a space for product and brand feedback for ages. More recently, review platforms like Amazon, Bazaarvoice, and TurnTo have been amping up customer Q&A for online retailers. These features allow customers to ask questions directly on retailer sites and receive answers from the best possible source: people who actually own the product. Figure 2.4 shows an Amazon solicitation for an answer about a product.

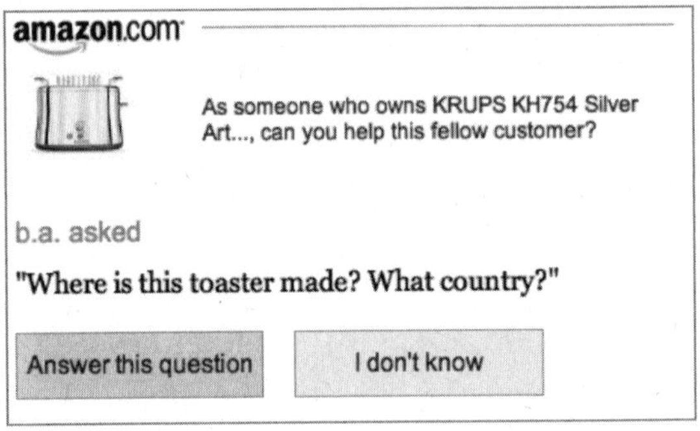

Figure 2.4 Solicitation for customer answer

Customer Satisfaction Surveys Some businesses collect customer feedback for internal use, either via email, at kiosks on-site, or at the point of sale. This feedback is usually collected just for the company's own learning process, but some services such as Revinate and Market Metrix provide technology that can feed customer surveys into public review venues. Reputation.com, which provides broader reputation management services, also offers an in-house, private review gathering capability. Figure 2.5 shows an example of an email for a customer satisfaction survey.

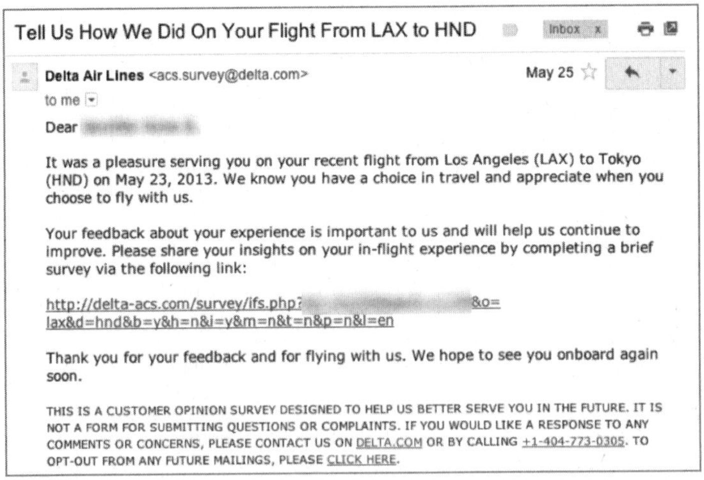

Figure 2.5 Customer satisfaction survey

Complaint/Scam Reports Some websites are built just for those consumers whose pastime of choice is unfettered venting about poor customer experiences. ripoffreport.com (Figure 2.6), pissedconsumer.com, and complaintsboard.com overflow with customer rants about business misconduct ranging from fraud to fornication. These reviews teeter on the edge of defamation and are often guilty of unforgivable grammar and spelling crimes. The hosting sites are perennially accused of extortion by business owners. You may not love these sites, but that doesn't mean you can ignore them. You'll learn more about responses to negative reviews in Chapter 7, "Navigating Negative Reviews."

Figure 2.6 Customer complaint on ripoffreport.com

Peer-to-Peer Buyer and Seller Ratings Marketplace sites such as eBay and Etsy and peer-to-peer platforms including Airbnb will typically allow both parties in a transaction to rate the other with positive or negative feedback plus a text comment. These ratings are associated with the user profile and are a crucial factor in gaining trust for future transactions. These sites are in the realm of the micropreneur, the *very* small business owner who has likely been communicating on a one-to-one basis with his or her customer from sale to transaction to review solicitation. Many books have been written about thriving in these marketplaces. We won't talk about the inner workings of these sites in this book, but if you're working on getting more and better reviews in these environments, much of the advice in this book is relevant to you.

Professional Reviews and Press Coverage The types of reviews listed so far can be posted by just about anyone with a keyboard and an opinion. If you're lucky, your business or product will also be scrutinized and reviewed by professionals: journalists, bloggers, product testers, industry experts, or other influencers in your space. This book is focused on the online voices of average consumers. Getting the attention of high-stakes professional reviewers is another animal, often requiring a specialized social media or public relations effort and a generous handout of freebies. By all means, pursue expert reviews, but keep in mind what the *American Journalism Review* said back in 2011: "Expert reviewing is plainly on the wane in the digital environment." The consumer's word is taking over online, and you should focus your attention accordingly.

Now that you know the various types of online reviews, we'll walk you through the many paths that an opinion can take on its way from one customer's thought bubble to another's computer screen.

Jargon Demystified

We've always disliked jargon, but the world of online marketing is lousy with the stuff. Here, we hope to demystify some of the terms you may come across in your online review management efforts.

Showrooming   When a consumer goes into a store to look at an item, then purchases that item online from another seller, that consumer is a *showroomer*. Brick-and-mortar retailers are scrambling to address this phenomenon and keep those showroomers' dollars in their own stores. A 2013 study by the location analytics firm Placed says that Amazon typically benefits from showrooming, while Bed Bath & Beyond was named the retailer most at risk from showrooming behaviors. According to a 2013 study by the Interactive Advertising Bureau (IAB), 31% of electronics shoppers use a mobile device for shopping activities in a store. Most check prices, and about half read online reviews.

Social Commerce   This phrase has taken hold with review services such as Bazaarvoice and Reevoo to describe how consumers check with other consumers before making a purchase. *Social commerce* refers to customers reading reviews, discussing products on forums, or accessing any other form of user-generated discourse about a product or company.

Sorting Algorithm   On many review sites and services, software-driven logic determines which customers see what reviews and the order in which they are displayed. On Yelp, the algorithm is called Yelp Sort, and on TripAdvisor, it's called a Popularity Index. Other services haven't necessarily given their algorithm a name, but all sites apply some sort of logic to displaying reviews, even if it's just chronological order or reviewer status.

Filtering Algorithm   Every site that displays reviews must take steps to avoid displaying fake or fraudulent reviews. They accomplish this with a *filtering algorithm*. Yelp's in particular is the subject of all sorts of speculation and superstition. Just as search engines keep their ranking algorithms secret, review sites do not reveal the details of their filtering algorithms for fear that spammers will use that knowledge to skirt the rules.

Paid, Owned, and Earned Media   Marketing folks have been using "paid, owned, and earned" for years to describe the channels by which businesses can communicate with their customers. On the Web, *paid media* refers to ads such as banner ads or pay-per-click (PPC) ads; *owned media* refers to your own website or other channels that you have significant control over, such as your Twitter or Facebook account; and *earned media* refers to press mentions and word-of-mouth, which includes social media chatter and online reviews.

Continues

Jargon Demystified *(Continued)*

Claiming a Listing Review sites such as Yelp and local search services such as Google+ Local offer businesses the ability to claim, or verify, their business listing. Claiming a listing gives the business owner access to helpful features, such as being able to edit the listing, receive alerts, publish promotions, and see reports.

Impressions In marketing lingo, *impression* just means *view*. People measure ad impressions (how many times people view online ads), but impression counts can also apply to other types of views— for example, views of your website's search engine result in Google or views of your Facebook post. If you've claimed your business listing, you might get access to reporting that tallies impressions for your business profile.

Rich Snippets Some search engine listings are dressed up with *rich snippets*, images and text that provide more context than just the link and description of the site. Examples of rich snippets include a product's availability and price, or a recipe's preparation time and calorie count. In online review management, you care about rich snippets that display the little yellow stars, as seen in these Google results for a Citysearch profile page:

Modern Cafe in **Minneapolis**, MN - Menu, Reviews, and ... - **Citysearch**
twincities.citysearch.com › Minneapolis › Restaurants ▾
★★★★★ Rating: 78% - 37 votes
Thirteenth Avenue in Northeast **Minneapolis** is busting at the seams with new and cool coffee shops, ... And while the Modern's décor is 1940s-diner inspired, the **food** is anything but. .... The **food** is hearty and the atmosphere **comfortable**.

Review sites aren't the only ones lucky enough to get bedazzled search listings. Any site can get rich snippets by constructing its pages in a way that the search engines can interpret, for example, by using schema.org markup. (We'll describe this in Chapter 8, "Showing Off and Being Found.")

Big Data When you have more information than you could possibly manage using 20th-century database methods, you've got *Big Data*. With the right tools, companies are learning how to wrestle meaning out of mountains of data, such as millions and millions of pieces of user-generated content. Big Data may also be remembered as the turning point when the Web started getting creepy: When Facebook figures out what kind of toilet paper you prefer, that's Big Data analysis at work.

Types of Review Sites, Platforms, and Services

Different types of reviews are often collected and displayed via entirely different processes or services, so it's time to familiarize yourself with the types of review sites and platforms that you might need to work with for your business's online reviews management efforts.

This is a dynamic, evolving, and sometimes overlapping industry. The following businesses have their own ways of describing themselves, but we've grouped the various review sites and platforms into categories that we think will be most helpful to *you* as a business stakeholder.

Review Sites

Imagine a large party, with lots of folks milling about. The hosts have one important rule: Gossip all you want, but tell the truth. Throughout the evening, partygoers are dishing the dirt: "Did you hear about the cupcakes at CakeNation? They're exquisite." "They're delicious, but stay away from the carrot cake cupcakes—too many raisins!" "Are you kidding? The donut place across the street is just as good—and half the price." This is the kind of party being thrown by Yelp, TripAdvisor, and other review sites that primarily exist to showcase consumer-generated reviews. Table 2.1 shows a selection of popular review sites.

▶ **Table 2.1** Review sites

Examples of review sites	Yelp
	TripAdvisor
	Citysearch
	Urbanspoon
	Insider Pages
	Angie's List
Who is reviewed?	Any business with a physical presence, including service providers, such as roofers, who travel to their customers' locations.
Where they stand on businesses encouraging reviews	Generally opposed to businesses offering incentives for reviews. Most are okay with asking, but Yelp is a notable exception.
Where reviews are seen	Reviews are displayed on the review site and affiliated mobile apps. Reviews often feature prominently in search results.
How they work with businesses	Review sites will list a business regardless of the business's intervention. Businesses can often claim and improve their listing and may be able to respond to reviews. Promoted placement and advertising is often available.

To succeed, these sites rely on gathering and displaying as many reviews as possible, and developing the perception that these reviews are trustworthy, to foster the virtuous cycle of more site visitors and more reviewers.

Since trustworthiness is key, these sites work hard to moderate and filter reviews that seem iffy. Back to our party metaphor, if a celebrant has a bit too much champagne and says something out of line like "CakeNation? That place only lets you in if you're one of those Green Party nutjobs," the hosts of the party will come along and hush that type of talk. In other situations, someone may drop a fib into the conversation. For example, if a guest is dripping with diamonds, you may not believe her when she says, "Oh, CakeNation! I go there because it's *such* a bargain, and I am always pinching my pennies." Our party hosts will shoo our spurious socialite out of the room to keep the integrity of the party intact. Just like our party hosts, review sites try to filter out reviews that appear fake or fraudulent or are generated in an unnatural way.

How They Work

For companies like Yelp and TripAdvisor, visitor engagement is the primary asset, and reviews keep the visitors engaged. These sites need a certain volume of reviews to stay healthy, which is why the following factors are typically true about review sites:

- Individual reviews are accessible via the search engines, providing a path for visitors to enter the site.
- Business owners can't opt out. Any user can add a business, and although business owners have the power to claim their profile, they do not have the power to delete it.
- The sites sell advertising and enhanced listings to businesses.
- The site rewards heavy reviewer participation with badges, labels, or real-life perks.

Studies show that, in order to trust reviews, people need to see volume and diversity of opinion. This is one reason review sites work so hard to filter out fake reviews, and businesses often find their legitimate positive reviews caught in that net. Site visitors will trust the review site less if they feel business owners can manipulate reviews.

Although credible review sites do care what business owners think, customers—not businesses—have to trust these sites, and use them in bulk, in order for the review sites to thrive and make money. It is the volume of reviews that drives the ability to charge for advertising, because where customers go, the advertisers (the businesses who are trying to attract these customers) will follow.

Visibility for the Reviews

Review sites typically have a lot of visibility in search engine results. These sites work hard at search engine optimization (SEO) techniques to make sure that individual reviews display in the search results, decorated with those lovely yellow stars (Google calls these rich snippets). Review site pages commonly get top Google spots for brand-agnostic searches such as <pet grooming> or <miami pet grooming> as well as branded searches such as <st judes mobile pet grooming>. Figure 2.7 shows one such Google listing with rich snippet review stars.

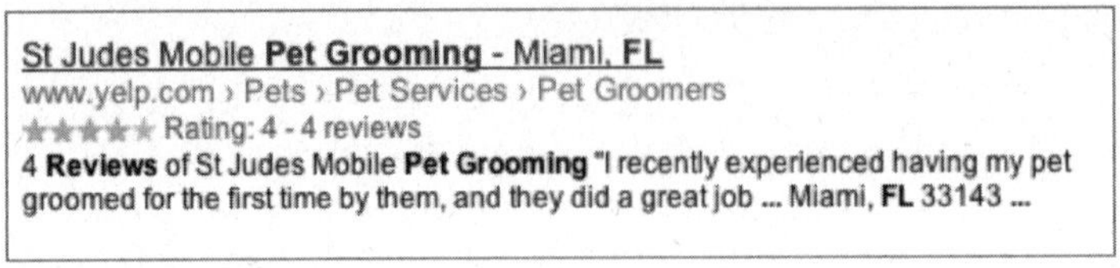

St Judes Mobile **Pet Grooming** - Miami, FL
www.yelp.com › Pets › Pet Services › Pet Groomers
★★★★☆ Rating: 4 - 4 reviews
4 **Reviews** of St Judes Mobile **Pet Grooming** "I recently experienced having my pet groomed for the first time by them, and they did a great job ... Miami, **FL** 33143 ...

Figure 2.7 A listing for a review site in Google's search results. The stars and the breadcrumb navigation links are examples of rich snippets.

To foster increased usage, review sites have also dedicated resources to perfecting their own mobile apps and search capabilities. This encourages users to go straight to the source, bypassing the search engines, who are, after all, displaying competing reviews. Yelp, OpenTable, Urbanspoon, and TripAdvisor offer intuitive, convenient mobile experiences, and Foursquare and Facebook check-ins are inherently mobile. Apps such as Raved are at the busy intersection of local and social, aggregating Facebook likes and check-ins and Foursquare check-ins from friends.

Businesses of the brick-and-mortar persuasion have a seemingly endless array of review sites to think about. To help you get your bearings, we've compiled a partial list of review sites in Table 2.2.

▶ **Table 2.2** Online review sites applicable to local businesses

Site name	URL	In a nutshell
ALL KINDS OF LOCAL BUSINESSES AND SERVICE PROVIDERS		
Yelp	`www.yelp.com`	Popular review site includes a wide range of local businesses, from pizza joints to podiatrists.
Google+ Local	`plus.google.com/local`, `maps.google.com`, and integrated into results on `google.com`	Google's own environment for reviews of local businesses is integrated with Google Maps and Google+. Includes Zagat reviews, reviews posted on Google by users, and links to reviews posted elsewhere.
Yahoo! Local	`local.yahoo.com`	Integrated with Yahoo! maps and local business listings. Hosts its own reviews and also aggregates reviews from elsewhere on the Web.
Citysearch	`citysearch.com`	Longstanding local business site features elite "scouts" offering reviews in addition to submissions from the public.
Foursquare	`foursquare.com`	Location-aware check-in site allows customers to post 200-character tips for businesses with a physical location.

Continues

Site name	URL	In a nutshell
YP.com	www.yellowpages.com	Old-school Yellow Pages listings are sparsely sprinkled with customer reviews.
Superpages	www.superpages.com	Yellow pages–style directory has space for local business reviews.
Judy's Book	www.judysbook.com	User reviews of businesses in wide-ranging categories from dining to school to health care.
MerchantCircle	www.merchantcircle.com	Merchant directory with user reviews.
FindTheBest	www.findthebest.com	Data-driven comparisons of pretty much anything you can think of, businesses and products included. Some user reviews.
RESTAURANTS		
Urbanspoon	www.urbanspoon.com	Popular restaurant review site aggregates critic, blogger, and diner reviews.
OpenTable	www.opentable.com	Primarily a restaurant reservation platform, but displays and collects reviews from diners.
Seamless	www.seamless.com	Online ordering for delivery or pickup. Customers can rate and review restaurants.
MenuPages	www.menupages.com	Menus, reservation info, and reviews for restaurants in a select list of cities.
GrubHub	www.grubhub.com	Site for ordering delivery from nearby restaurants includes restaurant reviews posted by its users. Also aggregates Yelp reviews.
Eat24	eat24.com	Includes restaurant reviews in addition to delivery order service.
Restaurantica	www.restaurantica.com	Local restaurant and nightlife guide with user reviews.
HOTELS, TRAVEL, AND ATTRACTIONS		
TripAdvisor	www.tripadvisor.com	Popular review site is focused on hotels but also includes reviews of destinations, attractions, and restaurants.
Hotels.com	www.hotels.com	Major hotel review site includes user reviews and TripAdvisor ratings.

Continues

Site name	URL	In a nutshell
Travelocity	www.travelocity.com	Major online travel agent (OTA) allows travelers to post reviews of hotels, cruises, and activities on a scale of one to five smiley faces.
Orbitz	www.orbitz.com	Major OTA allows travelers to post thumbs up/down reviews of hotels and cruises.
Expedia	www.expedia.com	Major OTA allows verified guests to post reviews of hotels and cruises.
Booking.com	www.booking.com	Hotel booking site allows travelers to post reviews.
Skytrax	airlinequality.com	Airline and airport reviews from travelers.
HEALTH		
Healthgrades	www.healthgrades.com	User reviews for doctors, dentists, and hospitals.
Vitals	www.vitals.com	Physician reviews from patients.
Wellness	www.wellness.com	Site for finding health, wellness, and lifestyle information. Contains some provider reviews.
RateMDs.com	www.ratemds.com	User reviews for doctors, dentists, and hospitals.
HOME SERVICES		
Angie's List	www.angieslist.com	Popular site charges a fee to access reviews. Focuses on home services but also includes health, automotive, and other categories.
Kudzu	www.kudzu.com	Reviews compiled from around the Web for local home and health services.
Insider Pages	www.insiderpages.com	Citysearch partner includes all types of local businesses but with an emphasis on health and home services.
AUTOMOTIVE		
DealerRater	www.dealerrater.com	Automotive dealership reviews.
Edmunds.com	www.edmunds.com	Popular site for new and used car information. Includes dealership reviews.

Continues

Site name	URL	In a nutshell
Cars.com	www.cars.com	Major site for automotive information allows users to post reviews of dealers.
LEGAL		
Avvo	www.avvo.com	Lawyer reviews posted by both clients and peers.
Lawyers.com	www.lawyers.com	A resource for legal information; uses both client and peer reviews to rate lawyers.
Super Lawyers	www.superlawyers.com	Rates outstanding lawyers based on peer recognition and professional achievement. No user reviews.
SCHOOLS AND NONPROFITS		
Charity Navigator	charitynavigator.org	Nonprofit charity evaluations based on financial and other data.
GreatSchools	www.greatschools.org	User reviews for educational facilities from preschool through college.
ChurchRater	churchrater.com	User reviews and ratings for local churches.

Social Commerce/Product Review Platforms

Almost any website that sells products can integrate product reviews into its shopping experience. This can be done by setting up the review collection and display features that come with your e-commerce platform (or its compatible add-ons), or by integrating a social commerce platform such as Bazaarvoice or Reevoo. Social commerce platforms may be the biggest review venue that you haven't heard of. From the consumer's point of view, the platforms are often invisible, because the reviews that they host are seamlessly integrated into the design of product pages on e-commerce sites.

Product reviews collected on your site will not make their way onto review sites like Yelp and TripAdvisor. But they reach far and wide, and Bazaarvoice in particular is a behemoth. In a 2013 keynote speech, Bazaarvoice's CEO and President Stephen Collins claimed that Bazaarvoice connects monthly with 400 million unique shoppers worldwide and described Bazaarvoice as the world's largest consumer network. Table 2.3 shows platforms that handle product reviews.

Examples of social commerce and product review platforms	Bazaarvoice
	Reevoo
	Feefo
	Pluck
	eKomi
	PowerReviews (acquired by Bazaarvoice)
	Google Shopping
	Review functionality features of e-commerce platforms such as Shopify or Volusion
Who is reviewed?	Primarily products.
Where they stand on businesses encouraging reviews	Asking customers for reviews is a key service offering of many social commerce platforms.
Where reviews are seen	Product reviews, Q&A, and other user-generated content are displayed on product pages on retailers' or manufacturers' websites where products are sold. Product reviews from various sources are displayed in the Google Shopping interface.
How they work with businesses	Social commerce and product review platforms are integrated with e-commerce websites and connect with your customers to encourage new reviews, as well as discussion and interaction around your products. They can require extensive implementation with varying features and fees.

How They Work

When a store or manufacturer hires a social commerce company or implements review functionality from their e-commerce platform, software is integrated on their website to perform some or all of the following functions:

- Send post-purchase emails to customers
- Collect verification information from reviewers and purchasers
- Moderate reviews
- Populate the reviews onto the seller's or manufacturer's website
- Provide insights, alerts, and communication pathways that allow businesses to better understand and engage with their customers
- Control the display of reviews and other user-generated content

Features vary widely among product review platforms. Some include only basic review capabilities, while others—sometimes giving themselves the "social commerce" moniker—offer a more sophisticated social platform, providing a technical backbone for brands or retailers to strategically place opportunities in front of customers to read and write reviews, ask a question, or otherwise connect around a product.

Even if your business is small, don't assume you can't afford to have product reviews on your site. Platforms known for high-end enterprise integration often offer solutions with prices that are within reach for small business.

Gathering Reviews

Many of these platforms gather product reviews by sending post-purchase emails to customers. In some cases, site visitors can initiate the reviewing process by navigating to product pages on e-commerce sites that have integrated product review platforms and then clicking a "write a review" link. Some benefits of this type of review-gathering process include:

Authenticity Details vary among implementations, but many social commerce companies tend to claim that real customers (or at least, real people) are behind the reviews they collect. Bazaarvoice displays verified buyer and verified reviewer badges next to certain reviews, while Reevoo and Feefo claim that all of their reviews come from verified buyers. Moderation features are available, ranging from automated removal of inappropriate content such as spam or vulgarity to manual review and removal by the business.

High Volume By connecting directly with customers and grabbing their opinions while their recent purchase is top of mind, these platforms can drive an increase in review volume that would be difficult to replicate using your own labor. And these services claim that because they gather reviews from a cross-section of customers, not just those self-selecting reviewers seeking out an opportunity to offload the bees in their bonnets onto your product page, your reviews are more likely to skew toward the positive.

Visibility for the Reviews

One big advantage of using social commerce and product review platforms is that the reviews they collect are integrated into the seller's or manufacturer's website (see Figure 2.8). Study after study has shown the benefits of customer reviews on e-commerce sites: Reevoo reports that reviews result in an 18% average uplift in sales, and an iPerceptions study found that 63% of customers are more likely to make a purchase from a site with user reviews. Marketers call this effect *social proof*, which is a fancy way of saying that people do what they see other people doing.

Many social commerce platforms claim that the reviews they generate are great for SEO, improving ranks and search engine traffic to product pages. The logic behind this claim is that the search engines tend to favor pages with fresh content, so the constant influx of new review text will be a boon for a product page's ranks. We don't disagree with this in principle, but we don't think you'll achieve your SEO goals with online reviews alone.

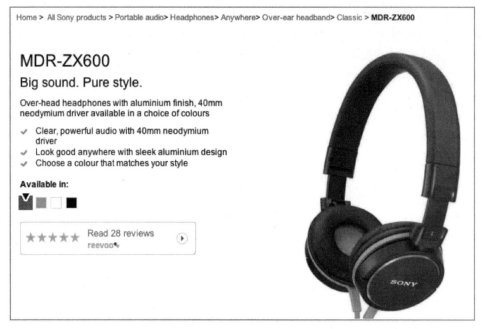

Home > All Sony products > Portable audio> Headphones> Anywhere> Over-ear headband> Classic > **MDR-ZX600**

MDR-ZX600
Big sound. Pure style.

Over-head headphones with aluminium finish, 40mm neodymium driver available in a choice of colours

✔ Clear, powerful audio with 40mm neodymium driver
✔ Look good anywhere with sleek aluminium design
✔ Choose a colour that matches your style

Available in:

★ ★ ★ ★ ★   Read 28 reviews
reevoo

Figure 2.8   Reviews from Reevoo integrated into a product page on sony.co.uk

Social commerce platforms tend to make strong claims about SEO benefits, and we encourage you to take this talk with a grain of salt.

E-Commerce Merchant Review Collection Services

For companies hoping to jump-start the collection, display, and management of online merchant reviews, e-commerce review collection services offer some reasonably affordable and practical options. Table 2.4 shows a partial list of companies offering e-commerce review collection.

▶ **Table 2.4**   E-commerce merchant review collection services

Examples of e-commerce merchant review collection platforms	ResellerRatings
	Shopper Approved
	Trustpilot
	RateItAll
	eKomi
	Google Wallet
	BizRate Insights
	Reviews.co.uk
Who is reviewed?	Primarily e-commerce retailers, although some services review travel and local businesses. True to its name, RateItAll allows reviews of anything from jelly beans to Julius Caesar.

Continues

Where they stand on businesses encouraging reviews	Most offer customer outreach/review solicitation as a service.
Where reviews are seen	Reviews reside off your site on review destination pages managed by the service. Reviews can also show up in Google Shopping pages and in Google AdWords seller rating extensions.
How they work with businesses	Some allow businesses to get reviewed without taking any steps, whereas others require a paid account. Businesses must pay for customer outreach and other features. Google Wallet's review collection tools are a small component of its integrated e-commerce system.

How They Work

E-commerce merchant review collection services offer a variety of options, but in general, they provide tools to help businesses collect reviews from customers, widgets or badges to link to these reviews, and opportunities for responding to reviewers. Monthly fees can be low—or even free—but scale up based on review volume and other factors. These services may be particularly appealing to companies that advertise in Google Shopping and Google AdWords, where reviews may receive a lovely visibility boost (see "Visibility for Reviews," later in the chapter).

All of these services can help you collect reviews via your website or purchase process, whereas some, such as ResellerRatings, supplement this proactivity with passive review collection that takes place on their own publicly accessible review site. Google Wallet is a horse of a different color, offering not only review collection services but also sophisticated online and mobile in-store payment solutions for merchants.

Some reputation management services (described later in this chapter) also act as third-party collection services. In contrast to many reputation management services, e-commerce review collection services do not allow a business to moderate reviews or control which customers are approached for reviews, although they may offer a buffer period before reviews are published, during which businesses may be able to contact the reviewer.

Gathering Reviews

In a typical paid implementation, these services integrate with your purchase confirmation process to help you collect reviews of your company from customers who have engaged in recent transactions. These services can be quick and easy to implement. For example, some simply require you to paste a special email address into the BCC field of your customer emails, and they do the rest, reaching out to customers post-purchase and encouraging reviews. The "real person" factor varies greatly from service to service, with some allowing reviews from anyone who stumbles across the "post a review" link, and others requiring purchase verification. Most provide some ability for businesses to respond to reviews, either by posting online or by emailing the reviewer directly.

Social Media Commentary: Reviews in Real Time

Here's a familiar scenario: A woman has a mediocre repast at an overpriced coffee shop and tweets about it:

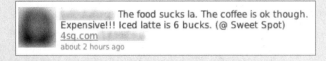

The food sucks la. The coffee is ok though.
Expensive!!! Iced latte is 6 bucks. (@ Sweet Spot)
4sq.com
about 2 hours ago

Opinions on the social web are real reviews, even if they are not curated, regulated, and aggregated in the same ways that reviews are on other venues. Social commentary is seen primarily by people who are connected to the reviewer, and studies show that that "someone I trust" is commonly identified as one of the most influential factors in making a purchase decision.

Here are some venues where that special someone can leave a social media review:

- Popped into the customer's own Facebook status. These are likely to be invisible to you, but plenty visible to the commenter's friends.

- Dropped onto your business's Facebook page. These are easy for you to find, and just as easy for prospective customers to see.

- Uploaded onto YouTube as a video that might be one keyword search away from the eyes of a stranger.

- Tucked into a check-in on Foursquare, where anyone who wanders by can enjoy reading tips about your business.

- Tossed onto Twitter in the form of a tweet that mentions your Twitter handle or your company or product names. Tweets can be seen publicly, although direct messages (DMs) cannot.

- Cross-posted from one medium to another. This is the case with the pictured tweet, in which a tip originated in Foursquare but was published on Twitter.

A positive and engaged social following matters in terms of both word-of-mouth and sales. A 2011 study by Chadwick Martin Bailey found that Facebook fans and Twitter followers are more likely to recommend a brand to a friend, and purchase from a brand, after liking or following the brand. But when compared to other factors, social media reviews are not quite (or maybe not yet) a force to be reckoned with. A 2013 study by Baynote of holiday shoppers found that social media was less influential than online reviews—less influential even than print catalogs!—in influencing purchasing decisions. (Per this study, the age group most likely to be influenced by social media was 25–34.)

Social media commentary can be ephemeral, but comments can add up over time to create a positive or negative impression. And of course, unlike more static online reviews, they have the potential to go viral (can you say "United breaks guitars?"). Depending on how socially connected your customer base is, you may need to put a little or a lot of effort into monitoring, encouraging, and responding to reviews on the social web.

Be warned: Reviews gathered by these services or using their tools are not necessarily the property of your business. Once you cancel your subscription, reviews may even be removed. You may not be able to respond to your business's reviews unless you are an active subscriber to the service. Before you sign up with a service, it's worth your while to investigate what will happen once you cancel your monthly fee.

Visibility for Reviews

There are several ways that reviews gathered by e-commerce collection services can be seen online:

Standalone Review Sites Consumers can search or browse reviews for thousands of companies on sites like www.resellerratings.com or www.trustpilot.com. Typically, these sites follow the Yelp-like practice of letting anyone create business listings and allowing businesses to verify their listings but not delete them.

Review Pages Linked from Your Site The reviews you collect through these services do not reside on your site. Typically, businesses can add a widget or a badge to their site that links to a special reviews page on the review collection service's domain. Figure 2.9 shows a Shopper Approved badge.

Integration into Google Shopping and AdWords Reviews from many of these services can be collected by Google and aggregated into its Google Shopping Seller Ratings (see Figure 2.10) as well as displayed as star ratings in AdWords ads. This Google integration amplifies their visibility and influence.

Figure 2.9 The Shopper Approved badge adds a trust signal to an e-commerce site.

```
eBags

Seller rating: 4.7 / 5 - Based on 373 reviews from the past 12 months

What people are saying
price                      ▌▌▌▌▌    "Good site, fast response and great prices!"
customer service           ▌▌▌▌     "Great bag and great service."
shipping                   ▌▌▌▌     "Super Fast shipping!!!"
selection                  ▌▌▌▌     "Fast, good selection."
ordering process           ▌▌▌▌     "Very good and smooth transaction."
return policy              ▌▌▌      "Good return policy and easy of returns."
packaging                  ▌▌▌      "They are a great way to organize when packing."


★★★★★   Timely delivery                                           Show reviews by rating
5 / 5    By Samrat - Feb 19, 2013 - Google Wallet Reviews
                                                                   1 star (368)
         Was this review helpful? Yes - No                         2 stars (188)
                                                                   3 stars (458)
                                                                   4 stars (1,874)
★★★★★   Excellent. They delivered in perfect condition exactly when they said they would.   5 stars (10,374)
5 / 5    By Don - Feb 27, 2013 - Google Wallet Reviews
                                                                   Sort reviews
         Was this review helpful? Yes - No
                                                                   Sort by relevance
                                                                   Sort by date
★★★★★   Very efficient and expeditious transaction! Great products at very reasonable prices. A repeat
5 / 5    customer, we will be back for additional travel and similar needs!   Show reviews by source
         By STEVEC - Feb 26, 2013 - Google Wallet Reviews
                                                                   Bizrate (423)
         Was this review helpful? Yes - No                         Ciao UK (1)
                                                                   Epinions (280)
                                                                   Google Wallet Reviews (11999)
                                                                   PriceGrabber.com (351)
★★★★★   "Don't hesitate to order from this company!! I have ordered many items online and have   ResellerRatings.com (128)
5 / 5    never had such a quick response . I ordered and received exactly what I... Read full review   TRUSTPILOT (22)
         By Jhurney - Jan 3, 2013 - ResellerRatings.com            Viewpoints (44)
                                                                   Yahoo! (28)
         Was this review helpful? Yes - No
```

Figure 2.10 Google Shopping seller ratings for eBags are aggregated from numerous sites and review collection services.

Shopping Comparison Sites and Online Travel Agents

Comparison sites like Shopping.com, Epinions, and NexTag, and OTAs like Orbitz, Expedia, and Booking.com, offer customers a convenient way to compare products for sale from different providers side by side. One way these sites add value is by displaying customer reviews so site visitors can feel great about making an informed purchasing decision. Table 2.5 provides a partial list of shopping sites and OTAs.

▶ **Table 2.5** Shopping comparison sites and OTAs

Examples of shopping comparison sites and online travel agents	Bizrate
	Shopping.com
	NexTag
	Google Shopping
	Orbitz
	Travelocity
	Expedia
	Hotels.com
Who is reviewed?	E-commerce retailers, products, hotels, cruises.

Continues

Where they stand on businesses encouraging reviews	All for it! These services generally seek reviews after the transaction.
Where reviews are seen	Reviews are primarily seen in the shopping site or OTA interfaces.
How they work with businesses	Businesses that pay to sell products or services via these sites have the opportunity to be reviewed there; Bizrate also offers a free option.

How They Work

To be listed in a shopping comparison site or OTA, providers must have a relationship with the site. For shopping comparison sites, the relationship is simple to set up: A retailer signs on the dotted line and submits a product feed to the shopping site. When a customer clicks from the comparison site to the retailer, the retailer pays a fee, usually calculated on a pay-per-click basis. In most cases a retailer must sell products via the comparison shopping site in order to be included there.

OTAs run on a similar model in which providers such as hotels, cruise lines, and tour operators pay a commission to the OTA on any transaction that the OTA completes on their behalf (through some sort of negotiation wizardry, airlines and car rental agencies get a free ride and don't pay these commissions). One big difference between OTAs and comparison shopping sites is that OTAs complete the transaction themselves, rather than passing the customer over to the service provider. In other words, if the Griswold family books a hotel through Orbitz, then they pay Orbitz, and Orbitz pays the hotel. If the Griswolds have a complaint or accolade to share, they may be confused about whether to communicate it to Orbitz or the hotel manager.

Shopping comparison and OTA sites make money by maximizing the volume of traffic and sales that visitors initiate from their sites, and research shows that a person is more likely to convert from a "looky-loo" to a purchaser after reading reviews. It doesn't take a rocket scientist to connect the dots: More reviews mean more revenue for the shopping comparison or OTA site. And they know it: According to research by PhoCusWright, OTAs have become aggressive about pursuing additional customer reviews on their sites, and as a result, more than two-thirds of all hotel reviews were posted on OTAs in 2010. Expedia alone reported that it had over 7.5 million guest reviews in 2012, with 500,000 new ones added per year.

Gathering Reviews

Merchants who sign up to list products on a comparison shopping site usually have the opportunity to set up a customer feedback component. This system reaches out to buyers immediately after the sale, and again after the expected delivery date, to request that the customer post a review.

Google Shopping is a special case: It is essentially a comparison shopping site integrated into Google search results. Merchants create product listings by providing a feed via Google AdWords, and pay on a per-click basis each time a visitor clicks on a product listing. However, unlike other comparison shopping sites, Google Shopping does not reach out to request reviews from buyers after the purchase is complete. Instead, Google Shopping displays product reviews that merchants have gathered on their own sites. Because the same product can be sold by several different vendors, Google Shopping sometimes aggregates product reviews from more than one seller. In Figure 2.11, Google Shopping shows reviews for a digital camera available from both Best Buy and Adorama.

> **Nikon D3200 24.2 MP Digital SLR Camera - Black - AF-S VR DX 18-55mm lens**
> $480 online   ★★★★★ 228 reviews
>
> ---
>
>   - Full review provided by ⬡ Best Buy
> ★★★★★ **Great Camera** - Nov 3, 2012
>
> Pros: Picture Quality, Lens Options, Pictures per second
>
> Cons: Kit lens could be better, but still not bad
>
> So far I love it. I'm a novice when it comes to taking pictures, so the auto feature is great. One of my neighbors has the 3100, so he was able to show me quite a bit about the camera that i would have otherwise not known. Once he pointed a few things out to me, my manual pictures are starting to turn out a lot better. I don't know enough about it to point out any negative features, but so far i have been very impressed. I can't wait to go shoot some deer with it!
>
> I went to an airshow the first weekend after purchasing, and even at a pretty good distance the planes look pretty crisp. The pictures per second is fast enough that it almost looks like a video in rapid ...
> expand »
>
> Helpful?   Yes   No
>
> ---
>
>   - Full review provided by ⬡ Adorama
> ★★★★★ **Fantastic Value For The Money,** - Aug 30, 2012
>
> Pros: Good Image Quality; Large Clear LCD; Quiet; Fast / Accurate Auto-Focus; Fast Shutter Speed; Easy To Use; Good Image Stabilization
>
> Image quality is just wonderful! I have been very favorably impressed with the camera in terms of the final image product that it produces. Even the 18-55mm lens, at F/8 turns out really great images. Put on some really sharp glass and the image quality just keeps getting better. Fantastic enlargements (16x20 and beyond are possible) with little if any post processing. Even major cropping, depending on subject material, while using really sharp optics, will still yield a nice 16x20 print. I wish there was a higher capacity battery, however, I realize that would have necessitated a larger camera body in some way. I typically shoot at ISO 400, beca ...
> expand »

Figure 2.11 Product reviews displayed in Google Shopping results

OTAs follow yet another procedure for building their portfolio of customer reviews. Because OTAs complete transactions in a direct relationship with customers, they have easy access for gathering reviews. OTAs will typically follow up a customer's hotel stay with a feedback survey sent via email. OTA reviews come from verified purchasers, so they get bonus points in the credibility department.

Visibility for Reviews

Customer product reviews are integrated with the shopping experience on shopping comparison sites, looking and behaving like product reviews that you've seen on individual retailer sites. An example of a product page on Shopping.com featuring reviews is shown in Figure 2.12.

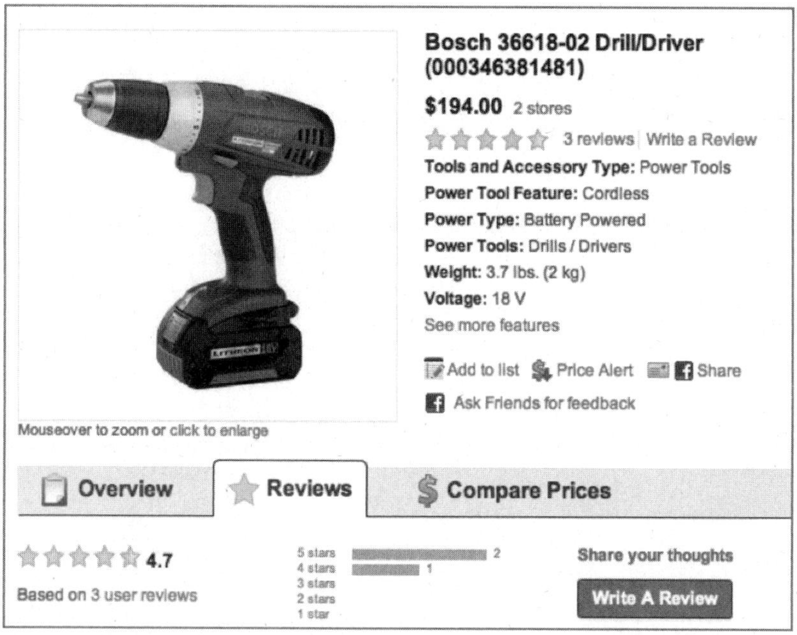

Figure 2.12 Product reviews on Shopping.com

In addition to product reviews, customers can leave seller reviews to describe their experience with a retailer's customer service. With this info, a customer might decide that a rock-bottom price isn't worth the risk of buying from a 1-star seller. Seller ratings can be seen on PriceGrabber.com in Figure 2.13.

Online travel agencies show reviews on hotel profile pages and throughout the site, as seen in Figure 2.14.

Figure 2.13 Seller ratings on PriceGrabber.com

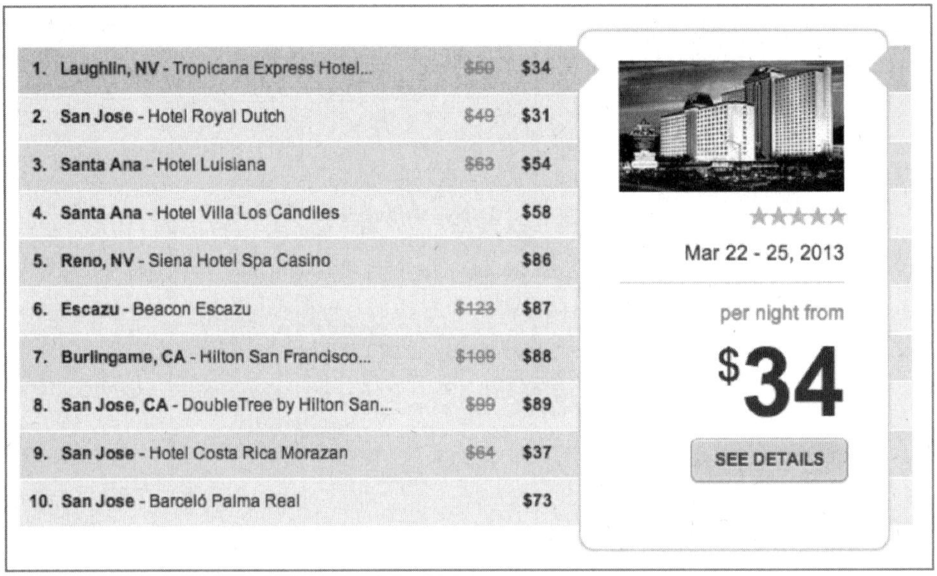

Figure 2.14 Hotel reviews on Expedia

Seller ratings posted on shopping comparison sites can find their way into Google Shopping, as you saw in Figure 2.10, and Google also throws these reviews into its calculation for star ratings in AdWords ads. Shopping comparison sites also feature prominently in Bing paid search results, as shown in Figure 2.15.

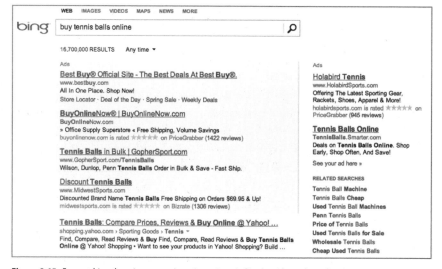

Figure 2.15 Eye-catching shopping comparison site reviews in Bing's paid search results

Reputation Management Services

You're probably reading this book because you're feeling some level of concern about your online reputation; perhaps for that very same reason, your curiosity has been tickled by ads from reputation management companies such as Reputation.com, Customer Lobby, and Demandforce. Among other things, these firms give customers the opportunity to bulk up on customer reviews and gain some control over the gathering and display of their reviews. Table 2.6 shows features of reputation management services.

▶ **Table 2.6** Reputation management services

Examples of companies offering reputation management services	Reputation.com Customer Lobby Demandforce Presto Reviews Genbook
Who is reviewed?	Primarily brick-and-mortar businesses, but a growing number of services exist for e-commerce sites and brands as well.
Where they stand on businesses encouraging reviews	All for it! Encouraging reviews is at the heart of their offerings.
Where reviews are seen	Posted on the business's own website and on the reputation management service's site. Reviews can show up in search results and may be syndicated to other review sites as well.
How they work with businesses	Businesses hire these services to help them monitor and generate reviews. Reputation management may also be part of a broader service, such as appointment management.

How They Work

With offerings ranging from automated tools to consulting services, these companies are difficult to lump together into a single category. Similar to the e-commerce review collection services described earlier in this chapter, these firms often function as third-party review collection services. However, reputation management comes into play with additional services such as syndicating reviews to review aggregator sites, strategically encouraging customers to post reviews in certain venues, and, in some cases, providing business owners with control over the review content that is published.

The relationship between a business and a reputation management company begins when the business signs up for a service package. The charge is likely to be a flat monthly fee for access to a suite of tools, which can start under $100 but can get quite pricey when optional add-ons such as consulting services are purchased.

Gathering Reviews

Businesses that sign up with this type of service will usually get a profile page on the service's website. This page displays reviews that can be collected in a number of ways, including email solicitations, in-house collection (for example, on a smartphone or a kiosk), or via a survey by phone or mail. Figure 2.16 shows a profile page for a mechanic on the Customer Lobby website.

Figure 2.16 Customer Lobby business profile page

Typically, a business has no control over which reviews get published and which don't. But some services offer measures of control that are a bit more business-centric than you'll find elsewhere in the reviewscape. For example, a business may be able to challenge a review it doesn't think is real, clear up a problem and request withdrawal of a negative review, or even specify which customers it wants the reputation management service to approach when seeking reviews.

Although most of these services do not offer outright rejection of reviews, some do, and this, along with some of the more outrageous promises made by a few unscrupulous firms, is one reason that reputation management services tend to have reputation management issues of their own.

Details of the review-gathering process vary among the various reputation management firms. Reputation.com offers a smartphone-based system for on-location review gathering. At Genbook and Demandforce, review gathering is integrated into an appointment management system—a good choice for service providers such as dentists and hair salons. Presto Reviews even offers a freestanding reviews kiosk, as seen in Figure 2.17.

Figure 2.17 Presto Reviews kiosk

Some reputation management firms take review gathering a step further by posting reviews on behalf of customers. For example, a company may send out survey cards to customers and then "digitize" them by posting onto Google+ Local or other review sites. Google explicitly warns against this practice. We believe the reputation management services we've named in this chapter don't do this, but be sure to double-check when you're hiring.

Despite the variations between services, the basic foundation remains the same for them all: Your business gains a system for requesting reviews from customers and also gains some degree of control over the customer review-gathering and display process.

Visibility for Reviews

So you've signed on with a reputation management service and your collection of customer reviews is growing fast! Congratulations—but who is seeing the reviews? Although reputation management services would like you to think that these reviews are being published far and wide on the Internet, the truth is that visibility can be a bit more limited. Here are places where potential customers can see these reviews:

Linked from Your Site and Social Media Properties Like other third-party review gathering services discussed in this chapter, these services typically post your reviews onto their own site and offer a widget or badge for businesses to post links to their reviews, as seen here:

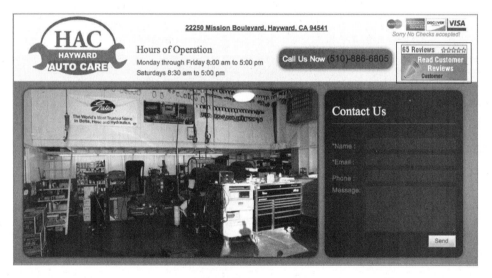

Similarly, new reviews can be published to a Facebook or Twitter account that you control or that the service makes on your behalf.

Reviews are a fantastic trust signal, and positive reviews displayed prominently on your site can help turn a buyer's decision in your direction.

 If you engage in the practice of curating or rejecting negative reviews, most of your site visitors probably won't know it, so this is not necessarily the most authentic and transparent business practice you can undertake. And savvy shoppers can figure it out—all it takes is a quick comparison of your posted reviews against a less malleable site like Yelp, and your customers' trust in you could be eroded.

On the Reputation Management Company's Site Reputation management firms generally post reviews on a profile page within their domain, such as demandforce.com/b/zanyaspasalon, or they will assist clients with creating a domain specifically to hold reviews, such as frankmyersautoreviews.com.

In Search Engine Results One of the major goals of reputation management services is to flood search results with positive information about their clients. Like any other page on the Web, review pages generated by reputation management services can be indexed by search engines and show up in results. Figure 2.18 shows an example of Demandforce reviews in Google results.

Queen Anne Eye Clinic
www.qaeye.com/
Your eyes work hard for you, all day, every day. At **Queen Anne Eye Clinic**, we give your eyes the care and attention they deserve, with comprehensive eye ...
4 Google reviews · Write a review

20 Boston St Seattle, WA 98109
(206) 282-8120

Contact us
Phone (206) 282-8120. Fax (206) 282-8046. Phone Queen Anne ...

The Doctors
Dr. Eric Bergstrom grew up in the Chicagoland area before ...

About Our Clinic
Queen Anne Eye Clinic provides high quality, personalized eye ...

Welcome to the Office Form
Queen Anne Eye Clinic. Eric J. Bergstrom, O.D.. Philip Lo, O.D ...

More results from qaeye.com »

Queen Anne Eye Clinic - Queen Anne - Seattle, WA
www.yelp.com › Health & Medical › Optometrists
★★★★☆ Rating: 4.5 - 22 reviews - Price range: $$
22 Reviews of **Queen Anne Eye Clinic** "**Queen Anne Eye Clinic** is the best experience I've ever had with any type of doctor or clinic anywhere ever, in a nut shell.

City Eye Care - Queen Anne - Seattle, WA
www.yelp.com › Health & Medical › Optometrists
★★★☆☆ Rating: 3.5 - 9 reviews - Price range: $$$
9 Reviews of City **Eye Care** "Dr. Dubicki and his team took great **care** of me. The combination of staring at a computer all day and turning 40 I thought it would be ...

Queen Anne Eye Clinic - Seattle, WA - 98109 - (206) 282-8120 ...
www.demandforce.com › ... › Washington › Seattle › Optometrists
★★★★★ Rating: 5 - 158 reviews
Queen Anne Eye Clinic provides high quality, personalized eye care to people of all ages and walks of life. Both Dr. Bergstrom and Dr. Lo, along with their ...

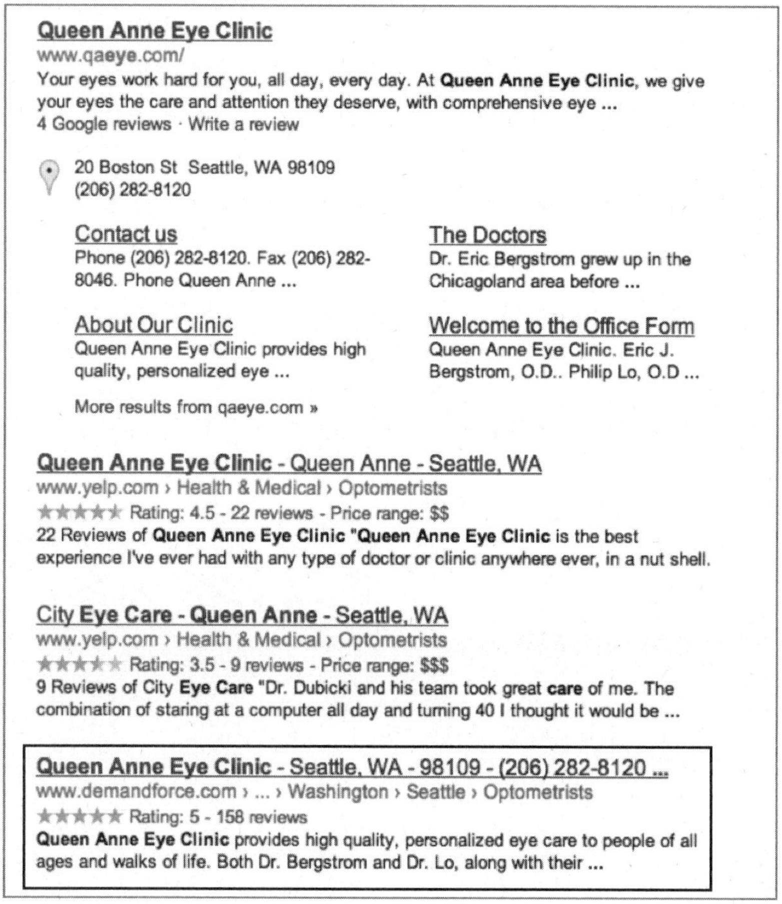

Figure 2.18 Demandforce reviews in Google results

Despite what some reputation management companies may proclaim, they do not have "partnerships" or other special relations with Google, Yahoo!, or Bing. Your review pages will compete in search results just like any other page.

Syndicated on Other Review Sites Reputation management firms have relationships with other review sites that allow them to expand the reach of your reviews. For example, reviews posted via Customer Lobby are purportedly percolated onto Citysearch, Judy's Book, Kudzu, and others. Figure 2.19 shows customer reviews that were generated in Demandforce being displayed in Judy's Book.

This syndication can be a helpful source of new eyeballs looking at your reviews.

Other Reviews for FoxFire Salon & Spa

NO PHOTO **"Great"**
☆☆☆☆☆ **by anonymous at Demandforce**

Provided by Demandforce

Wonderful experience and extremely happy with my hair. Would recommend Brittney to anyone! More >

Was this review helpful to you? Yes (0) | No (0) | Permalink

NO PHOTO **"A wonderful experience"**
☆☆☆☆☆ **by ▮▮▮ at Demandforce**

Provided by Demandforce

So appreciative of the staff, especially Topie and Theresa. Make me feel wonderful, worth every minute! A Merry Christmas to all! More >

Was this review helpful to you? Yes (0) | No (0) | Permalink

NO PHOTO **"appointment"**
☆☆☆☆☆ **by ▮▮▮ at Demandforce**

Provided by Demandforce

Always love coming there. Good atmosphere. Each girl is their own artist and feels confident about their work. Brittany does my hair and I just love... More >

Was this review helpful to you? Yes (0) | No (0) | Permalink

Figure 2.19 Demandforce reviews syndicated to Judy's Book

Local Search

The local search venues described in this section are not standalone sites. They exist as the local business listings—complete with owners' profiles, customers' reviews, and pins on a map—within major search engines. Search engines get a chance to show off their local business listings every time a searcher's query has a local-business focus. For example, <locksmith> and <plumber> typed into Google's search box will bring up local results, as will <lawyer san diego> and <schools 02134>. With growing visibility of business listings and reviews in search results, local search is a major channel for both customer acquisition and online reputation. Table 2.7 shows features of local search venues.

▶ **Table 2.7** Local search venues

Examples of local search venues	Google+ Local Yahoo! Local
Who is reviewed?	Brick-and-mortar businesses and businesses whose workers travel to local customers.
Where they stand on businesses encouraging reviews	Generally okay with encouraging reviews, although Google frowns on incentivizing reviews or in-store collection of reviews by business owners.
Where reviews are seen	Search engine results and mobile apps.
How they work with businesses	Businesses can create or claim a free listing. Google offers free reporting tools and listing enhancements such as photos, videos, and promotional offers. Yahoo! Local offers similar reporting and enhancements for a monthly fee.

The local search reviewscape is dominated by Google, as all things involving search are. Smaller player Yahoo! Local (`http://local.yahoo.com`) is one feature that still remains vibrant within the Yahoo! brand.

Bing local search reviews are powered by Yelp at this writing, so Bing doesn't belong in the local search discussion today. (Fun fact: Google tried and failed to buy Yelp before building the local service it has now.) Smart money has Bing integrating the recommendation engine Facebook Graph Search into its search results in the near future.

Reviews on Google+ Local and Yahoo! Local can be highly visible. Due to their prominence on mobile devices, they can reach prospective customers at crucial moments in the decision-making process. It's typically a good idea to keep a close eye on these reviews.

How They Work

Like Yelp and other review sites discussed in this chapter, local search venues are fundamentally a collection of local business profiles with associated customer reviews. Local businesses can create a listing, but these sites also commonly generate listings without the business's knowledge or approval. Businesses can claim their listing to add supplementary information—we'll walk you through the process for Google+ Local in Chapter 6, "Review Venues: Need-to-Know Tips for Your Action Plan."

Local search review venues deserve your special attention because of their strong integration with the search engines. Whereas review sites tend to be standalone entities, Google+ Local reviews are integrated into its large, dynamic, and heavily trafficked search engine and apps, making it easier for these reviews to gain visibility both intentionally and serendipitously. See Figure 2.20 for an example of how reviews are integrated into a Google search result.

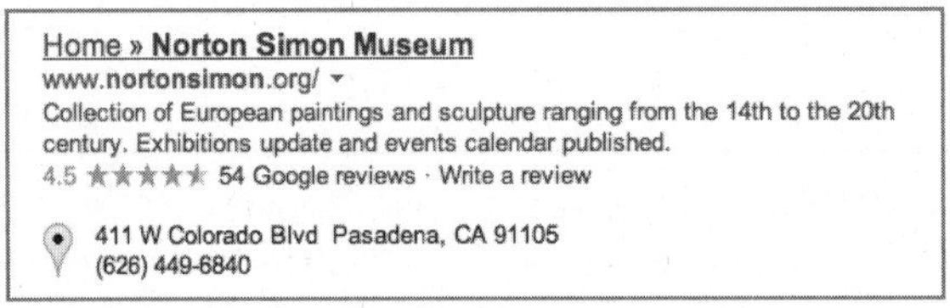

Home » **Norton Simon Museum**
www.nortonsimon.org/ ▾
Collection of European paintings and sculpture ranging from the 14th to the 20th century. Exhibitions update and events calendar published.
4.5 ★★★★★ 54 Google reviews · Write a review

411 W Colorado Blvd Pasadena, CA 91105
(626) 449-6840

Figure 2.20 This Google search result for the Norton Simon Museum incorporates review stars as well as links to read and write reviews.

As a result of the prominence of local listings within search results and businesses' inevitable lust for influence over this presence, an entire industry has sprung up around local search engine optimization. Local SEO encompasses efforts (some of which you'll learn about in this book) to improve ranks and listing quality for locally oriented searches.

Like most review sites, local search venues do not provide robust troubleshooting or mediation services for business owners looking for help with the reviews on their free listings. Their primary job is to serve their audience: the searching public, yearning for easy-to-find, comprehensive, and trustworthy local business information. And like review sites, local search venues are always happy to accept advertising dollars from business owners. We'll visit Google+ Local advertising options in Chapter 6.

Gathering Reviews

For Google, the container for its local business reviews is its social network called Google+ (pronounced "Google plus"). Google's local business listings have undergone such rapid evolution that, in addition to the current name (Google+ Local) you may still find people referring to them as Google Maps or Google Places. Business listings are created within Google+ and reviewers must be signed in with a Google+ account and use a real name. Far from an exclusive club, Google+ has accounts numbering in the hundreds of millions.

Google+ Local and Yahoo! Local count on strong search and social integration to encourage reviews. They recognize but don't particularly relish the fact that businesses will solicit reviews from customers. To bulk up its review library, Google+ Local also incorporates scores and summaries from venerable local ratings company Zagat (which Google owns) and links to a large number of sources such as Urbanspoon, Foursquare, Judy's Book, and Demandforce.

Visibility for Reviews

Google did not arrive first to the reviews game, but it has successfully insinuated itself onto the playing field. Whether the intention of the searcher is to find a business's address and phone number or to locate a Yelp review, there's a good chance that Google will serve up its own review elements in search results. Google+ Local content will often be ranked higher, formatted more attractively, and presented in a more invitingly clickable way than listings from any competing local review site. See Figure 2.21 for an example.

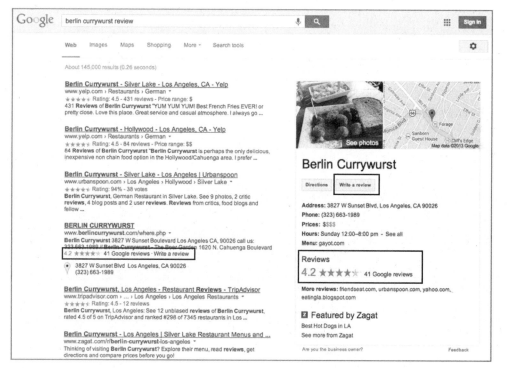

Figure 2.21 For the search query: <berlin currywurst review>, Google gives Yelp first billing but displays its own local review results in two other graphics-rich and colorful listings on the same page.

In 2011 Marissa Mayer, then Google's Vice President of Location and Local Services, said that 20% of Google searches are looking for local information (SEOs call this *local intent*). This number skyrockets to 50% or more in mobile search. With local info such a key interest for searchers, Google and Yahoo! are going to keep doing what they can to get the right stuff—not the least of which is reviews—front and center in search results.

As you may have guessed by now, you will probably need to analyze and engage with more than one venue in order to effectively monitor and manage your own online reviews. We hope you've got a general idea of opportunities that are well matched to your business, but we won't leave you with generalities! In Chapter 4, "Monitoring and Learning from Your Reviews," we'll show you how to identify specific venues that matter most for your business.

Fake Reviews

Consumers place a growing level of trust in online reviews, but is this trust deserved? With the explosive growth of online reviews and their unmistakable power to uplift or damage a business, inevitably some bad eggs are trying to cheat the system. Review sites like Yelp and Google+ Local are fighting back with every weapon they've got, both legal and algorithmic. As you boldly dive into your online reviews space, you may come face to face with fake reviews. And, let's be real, you might even be tempted to cross over to the dark side and generate some fake reviews yourself. Read on, and you'll be well versed in the who, what, and why of fake reviews.

The Scale of Fake Reviews

Bing Liu knows a little bit about fake reviews. He's a computer science professor at University of Illinois at Chicago, and he has been studying them for decades. When we spoke with Professor Liu, he shared a surprising piece of information with us: He estimates that *30% of online reviews are fake.*

Not every business or product will have this level of online shenanigans, but the alarmingly high 30% level is Liu's estimate for an overall average, based on his research. Gartner research puts the number lower, at 10%–15%. The highest estimate of the prevalence of fake online reviews we've seen is 40%, as estimated by HotelMe.com, specifically in the category of hotel reviews. Any way you slice it, the number of online reviews that are not genuine is much higher than most people realize.

The most common fake online reviews are positive ones that have been written or commissioned by the business itself. Businesses have so much to gain from positive reviews that the temptation to bend the rules and add a few positive reviews for themselves is strong. Anecdotal stories of fake online reviews abound: As far back as 2009, a cosmetic surgery company was busted by the State of New York for sending emails to employees instructing them to pose as satisfied customers online. An entrepreneurial if ethics-challenged fellow named Todd Rutherford unapologetically ran a bustling business writing fake Amazon reviews at the low price of 50 for $499. And online magazine Eater.com even runs a blog called Adventures in Shilling to publicly call out fake-looking restaurant reviews. Despite the fakery, trust in online reviews is growing, and according to a 2012 survey by LateRooms.com, 45% of consumers believe the reviews they read are real.

Fake negative reviews are much rarer than fake positive ones and do not seem to be the focus of the paid services that offer to write reviews on demand. If you think you're seeing a fake negative online review, it could be the handiwork of an individual with a vendetta or a competitor on a crusade. If your business has been victimized, either by a completely fake review posted by a competitor, or by a real but dishonest or inaccurate review posted by an actual customer, you may have some recourse. We'll discuss some options in Chapters 6 and 7.

Love for Sale

As the free market economy would have it, opportunistic companies have sprung up to cater to some businesses' desire for glowing reviews. Figure 2.22 shows an ad for an online review creation service that violates the terms of service for every review venue you should care about.

Figure 2.22 Advertisement for online review writing service

We don't think anyone knows exactly who is purchasing fake reviews, but Bing Liu's best guess is that mostly smaller businesses use these services, not large brands. Any company with a legal department probably has someone in a suit wisely putting the kibosh on this idea.

Small businesses, on the other hand, may not be sufficiently savvy to know the downside of faking online reviews. Feeling desperate and vulnerable is not the best condition under which to make a decision, and we beg you not to purchase fake reviews if this describes your mood right now.

Here are a few pros and cons of faking online reviews:

PRO Your business could see a lift in sales as a result of the fake online reviews.

CON Your business could get caught and publicly exposed (see the sidebar "Yelp's Sting Operation") or otherwise punished by the review site.

CON Your business misses out on the opportunity to genuinely improve in ways that will earn real reviews.

CON If your deception were to be exposed, your business reputation would suffer severe damage. And even if you're not publicly exposed, potential customers might sniff out the fakes and be turned off.

CON Customers with 5-star expectations will be sorely disappointed by a 2-star experience. A mismatch between expectations and experience is one of the triggers that cause people to write reviews, and you can bet those won't be good ones.

CON Did we mention that posting fake reviews violates the Federal Trade Commission Act?

We hope the cons listed here are convincing enough to dissuade you from commissioning fake reviews for your business. If you're dead set on purchasing fake reviews no matter what you read in this book, don't say we didn't warn you! We suggest that you dedicate at least a month to working on improving your genuine online reputation first. And for the sake of your business, be sure you continue to do the good work you need to also gain real ones.

On one end of the spectrum, some businesses are commissioning totally fake reviews. On the other end, some businesses are steering clear of doing anything to improve their reviews. In the space between, there is room to take some proactive steps to encourage reviews. Exactly when "proactive" crosses over the line to unethical is a subject of a great deal of discussion, which we'll cover in Chapter 5, "How to Get More Reviews."

Can You Recognize a Fake Review?

Recognizing fake reviews is a challenge. There are no simple linguistic giveaways that signify a fake review. Research shows that many people think reviews are fake when they are overly negative or outrageously positive, but neither of these is actually a reliable marker of a fake review. When we spoke with Bing Liu, he showed us some sample reviews. We've reproduced two of them here: one is fake, and one is real. Can you identify the fake review between them? (Reprinted with permission)

Review 1: I want to make this review in order to comment on the excellent service that my mother and I received on the Serenade of the Seas, a cruise line for Royal Caribbean. There was a lot of things to do in the morning and afternoon portion for the 7 days that we were on the ship. We went to 6 different islands and saw some amazing sites! It was definitely worth the effort of planning beforehand. The dinner service was 5 star for sure. One of our main waiters, Muhammad was one of the nicest people I have ever met. However, I am not one for clubbing, drinking, or gambling, so the nights were pretty slow for me because there was not much else to do. Either than that, I recommend the Serenade to anyone who is looking for excellent service, excellent food, and a week full of amazing day-activities!

Review 2: High Points: Guacamole burger was quite tall; clam chowder was tasty. The decor was pretty good, but not worth the downsides. Low Points: Noisy, noisy, noisy. The appetizers weren't very good at all. And the service kind of lagged. A cross between Las Vegas and Disney world, but on the cheesy side. This Cafe is a place where you eat inside a plastic rain forest. The walls are lined with fake trees, plants, and wildlife, including animatronic animals. A flowing waterfall makes sure that you won't hear the conversations of your neighbors without yelling. I could see it being fun for a child's birthday party (there were several that occurred during our meal), but not a place to go if you're looking for a good meal.

Having trouble identifying which one is fake? You're not alone—the review sites have trouble with this, too. The website reviewskeptic.com, designed by Cornell researchers for hotel reviews, can give you some insight into the process of identifying fake reviews—and we bet you can stump it if you try.

Answer: Review #2 is a fake, written by Professor Liu's staff, not a customer. A fake review often includes a mix of positive and negative remarks to throw you (and the review site) off its trail. Fake reviews are not easy to identify in a vacuum, which is why review venues look at several factors when they hunt for fakes, including the behavior and reviewing history of the reviewer.

The Fight against Fake Reviews

The success of review sites such as Yelp, TripAdvisor, and Urbanspoon depends on the quantity and credibility of their reviews. This means they have a strong incentive to root out and fight against fake reviews on their site—and also an incentive to downplay the scale of the fake reviews problem.

E-commerce sites, including Amazon, have much to gain and not as much to lose from the presence of fake positive reviews on their site. Positive reviews, after all, increase their bottom line by encouraging more purchases. Paradoxically, incentivized reviews (in which the reviewer receives discounts or some other form of compensation) have even been shown to be rated as more helpful by readers. This is not to say that these businesses don't have an interest in maintaining the credibility of reviews on their sites. Big retailers like Amazon and review platforms like Bazaarvoice state in no uncertain terms that fake reviews violate their terms of service and that action will be taken if fake reviews are discovered. Unfortunately, genuine reviews are often caught in the same net.

Here are some of the main ways that review sites and services are fighting the battle against fake reviews:

Filtering Out or Deleting Reviews The most common way for review sites to manage fake reviews is with a filtering algorithm that removes suspicious reviews from view. Yelp's filter is notorious with businesses and even some customers, who sometimes feel that their genuine positive reviews have been wrongfully filtered out. Google continually fiddles with its filter algorithm, sometimes setting the dial to extra-harsh and removing a large number of reviews, then bringing reviews back from the dead months later. Because it's unlikely that these sites can detect fake reviews solely by the content in the reviews, they are probably identifying fake reviews at least in part based on abnormal behavior patterns or inconsistencies from the reviewer, or review patterns for the business, including the timing of reviews. As Bing Liu described: "If a reviewer starts one review with 'My husband and I. . .' and another review with 'My wife and I. . .' that would be an inconsistency" that may trigger a filter. Google also advises against some practices that businesses take to encourage reviews, such as setting up a tablet on-site and encouraging customers to post reviews there. This results in many reviews coming from the same IP address, which may appear suspicious.

Posting Warnings or Alerts TripAdvisor, Yelp, and ResellerRatings have been known to post alerts on their own sites to call out reviews they did not consider legit.

Running a Sting Operation Beginning in 2012, Yelp has run a sting operation to catch businesses that attempt to pay for reviews on the site. See the sidebar "Yelp's Sting Operation" for details.

Verifying Reviewer Names Identifying reviewers by their real names helps review sites and review collection platforms increase the credibility of their online reviews. Amazon offers a "Real Name" label for reviewers who have agreed to display their names and verified it with a credit card. And though you may still see some older anonymous Google+ Local reviews, Google does not accept anonymous or even pseudonymous reviews. See Figure 2.23 for a peek into the strictly enforced Google+ names policy.

There's a problem with your Google+ profile

Our system has determined that the name you provided on your Google+
profile **Hieronymous Bollywood** may not actually be a name.

Figure 2.23 This notice from Google+ goes on to set a timeline for suspension of the user's
Google+ profile if a real name is not used.

Purchase Authentication Another way that review sites and platforms improve the credibility of their content is by verifying that reviewers have actually purchased the item being reviewed. Amazon labels these as "Amazon Verified Purchase," as seen here:

Many other services and sites, such as Seamless, HotelMe.com, ResellerRatings, Expedia, and others either identify verified customers or limit reviews to those with a confirmed purchase.

Allowing Users to Flag Reviews In addition to asking for readers to mark reviews as helpful or not helpful, many review sites allow visitors to flag reviews that appear suspicious or break the rules:

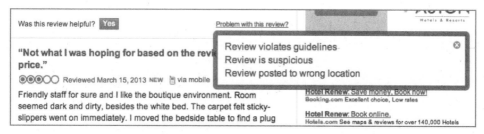

Unfortunately, as you learned in the sidebar "Can You Recognize a Fake Review?" most of us do not excel at recognizing fake reviews. As a result, flagging reviews probably doesn't accomplish much in the way of cleaning out the dross.

Yelp's Sting Operation

In late 2012, Yelp took a dramatic step in the fight against fake reviews: It launched a sting operation and caught eight businesses that were trying to buy fake reviews.

Here's how the bust went down: A Yelp employee posed as an Elite Yelp reviewer and responded to Craigslist ads seeking review writers. Once the Yelp employee received an offer of payment for reviews, Yelp posted a prominent warning on the Yelp page of the offending company, as seen here:

Consumer Alert

We caught someone red-handed trying to buy reviews for this business. We weren't fooled, but wanted you to know because buying reviews not only hurts consumers, but also honest businesses who play by the rules. Check out the evidence here.

Show me the reviews

Ouch, they weren't pulling any punches! The warning notices, aka public badges of shame, remained on Yelp for three months. Yelp calls this its Consumer Alerts program and posted a second round of alerts in 2013.

Yelp was quick to paint the review buyers as villains, but we think it's only fair to give them a tiny benefit of doubt. Many small businesses do not have the legal and social media savvy to understand that fake reviews violate terms of service as well as Federal Trade Commission guidelines.

This story could have gone another way. Consider what Google does when it catches a site in the act of flagrantly violating its terms of service: In most cases, it knocks the site down in the ranks and sends a private message to the website owner explaining what was found and offering tips on correcting the problem.

We hope that review sites will evolve to a point where improved algorithmic detection and more effective business education initiatives make sting operations like this unnecessary.

By now, you should have the knowledge you need to trace almost any review you encounter online back to its source. You might even feel like you have a pretty solid understanding of the technical underpinnings of the online review machinery. Now, get ready to learn about an even more complex machine: the reviewer.

Understanding Reviewers and Reviews

Even in the context of the Internet, online reviews are a new phenomenon, and researchers are still learning about the factors that influence reviewers and those who read reviews. Review sites and platforms are constantly tweaking their offerings based on the evolving understanding of consumer perception and behavior. We've gleaned helpful information from sources ranging from highfalutin academic studies to industry insiders who spend their days in the trenches. We hope you'll use the insights from this chapter to make smart decisions about how to connect with your potential reviewers, which reviews will do your business the most good, and which reviews are not worth stressing over.

In this chapter:

Who are the reviewers?

What triggers a review?

Influencing factors in reviews

Who Are the Reviewers?

Good businesses know their customers well: their likes and dislikes, needs, joys, and motivations. But for many businesses, online reviewers are a small, inscrutable subset of their customers—and this sample may or may not be representative of the group as a whole. To get the most out of your online reviews, you'll want to identify who among your customers is most likely to jump online and dish the dirt.

Once the realm of a limited number of in-the-know, uber-savvy consumers and wannabe insiders, the reviewscape is now home to a broad population of everyday folk. More than 78% of the U.S. population is online, according to the Pew Research Center. Business owners should assume that anyone they deal with has access to review venues that matter, regardless of age, income, race, and education level. Here are some insights into reviewers and reviewing habits.

Reviewer Demographics

Listen closely. Can you hear the Internet roaring? Research shows that women have an edge over men when it comes to posting online reviews. Reviews make online shopping more social and reduce the consumer perception of risk, both factors that research indicates are important to women (*Electronic Commerce Research*, 2011). Despite a gender gap putting men at the lead in online purchasing, a 2010 analysis by Revinate suggests that, at least among the married set, females were more likely to leave reviews on Amazon than males. And 2012 research by Olery looked at 50 million hotel reviews and concluded that 53% of reviews were posted by women. That said, if your business caters primarily to a particular gender, it's likely that group will dominate your online reviews.

Are online reviews the domain of the young? Consumer psychologist Kit Yarrow, author of *Decoding the Consumer Mind* (Wiley, 2013) and an expert in Gen Y buying behavior, told us, "Young people connect with other people online through their reviews—they get more emotional juice connecting and sharing online than an older person." But don't fall for the common misconception that all online reviewers are millennials who traded in their sippy cups for smartphones. A Nielsen study in 2011 found the age group doing the most online shopping was in the 35-to-54 bracket. As the Boomer generation ages, the number of online seniors shopping and reviewing their purchases is sure to grow.

Our roundup of online reviewers ends with a look at the ABCs (advocacy, bellyaching, and check-ins) of social media users. According to February 2013 research by the Pew Research Center, social media users tend to be under 50 years old, with 18-to-29-year-olds most heavily represented. More women than men use social media sites, and urban dwellers are significantly more likely to be found using social networks than those in rural settings. If your consumers' chatter has you believing that @NegativeNell's voice is louder than @PositivePete's, you may be on to something: A

March 2013 study by the Pew Research Center suggests that Twitter sentiment skews more negative than overall public opinion, at least for political chatter.

But luckily, social media advocates, those loyal customers and followers who feel passionate enough to broadcast their goodwill, tend to make a lot of noise, too. The social marketing company Dachis Group wrote that "while advocates make up just .001% of a brand's social subscribers, they're responsible for nearly 30% of the earned media impressions that a brand generates." In other words, your most enthusiastic social media supporters may be small in number, but they can be powerful contributors to positive information about your company.

Power Reviewers

Some people take an over-caffeinated approach to online reviews, generating a collection of commentary that would put the most prolific authors to shame. Review sites love these people because they keep the sites nicely populated with fresh, genuine material. Here's a rundown on some programs that cater to reviewers:

Yelp Elite Squad In Yelp's words, their Elite Squad consists of "stellar" community members who act as role models to other Yelp members. Anyone can apply to join the Elite Squad, but Yelp grants Elite status only to particularly active reviewers whose writing skills make the grade. Once on the team, Elite Yelpers receive a special badge next to their name and invitations to local events, aka "epic parties" featuring free food and drink. They are expected to use their real name, show their face clearly in their profile pic, and keep up the pace on posting new reviews. The quantity and quality of their reviews is reevaluated yearly.

Google+ Local Top Reviewers Google+ Local Top Reviewers can be found by selecting "from top reviewers" after performing a search in Google+ Local, as seen here:

Google appears to trust these reviewers more than others, and reviews from Top Reviewers may help a business's local search ranks. Additionally, reviewers who have written 50 "high quality" reviews and write at least five new reviews per month can receive the designation of Google City Expert and be rewarded with exclusive content and offers. Google+ Local is working hard to increase the volume of reviews on its site; we once stumbled upon a Google+ booth at a local street fair, where Google+ employees traded swag for reviews of local businesses. See Figure 3.1. A surprisingly offline tactic from the company that rules the online world, don't you think?

Figure 3.1 Google+ Booth at the Eagle Rock Music Festival in Los Angeles

Amazon Vine For this invitation-only program, Amazon selects from among the most trusted reviewers on its site. Participants, called Vine Voices, receive free products and pre-release evaluation copies of books. Vine Voices agree to review at least 80% of the materials they receive, but there is no expectation that the reviews will be positive. Businesses—mostly publishers—participate in the program by providing free products and paying a fee to Amazon.

Amazon Top Reviewers Although many of Amazon's top reviewers also participate in Amazon Vine, not all of them do. A 2011 study, "How Aunt Ammy Gets Her Free Lunch" by Trevor Pinch and Filip Kesler of Cornell, looked at the top thousand reviewers on Amazon and found that the majority of these reviewers, over 69%, were men. They lean toward the older side and hold occupations that heavily involve writing (writers, educators, and lawyers). Not surprisingly, retirees also feature strongly on the list.

TripAdvisor Status-Holders TripAdvisor reviewers can work their way up from Hotel Specialist (someone who has written at least three reviews) to Senior Reviewer (six reviews) all the way to Top Contributor (50 or more reviews). The badges appear next to reviews and posts to identify the site's most active members.

Foursquare Mayors Foursquare has been a pioneer in what is known as "gamification": providing badges and other virtual rewards for desired online activities. The best known among these is the mayoral status that Foursquare bestows upon the user who checks into an establishment more often than anyone else. To be sure, checking in is not reviewing, but it is a form of positive word-of-mouth. Foursquare mayors are likely to be accessible to business owners, unlike the elite reviewers we've just mentioned. If your business has a brick-and-mortar location, you should make a point of getting to know your mayors.

As a business owner, you will usually have no way of knowing when one of these prolific reviewers enters your establishment. It's definitely not acceptable to attempt to bribe them for a review, and they aren't likely to flash a card when they're being seated. (See the sidebar "Be Nice to Me, I'm a Reviewer" for more about self-identified reviewers.) If you have the right access and social skills for it, chatting up your customers may help you understand what kinds of customers tend to leave reviews. Other than that, the best path for gaining access to elite reviewers is to donate free items via established programs. Businesses that sell on Amazon can participate in the Amazon Vine program. Yelp Elite Squad parties also feature donated goodies—usually food or drink. You'll find options for connecting with Amazon Top Reviewers in Chapter 5, "How to Get More Reviews," and information on Yelp's Elite events in Chapter 6, "Review Venues: Need-to-Know Tips for Your Action Plan."

Paid or Fake Reviewers

No discussion of the reviewer population would be complete without a mention of the unsavory characters who write fake reviews for a fee. Writing *real* reviews for a fee is called endorsement, and there's nothing unethical about paid endorsement if it's properly disclosed. In Chapter 5, we'll help you understand where the lines are drawn.

As we've already discussed, as many as 30% of online reviews are fake, and the vast majority of fake reviews are positive reviews written by paid providers at the request of the business. The people posting these reviews may be freelancers, or they may be employed by review generation services (which may also call themselves reputation management services). They are, indeed, real humans and not spambots or software algorithms, and that is what makes fake reviews so darned difficult to detect.

Be Nice to Me, I'm a Reviewer

Picture a homeowner stuck at home after taking the day off, waiting for an electrician who hasn't shown up. As the clock ticks the afternoon away, she fumes: "If only they knew how active I am on Angie's List, they'd never leave me hanging like this!" In response to this situation, California entrepreneur Brad Newman had the devilish idea of selling the ReviewerCard, shown here:

Available at a cost of $100, the ReviewerCard gives customers the opportunity to, as Newman puts it, "enjoy premium service"—in other words, to pressure businesses to give them better than average service under threat of a negative review.

Other reviewers may employ a more innocent approach. Yelp Elite members can wear T-shirts that proclaim their special status. And TripAdvisor has given away free luggage tags to its reviewers; no doubt some travelers hope that hoteliers will notice the tags on their luggage and give them special favors.

Extortionist and unethical though this behavior may be, the implied threat of a bad review should be taken seriously. In a similar vein, any customer who mentions that they intend to post a review should be handled with care. A person who goes out of their way to inform businesses that they write reviews will likely have no problem following through and sharing their experience online—so try to make it a good one. You may have to grit your teeth to provide service with a smile, but think of this as an opportunity to make sure that *every* customer is getting a 5-star quality experience.

Another type of fake review is the one written by a friend or family member. If you've been asking those in your inner circle to send a little love your way in the form of online reviews, it's best to cut that out, or at least ask them to disclose the relationship. We know your peeps have the best of intentions, but this practice is risky because it's against any credible review venue's Terms of Service.

In a sense, employee reviews are another form of paid review. Reviews written by employees run the gamut from outright balderdash ("First time here—the manicure was amazing!") to perfectly legitimate advice ("I work at this hardware store. Take my advice and come on weekday mornings when it's less crowded.") Reviewing your own company is against the terms of use of many brick-and-mortar review sites, but reviewing a product your company sells is encouraged by some product review venues. What keeps an employee review on the virtuous end of the spectrum? It's all in disclosing the relationship.

We've spoken with small business owners who know the identity of everyone who posted a review, and we've spoken with larger businesses that have so much review data that they must use sophisticated reporting tools to get a handle on their reviewer demographics. If you are scratching your head about who's leaving reviews for your offerings, create a simple tally by doing the exercise in the sidebar "Identify Your Reviewers," later in this chapter.

Nobody Cheers About a Cell Phone Charger

Brent Franson, the VP of business products at Reputation.com, told us an interesting finding from his company's online reputation research: "We analyzed 10,000 reviews of cell phone chargers, and we found that they are rarely reviewed positively." This led Brent's team to wonder: Has something gone horribly wrong with cell phone chargers? Nope: "The reason is, a phone charger either does its job or it lets you down. You're never going to be ecstatic about your phone charger, but you might be disappointed." Without the opportunity to exceed expectations and knock the socks off their customers, cell phone charger makers and sellers are left getting reviews from only the underwhelmed portion of their customer base.

This issue can be extended to other utilitarian consumer ventures, such as a visit to Walmart or an oil change and lube job. Even worse, some businesses provide products or experiences that are inherently negative for many people, as Brent goes on to describe: "Even a great experience at a dentist is a tough experience! It's not fun to go to the dentist."

If your business or product falls into a category where exceeding expectations is unlikely, you'll need to make extra efforts to cultivate communication and proactively encourage a more representative cross-section of your population to post reviews. This could include all manner of nudging, which we'll talk about more in Chapter 5, and it may involve some brainstorming about improving your website interface or your post-transaction communications to simplify the reviewing process. Amazon shows an understanding of this phenomenon, and changes its review solicitation language depending on the item that was purchased. Customers may receive an email asking, "How do you like...?" for a clothing item, or, "How many stars would you give...?" for a digital video download; whereas for utilitarian purchases, the question is about expectations, for example, "Did 'CR2025 Energizer Lithium Batteries (1 pack of 5)' meet your expectations?"

As consumer psychologist Kit Yarrow told us, businesses may never find a way to improve the emotional connection with a mundane product or a utilitarian experience. So their goal should be this: Make the review process so easy that they will do it anyway.

What Triggers a Review?

Whole libraries' worth of books, blogs, and articles have been written on the question of how a casual browser, either in person or on a website, *converts* into a customer, and how businesses can tap into those motivations to maximize sales. Here, we look at a different set of goals and motivations: After the sale is made, what are the social, emotional, and logistical triggers that compel a client, patient, or customer to post an online review about your product or business?

Being Asked

You knew this already, of course, but asking for reviews and providing a convenient way to leave reviews increases the likelihood that you'll get them. Third-party collection services like ResellerRatings and Shopper Approved and social commerce platforms like Bazaarvoice and Reevoo are built on this principle. A 2010 study published in the journal *Computers in Human Behavior* revealed that "perceived pressure"—in this case, emailed requests for reviews from the seller or review venue—strongly influenced review writing.

Social and Emotional Motivations

After a product is purchased or a service is received, the customer forms an opinion of the experience, but will they express that opinion online? Several social and emotional conditions contribute to the decision to go public with an online review:

Social Connection Posting a review is a public and social interaction, and just like in the offline world, there are lots of different ways people like to get their social on. Some reviewers are posting to feel better about themselves; others genuinely wish to help fellow consumers. Some reviewers like to stand out in a crowd whereas others like to blend in. Research published in 2004 in the *Journal of Interactive Marketing* found that social connection and participating in a community are two of the most important factors influencing customers to post online reviews.

Quantity and Positivity of Previous Reviews A 2011 study in the journal *Marketing Science* looked at Bazaarvoice product review data and found that "consumers are more likely to post an opinion when the ratings already posted are more positive." Similarly, people are less likely to post new reviews into a negative ratings environment.

On the other hand, many people strive for the special status of discovering and writing about lesser-known products or experiences. As a 2010 study of movie reviews published in the *Journal of Management Information Systems* noted, "consumers prefer to post reviews for products that are less available and less successful in the market."

Review venues use language like "Be the first to leave a review!" to encourage visitors to jump into the coveted first position. As a result of these dual urges, people may be more likely to post reviews at the two ends of the popularity spectrum: supremely popular and deeply obscure.

Rewards A 2011 study by BrightLocal showed that 40% of customers would be more likely to promote a business if they received a reward, for example, a discount or free product or service. But tread carefully in this area; credibility of your reviews is of the utmost importance. Incentives should never be offered in exchange for *positive* reviews, and reviewers should disclose any freebies they have received. See Chapter 5 for more details on how to encourage reviews without crossing ethical red lines.

Ego, Altruism, and Equal Exchange Longstanding research by Teresa M. Amabile of Brandeis University has shown that people who want to show off their smarts and be seen as experts are likely to give more negative evaluations. Translate this into online reviews, and you're seeing some people posting negative reviews to make themselves feel smarter. Business owners often express vexation at how much negative influence a single blowhard can have on their reputation. But reviewers can use their powers to help others, too. Many reviewers are motivated by altruism to share helpful information with the community. Others may be motivated by a sense of fairness. Some researchers, such as Oliver and Swan (*Journal of Marketing*, 1989), propose that individuals have a basic desire for an equitable exchange. When customers receive something from a business that goes above and beyond what they've paid, they often feel an urge to pay the business back—possibly with a good review.

When It's Personal According to consumer psychologist Kit Yarrow, feelings of being "personally insulted or maligned" can be a catalyst in the decision to post a negative review. There are customers who leave negative reviews, and there are really angry customers who want to inflict damage. The article "When Unhappy Customers Strike Back on the Internet" (*MIT Sloan Management Review*, 2011) sheds light on the difference by making a distinction between dissatisfaction and betrayal. Dissatisfaction (for example, "the meal was bad") is associated with feelings of annoyance, whereas betrayal ("I bought this expensive product, it didn't work, and I called customer service five times before they finally told me they won't refund my money") results in anger. Annoyed folks may simply choose to stop being customers, but those who have entered the anger zone are more likely to wield the poison pen in public.

Helping Friends and Hurting Enemies According to a *New York Times* article, "Amazon Glitch Unmasks War of Reviewers," a bug on Amazon's Canadian site temporarily revealed the real names of anonymous reviewers. The result? Major embarrassment for several prominent authors who had given 5-star reviews to their own creations. Surprised? We didn't think so. A large portion of reviewers have a personal connection to the business or product being reviewed. For many businesses, the line between a friend and a customer or client is a blurry one, but there is nothing blurry about reviewing yourself under a cloak of anonymity—it's just plain unethical.

Customer Experiences That Trigger Reviews

Every customer experience could result in an online review, but there are some experiences that are more likely to cause a customer to spill his or her guts online. Here are a few triggers we've discovered:

Experience Not Aligning with Expectations A 1993 study published in the journal *Marketing Science* shows that customer satisfaction depends on the quality of the product or experience, and also on how closely it matches with the customer's expectations.

When there is a mismatch, buyer remorse, or more fabulously, *post choice dissonance*, may be a result. We believe that an experience that feels out of whack with what the customer expected prior to the purchase is likely to trigger the desire to "correct the error" via an online review, both as a pressure release for the reviewer's own pent-up frustration and out of concern for other consumers. See Figure 3.2 for an example.

1 Would not recommend

Anonymous
Central City, KY
Feb 28, 2011

"Looks Aren't What You Get"

We had a great time while in Goodlettville. We shopped and visited with family. But our hotel stay was awful to say the least. Our room was clean but that was about it. The pictures are NOT what you get in the superior king room. DO NOT EXPECT to get that awesome shower or the beautifully decorated room. The heaters in the room are up high on the wall, and there was parts of the ceiling falling into the heater. We won't be stay here again. We were completely disappointed in this hotel.

Hotel features (5 = best, 1 = worst):

	1	2	3	4	5
Amenities:					
Room cleanliness:					
Hotel staff:					
Room comfort:					
Location:					
Value:					

Figure 3.2 When an offering doesn't match a customer's experience, a negative review can result.

A Particularly Good or Bad Experience Maybe you've noticed that there always seem to be lots of 5-star and 1-star reviews, but not so many 2- and 3-star ones. If so, your observation is backed by research. A 2011 study published in the journal *Marketing Science* found that "Individuals with either high *or* low postpurchase evaluations are more likely to contribute ratings, whereas individuals with moderate postpurchase evaluations are less likely to contribute ratings."

A "meh" reaction won't carry you far when it comes to online reviews. On the bright side, this same study also found that overall, positive feelings about a product were more likely to result in the creation of a review than negative ones.

Lack of Other Communication Channels Some people post reviews as a way of contacting a company representative in the hopes of resolving a problem. This is one good reason to monitor your reviews and make contact when a response is requested. But one of the most powerful ways to positively affect your reviews is in *preventing* bad ones, by redirecting unhappy customers to express themselves in some other forum. As seen in

Figure 3.3, Amazon proactively offers customers two links: one to leave a review, and another to complain to Amazon directly and privately.

amazon.com.

So Jennifer Grappone, what do you think?
Tell others about your experiences with your recent purchases.

Reebok Men's Sublite Pro Rise Basketball Shoe
Fulfilled by Amazon. Problem with the order?

Review this product

Figure 3.3 The "Problem with the order?" link takes the customer to a form where they can submit a private complaint.

Unresolved Problems A study described in the MIT *Sloan Management Review* concluded that 96% of consumers who posted on complaint sites like ripoffreport.com did so after more than one attempt to resolve the problem unsuccessfully.

Statistically speaking, Hell hath no fury like a customer who reaches out for help with a significant product or service issue and is let down repeatedly by the offending company. According to the study, customers are most likely to vent online after bad experiences with automotive purchases; large retail purchases; credit, debt, and mortgage services; and cell phone providers.

Influencing Factors in Reviews

Most business owners can relate to celebrating over a single good review or despairing over a single negative one; it's human nature. If you're tired of living and dying by individual reviews, take heart: Review consumption is not a simple sentiment in/sentiment out process. There is no evidence that a typical reader of a single negative review will always come away with a negative opinion, any more than there is evidence that a single review's 5-star array will cause instant adoration on the part of the reader.

At the heart of online review consumption lies risk reduction. Consumers want to know: Should I buy this product or will it be a waste of money? Will I enjoy this travel experience, or will I have wasted my precious free time? Will I be proud of my landscaping, or will I want to run outside and cover it up next time the Google Street View van comes rolling through? To cut through that uncertainty, consumers want and need to trust the reviews that they read. But trust does not come easily; consumers are compelled to decipher a great number of signals every time they read a review. On a basic level, this involves forming an opinion about the author of the review and the site on which the review is seen. Contributing to this opinion are layers of judgment about the credibility, motivations, and biases of the reviewer and the site displaying the review, which in turn requires analysis of components of the review such as grammar, demographic information, and, of course, sentiment.

Let's delve into some of the factors that make some reviews more persuasive than others.

Variety and Volume

For the purposes of decision making, readers want to see a variety of reviews, both good and bad; studies have shown that consumers will seek out negative reviews if they encounter too many positive reviews in their research. Neville Letzeritch, Executive Vice President of Products at Bazaarvoice, told us, "People tend to distrust products with 100% positive reviews." Variety notwithstanding, is there a minimum number of reviews to strive for? A 2012 study in the *Journal of Hospitality & Management* suggested that consumers want to see approximately 5–10 reviews of a given hotel location in order to trust that the reviews are reliable. Another study from the *International Journal of Electronic Commerce* suggested that having a larger volume of reviews can convey a feeling of justification to a consumer, who may reason that if so many people bought a given product or service, it must be worthwhile. Neville put an interesting spin on this when he explained to us that in his experience, even if a large number of reviews are available, people tend to make up their minds after reading seven reviews.

Studies have come to conflicting conclusions regarding the effects of positive and negative sentiments on consumer perceptions. Are positive reviews viewed as more credible than negative ones? What about a positive review read by a neutral consumer, or a negative review read by an opinionated one? Since you're not in the position to craft your own reviews or handpick your potential customers, don't knock yourself out trying to follow every variable. Here are some of the more useful insights we've found:

- One study showed that, in cases where problems with service were described in a review, "consumers give higher helpfulness scores to reviews that document an effective recovery" (*Journal of Travel & Tourism Marketing*, 2009).
- A 2012 study examining the interdependency between trust, credibility, sentiment, and source found that "negative reviews with disclosed personal identification of the reviewer are perceived to be significantly more credible compared to other types of reviews" (*Journal of Vacation Marketing*, 2012).

- Researchers Susan M. Mudambi and David Schuff concluded in 2010 that Amazon reviews with extreme positive or negative ratings were less helpful to shoppers and consumers when compared to moderate ratings. These findings were specific to "experience goods," which is an economics term for purchases that a consumer must experience in order to determine their value, such as a bottle of wine or a book.

- In a sea of vague positive comments such as "We had a great time!" or "Would recommend this purchase," negative comments can be more useful in terms of evaluating a product or service. A helpful negative review ("The pump seems to be out of action. It just pumps very very slowly, and never actually finishes the brewing cycle. Amazing something that costs this much, has no longevity.") can be used for what one study described as a "diagnostic" function (*Journal of Hospitality Marketing & Management*, 2012).

- This study goes on to suggest that websites should not be afraid to allow visitors to sort reviews by negative or positive sentiment, and that allowing ratings on specific criteria (for example, parking for a brick-and-mortar or sturdiness for a product) will perform a useful function for the consumer. This may be something to keep in mind if you are shopping for a product review platform.

- Some studies suggest that first impressions count, with consumers holding onto an initial negative or positive opinion, even if they read the opposite sentiment later. One study found product reviews that were posted earliest had the largest long-term effect on product sales (*Marketing Science*, 2008)." We say: The earlier you focus on gaining and showing off positive reviews, the better.

Lest you worry that consumers are too easily swayed by stars, fear not. Studies show that shoppers do read the textual content of online reviews and respond to the text rather than relying solely on the star count. A 2010 study published in the journal *MIS Quarterly* found that longer reviews tended to receive more helpfulness votes.

Reviewer Identity

The more information a review shows about a reviewer's identity, the more credible it is. We don't think anonymous reviews will ever completely disappear, but the growing trend toward verified shopper and real name reviews provides a real benefit to both shoppers and businesses. Disclosing the source of a review gives the reader important context for judging whether the review is credible and useful. Yelp knows this—it requires its Elite reviewers to use their real names and display their faces clearly in their profiles, with the pronouncement, "Let everyone see your face so they know that you stand by what you say." Researchers Kusumasondjaja, Shanka, and Marchegiani actually found that a positive impact on sales was the outcome when demographic information about online reviewers was shared.

Here are some facets of reviewer identity that can make a difference:

Perceived Motivation   When reading online reviews, consumers' gears are turning as they consciously or subconsciously try to decipher the intentions behind the review. "What's in it for this reviewer? Does he have a personal vendetta against this brand? Did she get paid to write this? And does this website have something to gain from my purchase?" A 2012 study published in the journal *Computers in Human Behavior* considered the issue of trust in online reviews. Not surprisingly, the study concluded that a video review was found less trustworthy when the watcher thought it was made by the product manufacturer. A trusted review correlated with better feelings about the products being reviewed: "If the intentions of the original source seem genuine, people are more likely to trust the review and will have better product attitudes."

Perceived Expertise   When we spoke with Neville Letzeritch at Bazaarvoice, he mentioned that in-house product experts write reviews on the UK retailer John Lewis website and that these reviews tend to get high helpfulness marks by site visitors. This would seem to fly in the face of the finding we just described, in which people are less likely to trust reviews written by product stakeholders. It's important to note that these reviews disclose the relationship, as you can see in Figure 3.4, so in this case, the reviewers' motivation (an employee stands to make money if a product is sold) is counterbalanced by the reviewers' perceived credibility and expertise.

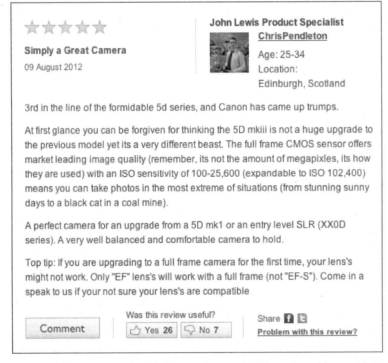

Figure 3.4   This review, written by a John Lewis employee, received 26 votes for usefulness on JohnLewis.com.

Review sites have clearly bought into the power of identifying expert reviewers, as evidenced by their special categories such as Yelp's Elite Squad, TripAdvisor's Top Contributor status, and Google+ Top Reviewers.

Shared Experiences/Similarity Studies show that consumers trust people who are similar to them, so they are more likely to trust advice from reviewers with shared experiences, similar values, and a similar social identity. It's no surprise that many review sorting algorithms, including those of Google+ Local, Yelp, and TripAdvisor, favor reviews from a reader's social connections. Many product review platforms collect and display location and demographic data about reviewers to allow consumers to see which reviews are written by people with shared experiences. See Figure 3.5 for the "people like you" concept in action on the Reevoo platform.

| All purchasers (240) | Budding chef (1) | Busy mum or dad (42) | Family cook (11) | Love to cook (22) | Occasional cook (3) |
| | | Occasional user (58) | Retired (63) | Other (40) | |

Figure 3.5 Reevoo's options for filtering microwave reviews by the reviewer's lifestyle

Exercise: Identify Your Reviewers

The "people like you" factor plays an important part in the credibility and influence conveyed by an individual review. Are your reviews written by the kinds of customers you are trying to appeal to? Your assignment for today is to compile a tally of the people who are writing online reviews for your business or products and determine how closely they match your desired customers. Forget the *what*—the compliments and complaints—and focus for now on learning about the *who*.

We'll use the example of the fictional restaurant Salad Hut, a lunchtime salad bar restaurant that's targeted to health-conscious office workers. Here's what to do:

Step 1 Write down your target customers' general characteristics in terms of demographics (gender, age, marital status, parental status, luxury- or bargain-minded, local or tourist, and so on) and interests. You may choose characteristics that match your existing customers or represent a goal.

Salad Hut might describe their customers as follows:

Most of our customers are men and women ages 25–45 who work in the neighborhood. They are mostly single and childfree, price-conscious but not to the point of bringing their own lunch to work. They're interested in fitness, health, ecology, and vegetarianism. They're active social media users and can help me spread the word about my business.

Continues

Exercise: Identify Your Reviewers *(Continued)*

Step 2 Navigate to the online review venue of your choice, and filter reviews of your business or a representative product from newest to oldest.

Step 3 Looking at a minimum of 10 of your most recent reviews; tally what information you can figure out about the writers. Start with the easy-to-find information first, and then dig deeper if necessary. You may not be able to determine all of the information you listed, but glean as much as you can:

- Check the profile details that display along with the review. For example, a reviewer with the screen name BBQLover is probably not a vegetarian, and a reviewer whose hometown is listed as San Antonio, Texas is probably not a Toledo office worker. A photo may give you a quick read on gender and age.

- If the profile details don't give much away, you can gather clues from the text of the review. For example, if you read "I don't go here because I like the food. I'm just trying to shed some baby weight," you've found a female. If you read, "The prices were outrageous! I can get a salad at McDonald's for half the price," you can guess that this reviewer might be pinching pennies a bit more tightly than your ideal customer.

- If a reviewer checked in at your location, that's an indication that they may have the social media skills you're looking for.

- If you can't find the identifying details that you're after, click through to the reviewer's profile to get hints from other reviews they've posted. (This option may not be available depending on the review venue.) Of course, your prospective customers are not likely to see this information, so their first impressions will not be influenced by any information you must dig to find.

Here's what the tally might look like for our restaurant:

▶ **The Salad Hut—Reviews on Yelp**

Description	Matched	Didn't match	Unknown match	Notes
Men and women ages 25–45,	✓✓✓✓✓ ✓✓✓	✓		One looked much older based on profile pic.
…who work in the neighborhood.	✓✓✓✓ ✓		✓✓✓✓	I suspect most do match— not enough information.
They are single…			✓✓✓✓ ✓✓✓✓	Not identified.

Continues

Description	Matched	Didn't match	Unknown match	Notes
…and childfree,	✓✓✓✓✓ ✓✓✓✓✓			Assuming yes to all for this exercise…none mentioned having a kid or bringing a kid in their review.
…price-conscious but not to the point of bringing their own lunch to work.	✓✓✓✓✓ ✓		✓✓✓✓	Four reviewers discussed our prices in a way that led me to believe they are price-conscious, others did not identify.
They're interested in fitness, health, ecology, and vegetarianism.	✓✓✓✓	✓	✓✓✓✓✓	One match each based on mention of "fat," "yoga," "diet," and "vegetarian." One non-match based on "lust for red meat." Others did not identify.
They're active social media users and can help me spread the word about my business.	✓✓		✓✓✓✓✓ ✓✓✓	Two check-ins

Step 4 Use the data you've gathered to assess whether your reviewers represent your target customers. In the Salad Hut example, we would say there is a good match between their customer description and the reviewers on the list.

If the people writing your reviews are representative of your desired customers, you can reasonably expect that your reviews will influence the opinions of the prospective customers you're trying to attract. (On the other hand, if your target customers are not represented among your reviewers, the customers you are trying to attract could be turned off: "This looks like a place for mostly college kids—I'll try somewhere else.")

Continues

Exercise: Identify Your Reviewers *(Continued)*

If you found a significant mismatch between your reviewers and your desired customers, ask yourself what this means for your business:

- If your reviewers are not a fair representation of your actual customers, ask yourself why your typical customer doesn't want to leave a review. Is it because they are concerned about anonymity? Could it be that they don't frequent review sites and aren't comfortable with the technology? This may be a sign that you need to work toward encouraging reviews from more representative customers.

- Based on the reviewers you identified, is there a particular group that is more engaged with your offerings than you'd originally thought? Perhaps this coincides with a possible new marketing or promotional focus.

- If the mismatch was caused by a temporary or unusual situation (for example, a tour group came through your restaurant, or your product was temporarily discounted), you now have a good understanding of how this situation affected your reviewscape and whether it's worth repeating.

- If you have reviews but could glean no information about your reviewers, why? E-commerce retailers might need to sign up with a product review platform that provides an opportunity for reviewers to disclose more about themselves.

Although this exercise won't give you all the answers, we hope it will help you start thinking more strategically about your own reviewscape.

Freshness

Some products don't change over time. For example, a cell phone stays the same until it is replaced by a newer model. For these products, shoppers don't particularly have a need for current reviews on which to base their purchase decisions. On the other hand, the customer experience at hotels and restaurants can change rapidly as the décor deteriorates or the menu modernizes. Prospective patrons of these establishments want and need current reviews in order to make educated decisions. Most online reviews come with a date stamp, and many sites allow the ability to sort by date. Yelp takes this further by displaying rating trends over time, as seen in Figure 3.6.

If current reviews are important to your business, you'll need to focus not only on gaining great reviews but also on encouraging your customers to churn out those reviews in a steady stream.

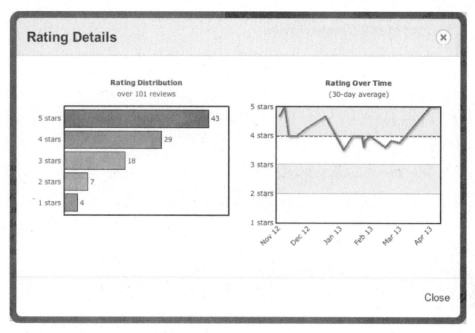

Figure 3.6 Yelp shows rating trends over time.

Now that you have some insight into what makes a review influential, you may be wondering what you can do with this information. For one, you can feel confident that you don't need to panic if the reviews you've accrued are not picture-perfect. Your prospective customers are reading your reviews with more intelligence and picking up more nuance than you might assume. Second, you can plan your review improvement efforts, which start in earnest in the next chapter, from a more enlightened perspective. Instead of scrambling to drown out negative reviews with rapturous ones, try instead to increase signals of trust and credibility in your review space. Finally, if you are evaluating platforms for product reviews on your own site, be sure to look for ones that are able to display an adequate assortment of useful information about the product and the reviewer.

You don't necessarily need to pile on more positive sentiment to make your reviews more appealing or credible or to help justify a shopper's purchase. Rather, you may need to pile on more information and more ways to sort that information. A larger number of reviews, along with information about reviewers, such as gender, occupation, and number of reviews posted, gives readers clues that lead them on the road to a purchase. Give consumers more information and more reasons to trust reviews and justify the purchase at hand, and everybody wins.

Although it's fascinating to dig into the general consumer psyche, we think you'll be even more captivated by your own customers. In Chapter 4, "Monitoring and Learning from Your Reviews," we'll show you how to keep your ear to the ground and your mind on improvement.

Anatomy of an Influential Review

"Loved it!" and "Hated it!" are just two pieces of information out of many that a consumer can pick up from a review. Here are some real-life reviews and possible interpretations.

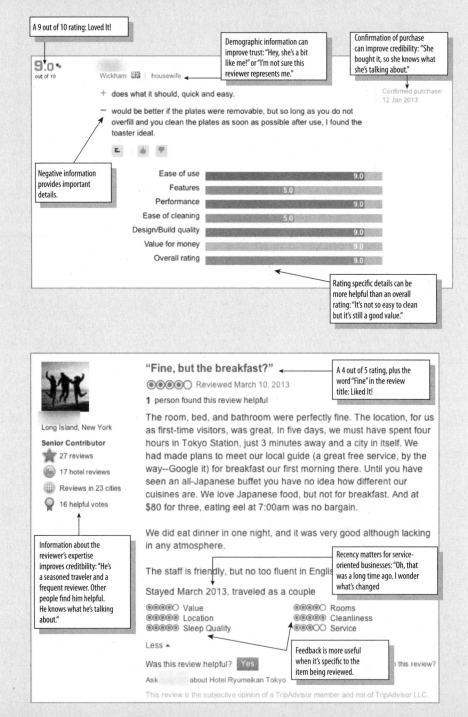

A 9 out of 10 rating: Loved It!

Demographic information can improve trust: "Hey, she's a bit like me!" or "I'm not sure this reviewer represents me."

Confirmation of purchase can improve credibility: "She bought it, so she knows what she's talking about."

9.0
out of 10

Wickham | housewife

Confirmed purchase: 12 Jan 2013

+ does what it should, quick and easy.

− would be better if the plates were removable, but so long as you do not overfill and you clean the plates as soon as possible after use, I found the toaster ideal.

Negative information provides important details.

Ease of use	9.0
Features	5.0
Performance	9.0
Ease of cleaning	5.0
Design/Build quality	9.0
Value for money	9.0
Overall rating	9.0

Rating specific details can be more helpful than an overall rating: "It's not so easy to clean but it's still a good value."

"Fine, but the breakfast?"

⊙⊙⊙⊙○ Reviewed March 10, 2013

1 person found this review helpful

A 4 out of 5 rating, plus the word "Fine" in the review title: Liked It!

Long Island, New York

Senior Contributor

★ 27 reviews

17 hotel reviews

Reviews in 23 cities

16 helpful votes

The room, bed, and bathroom were perfectly fine. The location, for us as first-time visitors, was great. In five days, we must have spent four hours in Tokyo Station, just 3 minutes away and a city in itself. We had made plans to meet our local guide (a great free service, by the way--Google it) for breakfast our first morning there. Until you have seen an all-Japanese buffet you have no idea how different our cuisines are. We love Japanese food, but not for breakfast. And at $80 for three, eating eel at 7:00am was no bargain.

We did eat dinner in one night, and it was very good although lacking in any atmosphere.

Information about the reviewer's expertise improves creditbility: "He's a seasoned traveler and a frequent reviewer. Other people find him helpful. He knows what he's talking about."

The staff is friendly, but no too fluent in English

Stayed March 2013, traveled as a couple

Recency matters for service-oriented businesses: "Oh, that was a long time ago. I wonder what's changed

⊙⊙⊙⊙○ Value
⊙⊙⊙⊙⊙ Location
⊙⊙⊙⊙⊙ Sleep Quality

⊙⊙⊙⊙⊙ Rooms
⊙⊙⊙⊙⊙ Cleanliness
⊙⊙⊙○○ Service

Less ▲

Was this review helpful? Yes

Feedback is more useful when it's specific to the item being reviewed.

Ask about Hotel Ryumeikan Tokyo

This review is the subjective opinion of a TripAdvisor member and not of TripAdvisor LLC.

Monitoring and Learning from Your Reviews

4

The best review monitoring process has a bit of jiujitsu in it: You need to deftly sidestep information overload, sweep aside emotional reactions, and efficiently gather wisdom from your reviews to improve your business. Here, you'll find practical advice for choosing which review venues deserve the bulk of your attention, how to keep track of your online reviews, and most important, how to incorporate what you learn from your reviews into your business practices, products, and policies.

In this chapter:
Why monitor reviews?
Review monitoring for best results
Review monitoring tools
Learn from your reviews

Why Monitor Reviews?

Consider the following real scenarios that illustrate common business concerns. A medical professional we know who had never given a moment's thought to Yelp was taken aback when a new patient asked him why his Yelp reviews were so bad. A resort owner we've worked with knows that TripAdvisor is delivering more reservations than her website but doesn't know whether that's a problem or an opportunity. Another destination client of ours has found strong complaints in their online reviews but lacks a functioning process to get that information into the hands of people who can address the problems that are driving the complaints. Establishing a business routine that includes monitoring and learning from reviews would help each of these businesses in different but powerful ways:

Avoid unpleasant surprises. A well-thought-out response is always better than a horrified gasp. If our medical friend had known about his bad reviews, he could have trained his reception staff to preemptively address common complaints.

Discover opportunities. A careful analysis of your reviews can help you understand both the venues that drive business and the kinds of customers who want more of what you're selling. The resort could play up its TripAdvisor page in marketing materials and encourage guests to post reviews on TripAdvisor to keep this marketing powerhouse fueled.

Fix problems and communicate that you care. As you may remember from Chapter 3, "Understanding Reviewers and Reviews," bad reviews can sometimes encourage more bad reviews. Our local destination client could improve in-house communication channels so that important online reviews get to the people who can fix the problem and work toward a public resolution.

You need to create processes to regularly monitor online reviews and translate your findings into customer service, marketing, and product improvements. Doing so may require a culture shift; for example, if your business has always run using the boss's gut-based decisions ("I know what's right for my business. Who are they to tell me what to do?"), removing emotion and establishing a meticulous data tally may help to make the case for change. It may also require you to put some thought into resource allocation. Far from being the sole dominion of your CEO or community manager, monitoring and alerting activities could be a good fit for any motivated soul in the marketing department or anyone on your team who has customer contact and knows your offering well, from a customer service specialist to a receptionist or greeter.

Businesses with a small number of reviews can work with a low-cost, mostly do-it-yourself method for keeping a handle on online reviews. We've included exercises in this chapter to get you started on this path. A larger enterprise may have too many reviews for a manual approach. Larger retailers, chains, manufacturers, and brands can benefit from a review tracking tool that provides alerts, summaries, and integrations with other business systems.

Review Monitoring for Best Results

A solid review monitoring process involves getting into a habit of looking in the right places and identifying actionable feedback. Your own process will fit your unique business needs and resources, but should include these components:

Understand which review venues matter most. Some businesses know which review venues are popular with their customers. Others have no idea where they can find reviews for their product or service—or if reviews exist at all. To put important context around your reviews, you'll need answers to a few questions:

- Which venues contain the highest volume of recent reviews?
- Which venues are the most visible in a typical Google search for your business or product?
- Which venues are used by your most desirable prospective customers?

The answers to each of these questions may point to different venues. For example, a hotel may have its highest volume of reviews on Expedia, while Google+ Local may deliver the most visible reviews when the hotel name is searched in Google, and TripAdvisor may be the primary driver of new reservations. In this example, the hotel has identified a short list of three review venues that matter, with TripAdvisor at the top because it's closest to the money.

Many review tracking tools will grab reviews from multiple locations around the Web and display them all together in a monitoring dashboard. Even if you're using one of these tools, it's still important to know which reviews merit the bulk of your attention so that you don't waste time on reviews that are destined to live out their days in obscurity. See the sidebar "The Bad Review Nobody Saw" later in this chapter for an example.

Watch for new reviews. Watching the Web for new reviews is an ongoing task, and the trick is to find the right rhythm for watching and a sane process for reacting, so that you aren't missing important developments or overinvesting your time and energy. Especially if you have a high volume of reviews, it's important to put the right people or tools on this job. Is it productive for the Big Boss to spend her time stressing over every review that comes in? Or would it be better to assign this to an administrative staffer or to choose a tool that organizes and prioritizes new reviews for you?

Catalog actionable feedback. Do people tend to love your [product attribute] but hate your [other product attribute]? Is your menu [something] but not [something] enough? Sometimes the big picture is easy to see, whereas other times you have to do some work, cataloging on a comment-by-comment basis, to find the signal in the noise. With a quantitative understanding of what aspects of your offerings are on the rant end of the rant/rave spectrum, and which are in the rave zone, the big question is: What can we do about it? Your clear-eyed analysis about what concerns are fixable and what compliments can be built upon, as well as the knowledge you gained in Chapter 3 about whether your reviewers represent the majority opinion, will help guide you in identifying actionable feedback.

Take action. Perhaps the most obvious but difficult step of your review monitoring process is to turn customer feedback into positive action. Challenge yourself or your team to create a process-driven habit of using actionable customer feedback to improve your business. Your options are as limitless as your own business, but possible actions can include the following:

- Responding publicly or privately to say thanks, apologize, provide a clarification, or take steps to resolve a problem
- Sharing a customer's glowing review on social media, on your website, or in your storefront, lobby, or waiting room
- Changing policies, reconfiguring staff, or otherwise shifting your resources to address a negative trend or reinforce a positive one
- Using your reviews to hone your marketing plan: Create personas based on who writes positive reviews, and market your products to that demographic
- Channeling information from a review to the appropriate internal team: product ideas to the product development team, service flaws to the staff supervisor, legal concerns to the legal team, and so on
- When a staffer is mentioned, following through on the complaint or compliment by issuing a warning, providing training, or rewarding a job well done

Your review platform or monitoring tools may significantly simplify this process. For example, some tools provide customizable alerts and allow you to visualize trends and sentiment and take actions with a few clicks. But even if it's just you, a browser, and a spreadsheet, you've got a winning combination: These are the only tools you'll need to complete the sample review monitoring exercise in this chapter.

Review Monitoring Tools

By now you know there are many venues that can display reviews of your business or products. Reviews can be found on third-party review sites, on search engines, within social media, on your own site, or on the sites of vendors who sell your products. Review monitoring tools can help businesses make sense of all of this information. Table 4.1 lists several tools and resources, including free and paid options, to get you started on your path to better understanding your reviews. Let's start with a quick roundup of some features to look for in review monitoring tools, ranging from basic to advanced:

- Sending alerts when reviews come in
- Providing measurement and analysis tools
- Providing a platform for following up and taking action on reviews
- Finding and aggregating reviews from multiple sources
- Providing views of the data that are tailored for different roles within the company
- Benchmarking your status among competitors
- Comparing between multiple locations of your business or retailers who sell your product

Here's an overview of review tracking products that may be useful for your business:

Review Site Dashboards One advantage of verifying your business listing on sites such as Yelp, TripAdvisor, and Angie's List is that you get access to reports about your reviews and visitors to your profile. Some information that you might not be able to glean elsewhere includes the number of mobile visitors, a breakdown of your visitors by location, and even competitor benchmarking data. Foursquare reports on the number of customers who checked into your location and how many of them are new customers. Depending on the review site, you may need to pay up or become an advertiser to get access to some of the juicier information. See Figure 4.1 for an example of a review site dashboard.

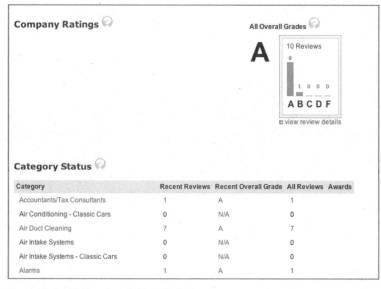

Figure 4.1 Angie's List reviews dashboard for businesses.

Basic access to your profile and dashboard is typically free.

Brick and Mortar/Local Business Review Tracking Products offered by Reputation.com, ReviewTrackers, and many others aggregate reviews posted online to Yelp, Google+ Local, and other venues. These tools generally provide a dashboard where business managers can see recently posted reviews assembled in one place for easy viewing. Various levels of analysis and reporting may be offered, such as metrics showing changes in reviews over time, or geographic distribution of reviews. ReviewPro, TrustYou, and Olery are specialized monitoring tools just for hotels. Revinate offers sophisticated monitoring and issue resolution workflow tools for hotels and restaurants. See Figure 4.2 for a sample Revinate dashboard.

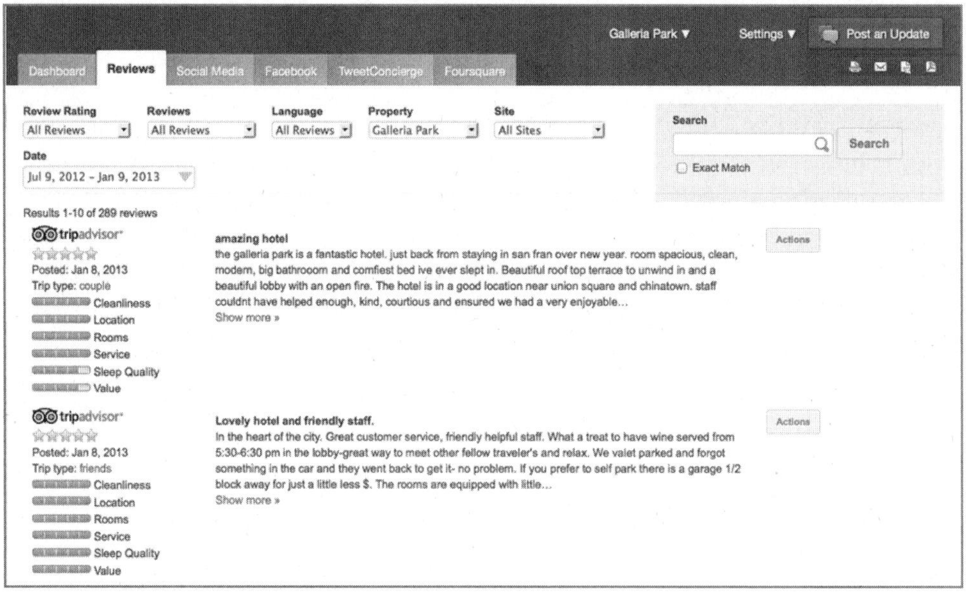

Figure 4.2 Revinate dashboard

 Recognizing their customer base, these services generally offer packages within reach for small businesses, in the $50- to $200-per-month range. Free 30-day trials are commonly offered.

These types of services are good for businesses that have a substantial number of reviews online and in-house staff capable of following up on the dashboard findings.

Social Media Listening Social media listening is a broad and manically fluxing space, with products that can be configured to scour the mass quantities of social media output and find mentions of your brand or products, including reviews. Social media monitoring is often just one component of broader social marketing functionality. Many social media tools help you publish to venues such as Twitter and Facebook, find influencers among your target audience, and measure the reach of your social media efforts.

Common features that you may find useful in your review monitoring activities include keyword-based monitoring, flagging and alerting, and functionality that allows you to respond to or share comments published on social media. There are so many tools out there that we can barely scratch the surface, but some well-known ones include Radian6, HootSuite, Sprout Social, and Raven. Figure 4.3 shows a dashboard from BrandsEye.

▶ **Table 4.1** Review monitoring tools

Name	Find it here	FYI
Brick and mortar/local business review tracking		
Brandify	www.brandify.com	Owned by Microsoft; provides a simple report card of brand presence; free trial available
Chatmeter	www.chatmeter.com	Geared toward franchises, agencies, and chains
GetFiveStars	www.getfivestars.com	Review tracking and customer relations tools for small businesses
GetListed.org	www.getlisted.org	Owned by Moz; a free tool that shows a limited list of reviews from around the Web
MDWebPro	www.mdwebpro.com	For doctors; offers free review tracking and a range of marketing services
Naymz	www.naymz.com	For individuals, particularly professionals and job seekers
Reputation.com	www.reputation.com	Offers a wide range of tools and services with many small business options
Reputation Ranger	www.reputationranger.com	Offers plans for lodging, restaurant/bar, automotive, and contractor
ReviewPro	www.reviewpro.com	For the hospitality industry; European-based company serving hotels worldwide offers review aggregation, alerts, dashboard, and analytics
ReviewPush	www.reviewpush.com	Startup priced for small business; free trial available
ReviewTrackers	www.reviewtrackers.com	Geared for small businesses; free trial available
Revinate	www.revinate.com	For the hospitality industry; official partner to TripAdvisor compiles reviews from TripAdvisor and many other sources with a user-friendly dashboard and workflow tools
TrustYou	www.trustyou.com	For the hospitality industry; headquartered in Germany; known for expertise in semantic analysis of review content

Continues

Name	Find it here	FYI
Product review tools (aka social commerce platforms)		
Bazaarvoice and Bazaarvoice Express (a small business product)	`www.bazaarvoice.com` `www.bazaarvoiceexpress.com`	Monitoring features ranging from basic to sophisticated
Pluck	`www.pluck.com`	Product Insights dashboard shows top/lowest rated products, keyword associations, review trends, and more
Reevoo	`www.reevoo.com`	Social commerce monitoring capabilities ranging from analytics dashboards to Reevoo Insights, a real-time business intelligence tool
Social media management tools		
BrandsEye	`www.brandseye.com`	Algorithmic analysis is combined with insights from a team of real people who evaluate online mentions
Brandwatch	`www.brandwatch.com`	Comprehensive brand monitoring tool well-suited to agencies and brands
Collective Intellect	`www.collectiveintellect.com`	Owned by Oracle; targets enterprise clients
HootSuite	`www.hootsuite.com`	Social media management dashboard popular with small businesses; free trial available
Lithium Social Web	`www.lithium.com`	Geared toward large teams handling social customer service
Meltwater Buzz	`www.meltwater.com`	Social media tool from PR-oriented creator focuses on listening and engagement
Radian6	`www.salesforcemarketing cloud.com`	Part of the Salesforce Marketing Cloud; a well-known and feature-rich social media listening tool
Raven	`www.raventools.com`	Internet marketing platform includes social media as well as SEO and paid search
SDL SM2	`www.sdl.com/products/SM2`	Formerly Alterian; comprehensive social media monitoring tool with entry level pricing options
Sprout Social	`www.sproutsocial.com`	Affordable tool for small businesses offers social media monitoring, posting, and reporting
Sysomos	`www.sysomos.com`	Multiple products including Heartbeat, a social media monitoring dashboard
Trackur	`www.trackur.com`	Focused on social media monitoring and analysis; priced for small business, free trial available

Continues

▶ **Table 4.1** Review monitoring tools *(Continued)*

Name	Find it here	FYI
uberVU	www.ubervu.com	Comprehensive monitoring platform geared toward enterprise clients; known for its competitor tracking
Viralheat	www.viralheat.com	Offers free personal account; free trial available
Visible	www.visibletechnologies.com	Comprehensive tool with an extensive feature set is geared toward larger businesses and agencies
Vocus	www.vocus.com	Social analytics is one component of this marketing and PR software suite
Wildfire	www.wildfireapp.com	A division of Google; offers enterprise-level social marketing software, advertising, and services for large brands

Figure 4.3 BrandsEye social media monitoring

Prices for social media listening tools range from under $50 per month all the way up to if-you-have-to-ask-you-can't-afford-it. Most have packages in the $500- to $1000-per-month range.

Search Engine Alerts One of the easiest tools for monitoring reviews online is a Google Alert.

It's free—you can't get cheaper than that!

We recommend that every business have a Google Alert for the branded terms that you choose in the exercise "Know Which Review Venues Deserve Your Attention." You don't even need a Google account; just visit www.google.com/alerts to set up your alert.

Product Review Tools Social commerce platforms such as Bazaarvoice, Reevoo, and Pluck are equipped with sophisticated review monitoring features that let you slice and dice your data. Curious what middle-aged women in Dubuque are saying about your products? Looking for an early warning system to tell you about problems with new products, weeks before returns start pouring in? These tools let you look at reviews through a wide array of customizable filters. See the sidebar "Brands Learn from Big Data with Bazaarvoice" for some examples of customer review intelligence at work in the real world. Finally, if you have configured your e-commerce platform to collect reviews for your own website, you'll most likely be able to set up alerts and moderation tools.

Other Review Venues Services that collect reviews of your business—even if reviews are not their primary function—will often supply you with reporting on the reviews they have gathered on your behalf. These services include small business software suites such as Demandforce and Genbook, reservation tools such as OpenTable, shopping comparison sites such as BizRate, OTAs such as Orbitz, and loyalty programs such as Rewards Network. When you are establishing a relationship with one of these entities, be sure you understand exactly how you'll be informed of reviews your business has received. See a reviews dashboard from Demandforce in Figure 4.4.

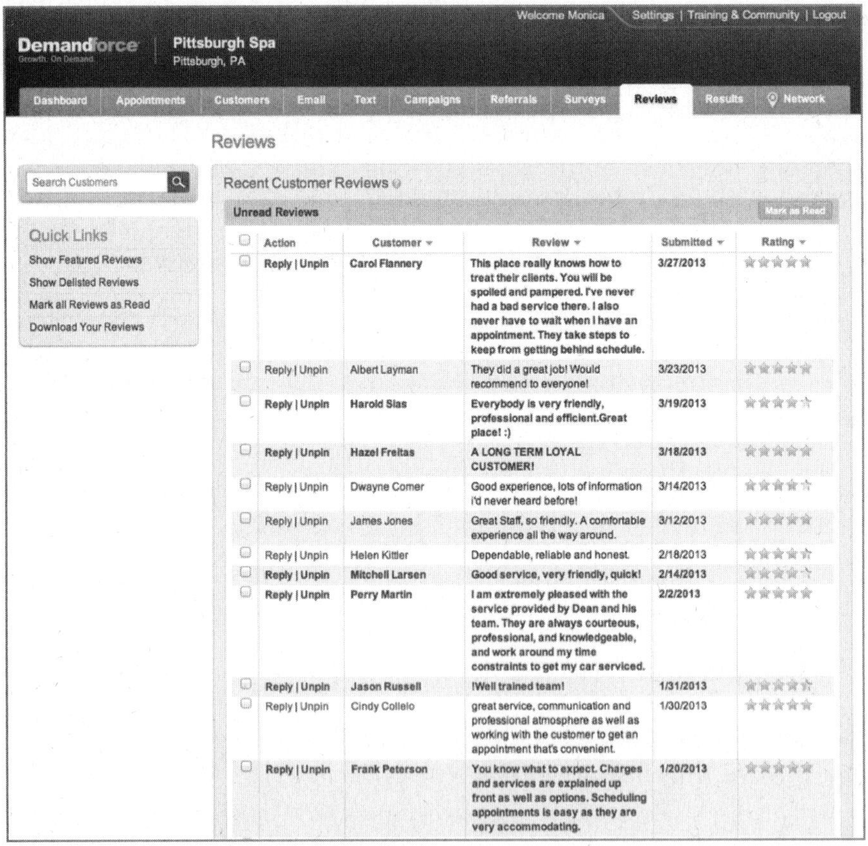

Figure 4.4 Demandforce's review monitoring dashboard

Brands Learn from Big Data with Bazaarvoice

If you've ever shopped online, we're pretty sure you've seen a Bazaarvoice-hosted review. The company provides a popular platform for e-commerce sites to gather and display customer reviews, and its sophisticated business intelligence functionality is closing feedback loops for many companies. We spoke with Neville Letzerich, Executive Vice President of Products, about some of the ways major brands and retailers use customer reviews to improve their businesses. At the heart of the process is the ability to configure alerts using customizable triggers. For example, wouldn't you like to be notified about the following:

- Reviews with fewer than 2 stars
- Reviews with 5 stars
- Reviews that contain legal concerns
- Reviews that mention a staff person by name
- Reviews that include product ideas or product flaws
- Any sudden change in a trend, for example, a spike in positive or negative reviews for a certain product, or a sudden increase in reviews from a particular customer segment

One Bazaarvoice client, a major sporting goods retailer, marries its product reviews with its client relationship management (CRM) system. With this information linked, a customer's likes and dislikes are part of the customer record, and customer service reps will have this information at their fingertips during future interactions. Pretty cool, right? Here are some more examples of smart ways businesses are using these tools:

- A perfume manufacturer noticed reviewers complaining that a scent was off, although they had not changed their formula. Putting faith in the word of their customers, they dug deeper and discovered that a supplier had changed an ingredient without informing them. The customer may not *always* be right, but if a big segment is trying to tell you something, even if it sounds crazy, you'd better be listening.

- A household product maker discovered that one of their highly rated products, a women's shoebox, could be improved. Women loved the plastic box, but didn't like that there were no holes in it allowing it to breathe. They were taking to the boxes with power drills and adding holes! Based on this information, the manufacturer changed the product to add the desired holes. Not only does this improve the product, it sends a strong message about how customer-centric a company really is.

- Another company set up their review tracking so that any 2-star or lower review automatically created a customer service ticket so that a staffer had to take responsibility for any needed follow-up.

The principle behind these stories can apply to businesses of all shapes and sizes: Listen to your customers. Their feedback is a gift—use it wisely.

Exercise: Know Which Review Venues Deserve Your Attention

Dedicating proper attention to every possible place where your business or products can be reviewed would take more hours than there are in a day, so we're going to make this simple for you, with four assignments for identifying the venues that matter most to you.

First, we describe a method that you can use to find your most visible reviews for your business in Google. After that, we break it down into specialized tasks, one for brick-and-mortar businesses (or any business with a Google+ Local listing) and one for online merchants. Finally, we help you find additional venues to consider based on where your competitors are.

Google Search Results for Your Branded Terms

Your first task is one you're already familiar with: Googling your own name. This exercise applies to any type of business. Here's the assignment in bite-sized steps:

Step 1: Remove personalization from your Google results.

Google search results are personalized based on the searcher's location, previous search behavior, and social profile. This can cause you to see wildly different results than your neighbors. If you're logged into Google you can easily turn off some personalization by clicking on the globe icon in the upper-right corner of Google's search screen. If you don't have a Google account or you're not logged in, visit www.google.com/history/optout, and click on the link "Disable customizations based on search activity," as seen here:

Google Web History

Your search and ad results may be customized using search activity from this computer.

Disable customizations based on search activity.

Sign in or create a Google account to get more personalized search and ad results using your signed-in Web History.

This will set a cookie preference to display depersonalized results.

Another way to remove personalization is by using incognito browsing mode. It's simple and will make you feel like a superspy. In Chrome, click File > New Incognito Window.

In Firefox and Internet Explorer, press Ctrl+Shift+P to enable private browsing.

Continues

File	Edit	View	History	Book
New Tab			⌘T	
New Window			⌘N	
New Incognito Window			⇧⌘N	
Reopen Closed Tab			⇧⌘T	
Open File...			⌘O	
Open Location...			⌘L	
Close Window			⇧⌘W	
Close Tab			⌘W	
Save Page As...			⌘S	
Email Page Location			⇧⌘I	
Print...			⌘P	

These exercises are Google-centric because Google is vastly dominant in the worldwide search market. If you have reason to think your target audience is using a different search engine, use it instead.

Step 2: Locate yourself.

When you perform a search, the location of your computer affects Google's search results, so you'll want to perform the search with settings that match your business's target audience. Google bases the location on your computer's IP address, but you can override this (perhaps not with 100% accuracy) by clicking the Search Tools button near the top of the Google search pane and entering a city and state.

Google — saab service above and beyond

Web   Images   Maps   Shopping   Videos   More ▾   Search tools

Any time ▾   All results ▾   Los Angeles, CA 90065 ▾

✓ Los Angeles, CA 90065
El Cerrito, CA
chicago, IL   Set

Service Above And B[...]i, Saab ...
www.serviceaboveandbe[...]
Specializing in European aut[...]
Google+ page · Write a revie[...]
150 Kuniholm Dr Hollis[...]
(508) 429-1993

Contact Us - Service - Schedule a Service

E-commerce businesses or brands that sell to any location don't need to worry about geographical settings. Businesses with an international customer base should perform these searches on all of the international Google sites that apply—for example, Google.de for Germany and Google.co.uk for UK—and should set the location to a city in the chosen country.

Continues

Step 3: Choose your branded search keywords.

In search engine optimization (SEO) lingo, search queries that include your business name are called *branded searches*. The branded terms you document today should include the following at a minimum: your business name, including all spelling variations; major product names; your personal name, if it is strongly tied to the business; and your business name or product name plus the word *reviews*.

You'll also want to include any related keywords that Google Suggest shows you. Google Suggest provides suggested search terms as you type based on common queries. Type your business name with a space after it and check to see if Google adds anything. If you find autocomplete text for your business, go ahead and perform those searches and document the top page results. Feeling ambitious? Type your business name, a space, and then a random letter to see what other suggestions you can find.

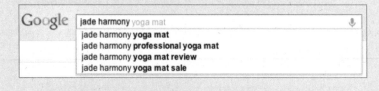

Step 4: Perform your branded searches on Google.

An example of Google branded search results is shown here:

> **Moving Reviews for TWO MEN AND A TRUCK**
> www.twomenandatruck.com/moving-reviews ▾
> ★★★★★ Rating: 4.5 - 152542 reviews
> Read unedited moving **reviews** of TWO MEN AND A TRUCK from real customers all
> across the United States.
>
> **TWO MEN AND A TRUCK**, Movers, Moving Company, Moving ...
> www.twomenandatruck.com/ ▾
> Get a FREE moving quote & read unedited moving **reviews** for your local movers. 3500
> movers, 1400 **trucks**, 96% referral rate. Residential & Commercial.
> Free Moving Quotes - Locations/Contact - Local Movers - Moving Terms
>
> **Two Men And A Truck** - Livermore, CA - Yelp
> www.yelp.com › Home Services › Movers ▾
> ★★★★☆ Rating: 3.5 - 12 reviews
> 12 **Reviews** of Two Men And A Truck "Another great move with **Two Men And A
> Truck**! Ditto to everything in my 2011 **review**, including the onsite estimate and ...
>
> **Two Men and a Truck** - Sacramento, CA - Yelp
> www.yelp.com › Home Services › Movers ▾
> ★★★★★ Rating: 4.5 - 62 reviews
> 62 **Reviews** of Two Men and a Truck "You don't always get professionals when you
> hire professional movers, but **Two Men and a Truck** deliver great customer ...
>
> **Two Men and a Truck** - Near West Side - Chicago, IL - Yelp
> www.yelp.com › Home Services › Movers ▾
> ★★★★☆ Rating: 3.5 - 31 reviews
> 31 **Reviews** of Two Men and a Truck "So glad I hired a moving company this time. So
> glad I hired THIS moving company. You can go to their website and fill out ...
>
> **Two Men and a Truck** Employee **Reviews** | Indeed.com
> www.indeed.com/cmp/Two-Men-and-A-Truck/reviews ▾
> ★★★★☆ Rating: 3.5 - 43 reviews
> 43 employee **reviews** of **Two Men and a Truck**. Indeed.com.

Continues

Snap a screenshot of the top page results in Google. You may see some bad reviews or upsetting reputation blotches along the way. Try not to get sidetracked on these, but do document them so you can go back and obsess over them later.

Since you're already on a review venue finding trip, any business with a physical location should take a quick detour to GetListed.org to see if this free tool serves up any other review venues that are getting a lot of action.

Step 5: List the review venues that you see in the results you've collected.

With the first four steps complete, you should have collected five or six screenshots showing top Google results. Now, look through those sheets and tally up any review sites that you see. To identify review sites, look for stars in the Google listings, or telltale titles that indicate customer reviews. Click through on any sites that you don't recognize to see if there are any reviews there. Sites with zero reviews, or with just one crusty review from 2009 or so, probably don't belong on your list, but use your judgment and add them if they convey any form of extreme sentiment, or if they are legitimate sites that are well targeted to your customers.

If you have more than five sites on your list, keep the ones that you found the most often. If you don't find any review sites, be sure to pay close attention during the step called "Where Your Competitors Are," because you'll likely identify some good venues for pursuing new reviews.

A dermatologist may end up with a list that looks something like this:

- Google+ Local
- Healthgrades.com
- Vitals.com
- Yelp.com
- Wellness.com
- Insiderpages.com

Well done! You have a starter list of review venues that deserve the majority of your attention.

Your Google+ Local Listing

Your second task is to find the reviews that are displayed on, or linked from, the Google+ Local listing for your business. Not every business will have a Google+ Local listing, so this assignment only applies to those of you with a physical presence. Here's what to do:

- Step 1: Click on "Maps" in Google and then search for your business name.
- Step 2: Click on "more info" to reach your business's Google+ Local page

- Step 3: Scroll down and look at the reviews. Reviews that were posted directly on Google will include text, like this one:

- Step 4: Continue scrolling down and look for links to reviews on external sites:

Reviews from around the web: yahoo.com - urbanspoon.com - centerstagechicago.com

Simple enough. Here is this restaurant's list from the second task:

- Yahoo.com

- Urbanspoon.com

- CenterStageChicago.com

Continues

Your E-Commerce Seller Ratings on Google

This task is just for those of you who have e-commerce sites and are advertising on Google AdWords (www.google.com/adwords) or promoting your products via Google Product Listing Ads (PLAs) (www.google.com/ads/shopping). As you learned in Chapter 2, "The Online Reviews Landscape," Google pulls in seller ratings from various review sources on the Web. We'll go into more detail on seller ratings in Chapter 8, "Showing Off and Being Found." In this task, you'll find the sites from which Google is pulling your reviews.

Step 1: Navigate to Google's seller ratings page for your site.

There are a few ways to get to Google's page showing reviews of your e-commerce site. If you have seller rating review stars on AdWords ads for your site, just click on the link next to them in your ad. In this example, CoffeeForLess.com would click on "44 seller reviews":

If your site hasn't been graced with star-spangled ads, here's another way to see your ratings: Visit Google Shopping at www.google.com/shopping and search for a product that you sell. You will need to be running Google PLAs for your products to show up in this search. Click the Compare Prices button.

Continues

Then, click on the ratings link next to your store name:

Keurig Vue Pack Green Mountain Breakfast Blend Coffee, Regular, 16/Pack

$11 online, **$12** nearby

★★★★★ 1 review   🔖 Add to Shortlist

« Back to overview

Online stores shipping to Richmond, CA

☐ 🕪 Google Wallet   ☐ Free shipping   ☐ Refurbished / used

Sellers ▾	Seller Rating	Details	Base Price	Total Price
Keurig.com	No rating	No tax	$10.79 $6.95 shipping	$17.74
Bed Bath & Beyond	13 ratings	Free shipping	$11.99 $1.08 tax	$13.07
Macy's	★★★★★ (46)		$11.99 $11.03 tax & shipping	$23.02
Totalvac.com 🕪	★★★★☆ (421)	No tax	$11.99 $6.95 shipping	$18.94

Step 2: Make a note of the review sources Google is using.

Now, you should be looking at a page that contains reviews and a list of sources:

Google [   ] 🔍   SIGN IN

CoffeeForLess.com

Seller rating: 4.4 / 5 - Based on 45 reviews from the past 12 months

What people are saying

price	▓▓▓▓	"Good coffee, good price, fast delivery!"
customer service	▓▓▓	"Great service , fair prices."
shipping	▓▓▓▓	"Impressed on the quick delivery."
selection	▓▓▓▓	"Nice selection of product."
ordering process	▓▓▓	"Quick and easy transaction."
communication	▓▓▓▓	"Great service and communication"
service	No rating	"GREAT SERVICE AND DELIVERY......."

★★★★★ 5 / 5   great service and fair pricing
By DavidT - Apr 18, 2013 - Google Wallet Reviews
Was this review helpful? Yes - No

★★★★★ 5 / 5   Fast shipping, easy ordering, good pricing and regular special offers make for an excelent experience.
By Shopper - Dec 28, 2012 - Google Wallet Reviews
Was this review helpful? Yes - No

★★★★☆ 4 / 5   Prices not special
By Stephen - Jan 13, 2013 - Google Wallet Reviews
Was this review helpful? Yes - No

★★★★★ 5 / 5   No problems. Fast shipping.
By msn - Feb 17, 2013 - Google Wallet Reviews
Was this review helpful? Yes - No

Show reviews by rating

1 star (74)
2 stars (38)
3 stars (57)
4 stars (159)
5 stars (1,026)

Sort reviews

Sort by relevance
Sort by date

Show reviews by source

Bizrate (127)
Epinions (2)
Google Wallet Reviews (1199)
PriceGrabber.com (23)
TRUSTPILOT (3)

Continues

In the case of CoffeeForLess.com, the seller reviews are being sourced primarily from Bizrate and Google Wallet, with Epinions, PriceGrabber.com, and Trustpilot contributing some as well.

Where Your Competitors Are

The tasks you just performed gave insight into sites where your business or products have already been reviewed. For your next assignment, you'll look for the venues where your competitors are listed.

- Choose three or four competitors. If your company doesn't have direct competitors, choose other businesses that are similar to yours.

- For each of the competitors, go back and rerun the tasks you just completed, but this time, do it for your competitors' branded names, and if applicable, their Google+ Local listing and Google seller ratings. Compare the list to the one you compiled for your business. Did you find any new sites that aren't on the list?

As an example, suppose you run a limo service in Oklahoma City and one of your competitors is Royal Limousine Services. Their Google+ Local page shows five Google reviews and also includes links to Superpages, Local.com, and Citysearch. You've already got Local.com and Citysearch on your list, but *Superpages*—that's a new one. Add it to your list now.

With your assignments completed, you've got a solid list of the review venues that matter the most for your business.

Keep this list at the ready as you learn more about monitoring and encouraging reviews for your business in Chapter 5, "How to Get More Reviews." We hope you won't need to use this list for crisis management, but if you do, you'll find some helpful advice in Chapter 7, "Navigating Negative Reviews."

Learn from Your Reviews

Learning from your reviews and taking action to change the problems at your business that are triggering negative reviews is a crucial element of any review management plan. Some businesses use sophisticated tools to sift through their reviews and parse out meaningful information from the resulting mountain of data, as we described earlier in the sidebar "Brands Learn from Big Data with Bazaarvoice." But even if you do not have access to these tools, you can still take a manual approach using the best semantic analysis tool there is: your own brain.

The Bad Review Nobody Saw

"This guy intentionally tried to hurt my business!"

This was our client's frantic comment when he found a scathing review about his services on Yelp. The reviewer, who won't be winning any awards for decency or reason, made false claims and accused our client of ineptitude.

This understandably caused a great deal of concern for our client, and as we advised him on how to address the situation, we provided some perspective. The Yelp activity panel showed that the number of people who looked at our client's profile in the span of three months could be counted on one hand. Sure, a single negative review has the potential to harm a reputation, but the likelihood of harm decreases when almost nobody's looking.

Before you lose sleep over negative reviews, take a few minutes to understand where your prospective customers might be looking:

- If you have access to statistics from a review site, look for a view count to see how many people are visiting your profile.
- Your website analytics can tell you how many visitors arrived at your site from review sites. (In Google Analytics, click Acquisitions > All Referrals.)
- Ask your existing customers whether and where they researched your company.
- Perform a Google search for your company name or product to see if your reviews are making their way into search engine results. This process is described in more detail in the earlier sidebar "Know Which Review Venues Deserve Your Attention."
- Investigate where your popular competitors are getting the most reviews, by performing the steps described in this sidebar in the section "Where Your Competitors Are."

Our client spent more time and energy trying to investigate and mitigate this one negative Yelp review than he'd ever spent on proactive tasks such as improving his website, showcasing his expertise in social media, or soliciting new reviews from happy customers. Happily, the review was eventually filtered by Yelp, and the entire team was able to direct its attention back to working on more useful marketing efforts.

An Honest Assessment

Your first step in learning from your reviews is understanding their content. If you've been obsessing over a single negative review for the last two years, or if you get so many reviews you have trouble keeping up, you need a way to get an actionable summary. Even if you think you already know everything about your reviews, using a formal process to tally them may cause unexpected patterns to emerge.

There is no one-size-fits-all approach here, so we won't tell you exactly how to do it. The ultimate goal is the same for all businesses: Look through your reviews on the venues that matter to you and identify and quantify the positive and negative mentions of your business, product, or services. For example, a restaurant might develop a simple tally like this:

	Positive mentions	Negative mentions	Notes
Service	✓	✓✓	Negative mentions of wait time for getting the check.
Taste	✓✓✓✓		The food itself is never a problem!
Price	✓✓		
Location		✓	One complaint that the neighborhood is too quiet. Well, we can't change that.
Cleanliness	✓		
Drinks	✓		
Wait time	✓	✓✓✓	Long waits for Sunday Brunch
Hours		✓✓	Closing too early, hours not clear on website

Logging the sentiment in your reviews can be difficult if you feel a negative remark is unfair or incorrect. We recommend including all reviews in this assessment and remaining as objective as possible. Many businesses, upon performing an assessment like this, will notice a handful of concerns rising to the surface. Fair or not, these need to be addressed.

Taking Action

Once you develop an assessment of your reviews, you'll probably see some familiar complaints and compliments. You may also see some surprises. Here are a few ways to frame your thinking around these findings:

- Look for easy wins. Are there any specific, easily remedied problems ("the waiting room is too cold") that came up more than once? Why not jump on making that change right now? And don't forget: If the review venue allows it, it's almost always a good idea to respond to these reviewers and let them—and anyone else who's reading—know you're listening.

- Any complaints that show up in multiple reviews deserve your attention, but for large or difficult changes, review sentiment will be just one of many factors that inform your business decisions. If you can't fix the problem right now, what can you do to improve upon it? For example, you may not be able to shorten your wait time, but can you think of ways to make the wait time more pleasant for your customers?

- Has a member of your staff been complimented, either by name or by role ("the concierge was so helpful!")? Figure out a way to acknowledge, or even reward, staff members who get recognition in online reviews.

- Can you incorporate your findings into your business processes on a regular basis? A monthly meeting or weekly write-up might do the trick. Connecting with your staff about online reviews also gives them a chance to tell you about offline complaints and compliments so that you can compare notes and identify high-priority concerns.

- One simple action you can take is responding to reviews. This doesn't have to be too time-consuming. As an example, the Revinate tool has a template feature that allows hotels to compose and store boilerplate responses to common remarks such as compliments on customer service. Obviously, you don't want to publish repetitive responses to multiple reviewers, but having starter text at the ready will help you maintain a cohesive voice and keep responses consistent with your company policies. (Pssst...you don't need a tool to create your own customer response templates!)

Even if your business uses more sophisticated review tracking tools, ultimately it's this kind of human analysis that garners meaning and points you toward business changes. You know your business, you know your customers, and you know what changes are possible in the short and long term. That's a trifecta no sentiment analysis algorithm can beat.

Creating a Boss-Friendly Weekly Reviews Digest

Claire Raben is an assistant manager at a bustling regional Italian restaurant (names and identifying details have been changed) and its sister cafe. Having worked there for many years, she knows all the business's ins and outs, including the sensitivities of its owner, Anita. Like many small business owners, Anita pours her heart and soul into this business, and she takes every negative review as a painful personal affront.

"We were spending too much time talking through every review, and she was getting really agitated about them," Claire confides. "Eventually I told her, 'Look, let me do this for you. I'll alert you if there's anything important.'"

Claire and her boss developed a review monitoring system that works for everyone: Claire monitors reviews manually and creates a weekly digest for the boss, summarizing important reviews. By evolving the process over time, they've established criteria for what's included in the digest, as Claire explains:

- Anything that mentions a staff member by name. "We always follow up on both the negative and positive mentions and make sure we address any problem with the employee."

- "Glowing reviews." Nobody minds a little morale boost!

- Any review that mentions a specific incident. "We talk about it with our staff to get a clear view of the situation."

Continues

Creating a Boss-Friendly Weekly Reviews Digest *(Continued)*

Claire feels her most important task is to weed out reviews that don't deliver useful information: "The goal is to not let the boss get upset about things when either they aren't really valid or there's nothing you can do about them. Sometimes a person is just having a bad day." Claire writes a short-attention-span-friendly summary, highlighting important quotes, and emails it along with the full text of key reviews, source venue, and URL. She and Anita then work together to decide on any follow-up actions to be taken, such as pulling a staff member aside to work out an issue or writing a private response to a reviewer.

Beyond the weekly reports, Claire's process also helps her internalize the Zeitgeist of her restaurant's reviews in an ongoing way. If she sees common issues repeating over time, she'll make changes at the restaurant to address them. "I might notice that a lot of people are mentioning they had to wait a long time for coffee refills, and I will be more aware of this on the floor—'Hey, we need to get the coffee refilled, people are complaining.'"

There's much to love about Claire's review monitoring process: It's low cost, it focuses on actionable information, and it is simple enough to be a long-term habit. Bravissima, Claire!

Now that you have a better understanding of the reviews you've got, let's work on getting more and better reviews. See you in Chapter 5!

How to Get
More Reviews

There's a well-kept secret about online reviews, and we're going to spill it now. The success of your business doesn't depend on getting 5-star reviews. Rather, it depends on getting more reviews, as many as you can ethically accumulate, so that the customer voice can tell the real story of your business to your prospective customers. In this chapter, we'll show you straightforward tactics for getting more reviews and a more representative sample of your customers, clients, or membership while remaining authentic and steering clear of review site filters. Put some energy into these efforts, and you may just feel sorry for your competitors by this time next year.

In this chapter:
Tools and techniques for getting new reviews
Cultivating a word-of-mouth mentality
Authenticity and ethics

It's easy to say "be great, and the reviews will follow." And maybe a business that does extraordinary, remarkable things every day or creates unbelievable, amazing, noteworthy products that never fail and always arrive on time doesn't need to spend a lot of time in the review cultivation effort. This chapter is not about how to be amazing. Rather, we give you real-world techniques for encouraging reviews and making it as easy as possible for people to write them. You want the path of least resistance to flow right to your online reviews, and here's how to make that happen.

Tools and Techniques for Getting New Reviews

Like so many things in life, online reviews follow the basic precept "Ask and ye shall receive." As you learned in Chapter 3, "Understanding Reviewers and Reviews," studies show that people who are asked to provide a review are more likely to write one. That finding? Pretty obvious. But the *right way* to ask may not be so obvious.

To be most effective, a method of asking for reviews should be…

Easy for the Customer The path to writing a review must be fast and easy. It should require the least possible effort on the part of the reviewer.

Easy for the Business You need a process that is simple for the staffers executing it and sustainable so that it can be performed consistently for the long term.

Broad-minded Target the largest number of customers or clients possible, not just the happy ones. Variation among reviews enhances credibility, and negative reviews are often informative and helpful.

No Pressure You're asking for a favor, not making a demand. Customers should know that there is no pressure to write a review, but their honest review would be much appreciated.

Timed Well Customers should be contacted quickly so that your transaction is fresh on their minds, but not before they've had the chance to receive a product or judge a service.

In Keeping with Your Image The way you ask for reviews should be consistent with your brand personality and marketing message. Don't rely on boilerplate messages from third-party services. Your requests should be customizable so you control what is said to your customers.

Ongoing Many review venues and prospective customers give more weight to recent reviews. For businesses like hotels and restaurants, current reviews are a must.

Measurable Whatever you try, be sure that you can measure whether it works and adjust accordingly.

If you are already asking for reviews, we applaud you. Read the information here to improve your requests so they can bring you even more online love.

If you're not asking for reviews, let us pull you aside for a quick heart-to-heart: *Pssst…. You know we love you. But if you've been holding back on asking for reviews because you feel shy or it seems weird or pushy, you really need to get over it. Try to think of the last time you were turned off or appalled by a business asking you for a review. What? That's never happened to you? Yep. That's the same for almost everyone else, too. Your customers can handle it, and so can you.*

There are many ways to ask for reviews and to provide a path for review completion. Here, we've assembled a list of techniques and tools that we've seen businesses use. We hope you'll read these with an eye toward the criteria listed earlier. Could any of them work for your business?

Personal Request This technique is well suited to contractors, auto mechanics, professionals, authors, and just about any service provider who offers work with a personal or face-to-face element. Here's an example: Not long ago, Jennifer had some work done on her house. After the service was complete, the contractor shook her hand, looked her in the eye, and told her it would be a big help if she could write an online review. Hours later, Jennifer had joined the 70 or so other folks who had written this company a review on Angie's List. The business owner took a fabulous first step by asking for the review. He even bolstered his position, appealing to Jennifer's good nature and desire to help others by saying how important her review would be to him.

Sometimes asking for and receiving a review really is that simple, but sometimes it takes a bit more finesse. Here are some things to keep in mind when asking for a review in person:

- Ask for the review after the service or transaction is completed.
- Let your customer know the importance of online reviews to the success of your business and to you personally. Many reviewers are motivated by a desire to reciprocate when businesses have served them well.
- You know which venues are most important to you from the exercise you performed in Chapter 4, "Monitoring and Learning from Your Reviews." Tell your customer the specific venue where you would prefer to be reviewed—but make it clear you'd be happy with a review anywhere.
- If you are seeking Yelp or Google+ Local reviews, it will be more fruitful to direct your requests to active reviewers on those sites. First-time reviewers who post on your behalf have a higher chance of being filtered out.
- If you make follow-up calls to check on customer satisfaction, that's a perfect time to ask for a review.
- People forget! Don't be afraid to ask more than once. Follow up your face-to-face request with reminders to complete the review. You can follow up

via phone or email a few days after your initial request or use a physical reminder. See more about physical reminders later in this chapter.

- Don't assume your customers know how to use online review tools. If you suspect that your clientele is not comfortable in the digital world, you can offer them clear instructions on how to write a review. Some businesses take this further: We spoke with a carpet cleaning company that tried a variety of ways to ask for reviews and found they were getting nowhere. Finally, the cleaning staff began gently offering to stand by and help customers through the review creation process. Don't get the wrong idea; this was tech support, not coercion. Their approach paid off, and using this method they have been able to develop a solid stack of reviews.

You're human, which means you're probably tempted to request reviews from only your happiest customers. Sure, you can leave out the tiny percentage of impossible-to-please customers and vindictive extremists, but we suggest you broaden the net wide enough to include a representative sample of your customers. As hard as it may be to hear it, your less-satisfied customers have valuable information to share, and as you learned in Chapter 3, studies show that having some negative reviews can help, not hurt, your business. If you're worried about your outreach resulting in negative reviews for your business, be sure your email also includes an option to contact you directly with concerns or complaints.

A Successful New Approach for an Old-School Business

Like many old-school businesspeople, Maryland mortgage broker Michael Mandis avoided Internet-based marketing for a long time. He runs a successful business that has, in his words, "always done the right thing for my customers for 20 years." Simply put, Michael is an old-fashioned businessman in an old-fashioned business, built on his honor and his handshake.

Michael may not have a lot of experience in online marketing, but his business wouldn't have succeeded for all these years if he didn't know how to focus on his clients and give them a top-notch experience. "I'm available evenings, weekends. I go the extra mile."

Recently, Michael decided to throw his hat into the online marketing ring, to translate his clients' excellent offline experience into an improved online presence.

What works for Michael? "Persistence is one of the main things. People intend to do it and then they forget." Michael asks for reviews from his clients after the home sale has closed. Here are some ways he helps them along:

- If a client has a Yahoo! email address, Michael asks for a review on Yahoo!. If they have a Gmail address, he asks for a Google+ Local review. "I'm looking for the path of least resistance."

Continues

A Successful New Approach for an Old-School Business *(Continued)*

- He always follows up. "A lot of times people leave reviews using screen names. Sometimes I can't tell who is leaving them. I say 'Thank you if you did, and if you didn't, here is the link again.'"

- Whenever Michael receives a referral, he sends a custom printed gift card that includes a QR code for Angie's List, Yahoo!, or Google+ Local. "I'm not bribing them for a review. It's a thank you for the recommendation, and just by virtue of the fact that you recommended me to someone, don't keep it a secret."

Michael's review cultivation strategies, combined with his business's commitment to impeccable customer service, have had fantastic results. "I can attribute $100,000 in additional revenue to leads that have been generated organically through my reviews in roughly the last year." Even better, the clients who are coming to him after looking at reviews are the kinds of clients he wants, "not rate-seekers. I'm attracting people who want someone they can trust." Michael also uses his reviews as a sales tool. On the phone with a prospective client, he'll encourage them to Google his name plus "reviews" and do the same for a competitor. "Ten minutes later they'll call me back and say, let's get started."

For Michael, his online reviews journey has been rewarding, not only financially but also emotionally: "It's an honor to be reviewed, and it's humbling, and it's touching."

Because he has embraced online reviews in an old-fashioned business niche, Michael is now well ahead of his competitors. With a year of effort and many reviews collected, Michael compares himself to his competitors who have not embraced online marketing: "I feel like I'm halfway through the marathon and they're just tying their shoelaces."

Post-Transaction Email to Review a Product If your business includes an e-commerce component and you have product reviews on your site, sending post-transaction emails is a great way to increase the number of reviews on your site. According to Bazaarvoice, clients who use what it calls a post interaction program "typically see more than 80% of their ratings & reviews volume generated through [post interaction emails]."

If you've been putting more time and attention into perfecting your email newsletters than you have into your transactional emails such as purchase confirmations, shipping notifications, or review requests, consider flipping this strategy on its head. Studies consistently show that transactional emails are much more likely to be opened than bulk emails. As a bonus, several case studies have noted that a surprising number—14% in one example—of customers who clicked back to the site from a review-request email went on to make another purchase.

Amazon is an example of an e-commerce retailer with a thoughtful and effective process in place. After a customer makes a purchase, the system waits a predetermined amount of time and then sends out an email, like the one seen in Figure 5.1, requesting a product review.

LOCS Sunglasses Hardcore Black Dark Lens 0103 Designer Stylish w Bag

Figure 5.1 Amazon.com post-transaction email offers a convenient link to review the product.

Amazon's post-purchase emails are brief and focused, with a prominent link to make it easy for customers to review the product. The email from Sierra Trading Post shown in Figure 5.2 goes a step further by offering to enter reviewers into a $1,000 giveaway contest as an incentive for writing a review.

Figure 5.2 Post-transaction email from Sierra Trading Company

Chewy.com combines Bazaarvoice-supplied boilerplate text with its own messaging to ask for reviews and encourage photo uploads. See Figure 5.3.

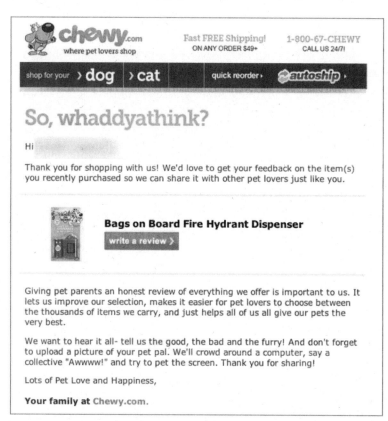

Figure 5.3 Post-transaction email from Chewy.com

Although they may seem ubiquitous, post-transaction emails requesting reviews are considered an underutilized tactic by many marketers. Implementing a post-transaction email request could be a great way for you to differentiate yourself from the competition. Here are some ways you can get a program like this off the ground:

- Consider using a social commerce platform that incorporates post-transaction emails as an integral part of the system, such as Bazaarvoice or Reevoo.

- Post-transaction emails may be a feature available in your e-commerce system. For example, Volusion allows you to send a customized email requesting a review a specified number of days after a product is shipped. WooCommerce has extensions called "Follow-up Emails" and "Review for Discount" that can be combined to create this capability. Look into the offerings of your e-commerce system by speaking to an account rep or searching its name plus <transactional email>.

- Many email service providers offer triggered email messages. Tools such as Constant Contact, VerticalResponse, Silverpop, and HubSpot can be set up to send fully customized post-transaction emails.

- If you have a small number of transactions, getting in touch via a personal email may be a viable option for you. Follow the guidelines listed previously under "Personal Request."

Experiment with your email content and timing to see what permutation gets the best results for your business.

Post-Transaction Email to Review a Business Automating the collection of business reviews is a well-established practice. Plenty of options are available for online merchants, and a growing number of options are available for brick-and-mortar establishments. For e-commerce sites and some service providers, tools such as ResellerRatings, Shopper Approved, Customer Lobby, and Demandforce can be configured to automate the process of sending emails to request reviews after an interaction with a customer or client or at other customer touchpoints. Amazon merchants can send a post-transaction email asking for customer reviews.

Shopping comparison sites such as Bizrate, online travel agents such as Booking.com, and restaurant reservation tools such as OpenTable also send post-transaction emails inviting reviews.

Figure 5.4 shows an example of a ResellerRatings email seeking reviews for a travel insurance company.

Figure 5.4 ResellerRatings post-transaction email

According to ResellerRatings, these emails are very successful, generating an average rating of 9.7 out of 10 for the business.

UK e-commerce site Appliances Online uses humor and a visual to engage reviewers with their post-transaction email, shown in Figure 5.5.

Figure 5.5 Appliances Online uses humor to engage potential reviewers.

Here are some things to keep in mind when writing post-transaction emails or considering a tool to generate them:

- The guidelines described in "Personal Request" also apply here. Give your email a personality and give the recipient a reason to take action.

- Many review-generation tools' outgoing emails only invite customers to review the business on their own venue: Demandforce on the Demandforce site, ResellerRatings on the ResellerRatings site, and so on. If you are considering investing in a review collection tool, first consider whether the reviews it collects will reside on—or feed into—the top review venues you identified in Chapter 4. If not, you should know that reviews on these sites may not be the most helpful for your business. Be sure to monitor, measure, and adjust if necessary.

- If you are in the habit of sending a "how did we do" email, find out if the survey responses can be published on a review venue. See "Integration of Surveys with Online Review Sites."

- To avoid confusion, provide separate links for product reviews and business reviews, or solicit product reviews and business reviews in separate emails.

- Don't expect a high response rate. As a point of reference, Bazaarvoice Express notes that "On average, retailers see almost 7% of their email recipients complete a review" with its email solicitation tool. A lighting business in a Google+ Local forum described a similar response rate: "Even though our customers have the best intentions to give us a review, out of 50 [requests] you may get 2 or 3." If your initial response is paltry, don't give up! Send more than one request if necessary. Try variations until your results improve, and use the exercise in this chapter to get an eye for the most effective emails.

Day-to-Day Correspondence There's no telling when a longstanding customer will decide to cross over into advocacy territory, so adding review links as a permanent feature of your routine customer communications is a smart strategy. In Figure 5.6, Demandforce's appointment reminder serves double duty as a review request.

Figure 5.6 This dental appointment reminder generated by Demandforce contains a review link.

Links to your review profiles can also be part of your business's email signature. These low-maintenance, always-on methods help ensure that every connection with your customers provides an easy opportunity for them to lay down their two cents.

Physical Reminder People are busy and forgetful. Any business owner can surely relate! It may not be enough to provide an emotional incentive or a perfectly timed email for people to leave reviews. You may also need to provide physical reminders.

Here are some examples of physical reminders:

- Shipping insert. Be sure your insert makes the case: Don't just say "Review Us." Explain why your customer should take the time to do it. And don't forget to provide a URL or instructions for finding your profile on the review site. Here's a good example of a shipping insert:

  www.smallbusinesssem.com/good-example-how-to-ask-for-a-review/7370

- Signs at your location. Figure 5.7 shows a sign in a wifi-enabled waiting room. Yelp, with its stance against asking for reviews, would rather the sign say "Find us on Yelp" and leave off the "Review us" part. Read about Yelp's review solicitation policies in Chapter 6, "Review Venues: Need-to-Know Tips for Your Action Plan," and later in this chapter.

Figure 5.7 A sign is a convenient reminder, especially if it is in a location with wifi.

- A reminder printed on your receipts, bags, napkins, menus, hotel binder, or anything else that your customer makes contact with.
- On-site kiosk. Presto Reviews is an example of a company that offers on-site electronic review stations. However, Google+ Local has specifically warned against this practice and it may put you at risk of having your reviews filtered.
- Printed take-home sheet with detailed instructions on how to leave a review.
- Some review venues offer free or low-cost printed reminders for businesses to use with their customers, including review forms, reminder stickers, and tear pads.

Calls to Action on Your Website If you are hoping to accumulate more reviews on a particular review site, consider grabbing one of the review site's widgets for your own website. A widget is a simple piece of code that you can embed on your website if you want to create an eye-catching link to your business profile on a review site. They can also display reviews that you already have; we'll talk more about that in Chapter 8, "Showing Off and Being Found." Many review sites offer customized widgets for free. TripAdvisor's widgets come in several variations, ranging from small, linked graphics to a form that allows the site visitor to start writing the review without leaving your site (see Figure 5.8).

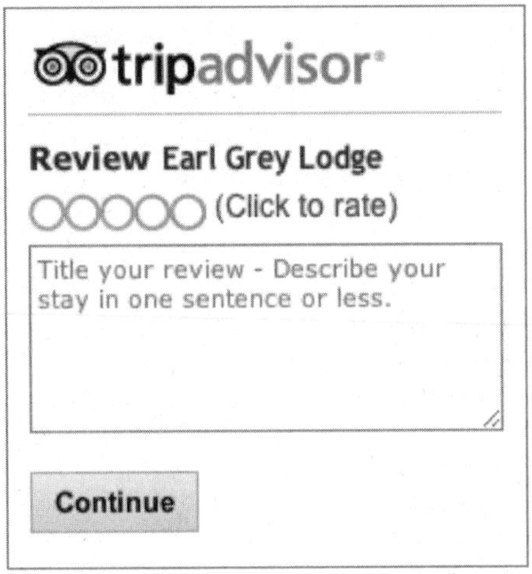

⊙⊙ tripadvisor®

Review Earl Grey Lodge
○○○○○ (Click to rate)

Title your review - Describe your
stay in one sentence or less.

Continue

Figure 5.8 TripAdvisor widget displayed on the Earl Grey Lodge site

If you're not keen on widgets, or your favorite service doesn't offer a widget, you can create your own link. Some sites create a page dedicated to review requests; others keep things minimal with a small "Review us" text link. Figure 5.9 shows a call to action from a catering company's home page that we like because it's simple and visually compelling.

HOW ARE WE DOING? - REVIEWS WANTED!
Are you a current or past customer?
Please let others know what you think
about

Review us on YELP!

Review us on GOOGLE+ LOCAL

Review us on YAHOO! LOCAL

Figure 5.9 Home page call to action

Before you incorporate any widget or link onto your site, keep in mind that this link will take visitors away from your site. Be sure you want reviews badly enough that you're willing to risk having your visitor forget whatever it was that they came to your site for in the first place. This approach is less of a concern if your company's profile on the review site is more compelling or useful than your own website.

Rewards Programs Some loyalty reward services, such as Royalty Rewards (www .royaltyrewards.com) and Rewards Network (www.rewardsnetwork.com), send out emails after a visit to your establishment, asking for customer reviews. Rewards Network, which administers rewards for dining in participating restaurants, displays reviews on its own site at www.idine.com, whereas other services may link to the business's profile on Yelp or Google+ Local. A business can even offer loyalty points as a reward for writing a review. Rewards programs can be used by restaurants as well as local merchants and service providers.

Product Giveaway Some marketers use giveaways or discounts to seek reviews from targeted individuals. There are myriad ways to formulate a product giveaway to encourage reviews; here are a few examples:

- E-retailer Battery World offers discounted prices to members of a "product review team," an invited list of past customers who agree to leave honest product reviews on its site.

- The Amazon Vine program allows businesses to give free products to trusted reviewers. (Some examples include free review samples of the Disney video game Pure and the Rosetta Stone Italian software.) In exchange, the reviewers agree to review 80% of the products they receive. Amazon marks these reviews with an icon and discloses the freebies.

- Business strategist Mike Michalowicz gives away free book copies to gain Amazon reviews. Here's the process he describes in his blog: First, he looks at a competing book on Amazon and lists the most recent reviewers. By looking at the reviewer's profies, it's often easy for him to find their website, Facebook page, or Twitter account and determine a way to contact them. Mike reaches out and offers a free book to each reviewer, with no obligation to write a review. Using this method, he receives roughly one review for every two free books he sends out.

  This approach may push the boundaries of your comfort zone, but many of the top reviewers on Amazon do welcome freebies. See the sidebar "Amazon—Tips for Authors" for more approaches. If you want to pursue this idea on other review venues, be sure to consult their rules first. And keep your politeness dial turned to 11 if you ever choose to send unsolicited emails so that you minimize the potential to annoy or offend anyone.

- Yelp community event giveaways can be an avenue for outreach to Yelpers (people who write Yelp reviews). Learn more about this in Chapter 6.

Integration of Surveys with Online Review Sites Customer satisfaction surveys and comment cards have traditionally been used to generate information that remains private—a confidential conversation between a company and those whom it serves. But recent innovations are changing that. We spoke with Mike Waite, VP Marketing at Market Metrix, about his company's customer-feedback survey system for hotels. Originally a tool that collected feedback for internal use only, Market Metrix is currently piloting a feature that allows hotels to embed a TripAdvisor form within their guest surveys. Results have been huge: According to Mike, a typical property can get 10 to 25 times as many guest reviews using this system as they would otherwise receive on TripAdvisor. In a similar vein, Revinate's inGuest surveys, seen in Figure 5.10, can be published to TripAdvisor, Facebook, and Twitter.

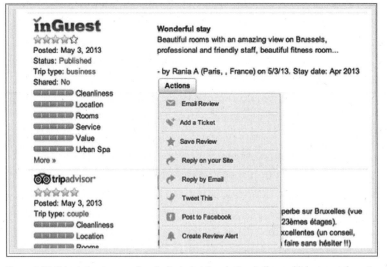

Figure 5.10 Using inGuest surveys from Revinate, hotel marketing staff can publish survey information to TripAdvisor, Twitter, and Facebook.

GetFiveStars offers a survey and review management system geared toward small businesses and brick-and-mortars.

We love the idea of getting your customers to shout from the rooftops rather than murmuring into their collars! If you're using a survey or comment card system, look into whether your vendor provides integration with online review venues.

Watch out for ethical slips in this area. We've seen some survey and feedback-gathering tools that funnel unsatisfied customers into a private dispute process, whereas satisfied customers can be asked to submit a public review online. This system has the potential for abuse, so pay attention to where these curated reviews are published and how they are labeled. Any site that misrepresents its curated positive reviews by implying that they are a complete or objective body of reviews is crossing the line.

Don't Ask, Don't Yelp

Yelp strongly discourages business owners from asking for reviews. In its FAQ, Yelp argues that it's a "slippery slope" from a happy customer's spontaneous review to a less-than-genuine positive review resulting from an incentive. According to Yelp, when businesses encourage reviews, a long-term bias results in the review landscape. The consequences of asking for Yelp reviews are laid out clearly: "Don't be surprised, then, if your solicited reviews get filtered by Yelp's automated review filter." Read more here: `https://biz.yelp.com/support/common_questions`.

We don't think asking for reviews is unethical, and we join the throngs of marketers and business owners who think Yelp's position is wrong-headed. But businesses need to spend their time on efforts that are going to pay off, and right now, we don't think asking a broad swath of your customers for Yelp reviews is likely to work well for you.

Here's Yelp's advice: Rather than trying to get more of your customers to write Yelp reviews, get more Yelpers to become your customers. To do this, you'll need to increase your visibility in Yelp overall. Options include advertising, Yelp deals, Yelp check-in offers, icons on your site and reminders in your physical location, and, if you're well connected or lucky, getting involved in community events. We'll walk you through all of these options in our close-up look at Yelp in Chapter 6.

Review Site Tools and Services Some review sites, such as TripAdvisor and Angie's List, are fans of businesses encouraging their customers to post reviews—and they even provide tools to help. Angie's List is a standout, offering business aids such as the printed handout shown in Figure 5.11.

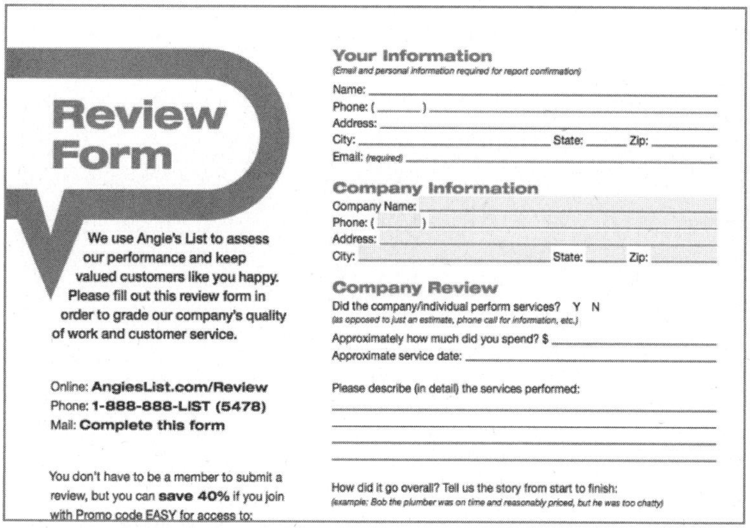

Review Form

We use Angie's List to assess our performance and keep valued customers like you happy. Please fill out this review form in order to grade our company's quality of work and customer service.

Online: **AngiesList.com/Review**
Phone: **1-888-888-LIST (5478)**
Mail: **Complete this form**

You don't have to be a member to submit a review, but you can **save 40%** if you join with Promo code EASY for access to:

Your Information
(Email and personal information required for report confirmation)
Name:
Phone: ( )
Address:
City: State: Zip:
Email: (required)

Company Information
Company Name:
Phone: ( )
Address:
City: State: Zip:

Company Review
Did the company/individual perform services? Y N
(as opposed to just an estimate, phone call for information, etc.)
Approximately how much did you spend? $
Approximate service date:

Please describe (in detail) the services performed:

How did it go overall? Tell us the story from start to finish:
(example: Bob the plumber was on time and reasonably priced, but he was too chatty)

Figure 5.11 Angie's List has helpful tools for businesses to encourage reviews.

Angie's List representatives will even call your customers to collect feedback for you as part of a free service called Fetch.

TripAdvisor's Review Express tool lets you build templated review emails and send them out to up to 1,000 of your guests or customers. An example can be seen in Figure 5.12.

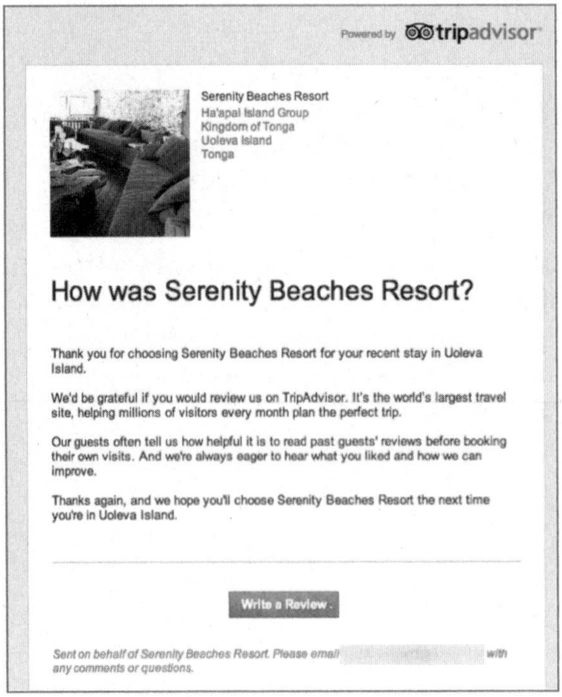

Figure 5.12 TripAdvisor generated this review request email with its Review Express tool.

Paper is also an option at TripAdvisor, with printed flyers and customizable reminder cards available free or cheap, as seen in Figure 5.13.

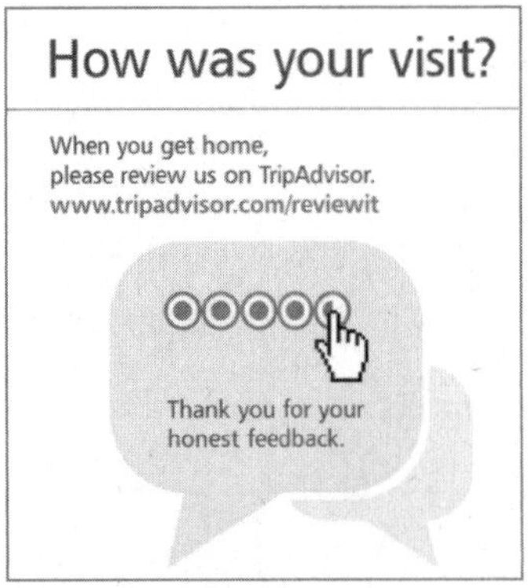

Figure 5.13 TripAdvisor offers a paper reminder flyer.

Healthgrades.com is another example of a review site that offers printed materials: Doctors can request customized postcards to hand out to patients.

We'll visit Yelp, Angie's List, and TripAdvisor again in Chapter 6, with more details and tips.

Paid Review Collection Services The idea is simple: Write a check, and someone else will make the calls, send the emails, and write the letters that bring you the online reviews you need. In practice, hiring a review collection service can land a business in complex territory. Services like ResellerRatings, Demandforce, and Shopper Approved, that only seek reviews on their own platforms, are in the safety zone. Reputation management services that reach out to your customers to ask for reviews on the venue of your preference deserve more scrutiny. Are you comfortable with them getting their eyes on your client list? How will your customers feel about being contacted by a third party? And are they scrupulously careful about complying with the review sites' terms of service, with no shenanigans like posting reviews on behalf of others?

Reviews from Friends Many businesses ask friends and family for reviews, especially when the business is just starting out or launching a new product or creative work. If this sounds like you, be sure to read the "Authenticity and Ethics" section later in this chapter to make sure you're avoiding any ethical, legal, or terms-of-service landmines when requesting reviews from people you know.

We may have overloaded you with options! Where to start? By all means, go with the review solicitation method that's most practical for you right now. But don't stop there. Be sure to vary your methods until you hit on one that produces results. Every business we know with a successful approach to review cultivation has evolved its practices over time and keeps an open mind about trying new ideas.

Cultivating a Word-of-Mouth Mentality

The steps described in the previous section will go a long way, but you can do even more. Many companies embrace word-of-mouth as a foundational element of their business culture, incorporating feedback opportunities into every customer interaction. If you're ready to take a more social, holistic approach to gaining online reviews, here are some ideas to get you started:

Social Media Conversations Are you looking for ideas to fill out your company's Twitter patter or Facebook fraternization? Why not ask for feedback? Any time can be a good time to ask, but a great time to ask is when you've gained new followers or have just had a good sales run (see Figures 5.14 and 5.15).

Rise Records @riserecords   9 May
we have a lot of new followers! Tell us where you're from and who
your favorite @riserecords bands are! RT!

Expand   ← Reply   t⊋ Retweet   ★ Favorite   ••• More

Figure 5.14 Rise Records reaches out to its new Twitter followers for feedback.

#NerdFashion @NerdFashions   3h
If you've ordered from us, and received your item PLEASE leave us
some feedback on our etsy page! etsy.com/shop/nerdfashi...

↳ View summary

Figure 5.15 NerdFashions solicits reviews for its Etsy shop (and doesn't forget the link!).

User-Generated Content If you've got a product that's great for show-and-tell, you could carve out a spot on your website where your customers can connect and share their love. Ducati North America (www.ducatiusa.com) has an active community called the Ducatisti that posts pics and Twitter-style comments such as this one:

I am glad I chose the trico the colors are fantastic

With its hip Customer Action Shots feature, ThinkGeek (www.thinkgeek.com) gets customers excited about uploading fun photos of its products—even products as mundane as office supplies. Social media sharing widgets accompany every photo.

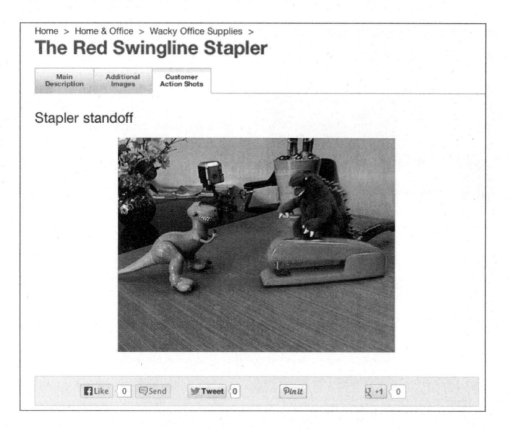

Home > Home & Office > Wacky Office Supplies >

The Red Swingline Stapler

| Main Description | Additional Images | Customer Action Shots |

Stapler standoff

If your offerings are complex or your customers tend to research before they buy, providing a forum can be just the ticket to more credibility and sales. One example is Amazon's Customer Discussions, forums that reside on product pages (including the Kindle Store) so that customers can, in Amazon's words, "read what others are saying about hot products, get knowledgeable answers, check out product comparisons, and swap comments." You can harness the power of customer advocacy on your own site inexpensively by adding an "Ask an Owner" section to your website's forum and inviting your customers to participate. Or you can pay to get the conversation started: Some review platforms such as Bazaarvoice can reach out to verified purchasers to request that they answer prospective customers' questions.

VideoGenie is a service that allows businesses to collect and display consumer-generated videos for a monthly fee (see Figure 5.16). Your more outgoing customers may jump at the chance to showcase their comments in these short, entertaining videos that you can add to your website or Facebook page.

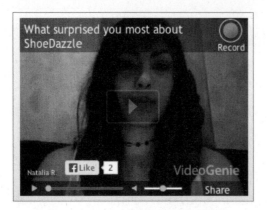

Figure 5.16 VideoGenie testimonial video for ShoeDazzle

Social Profiles Look at the social media properties that you control to see if there's a prime spot to incorporate a review request. Possibilities include your YouTube channel, your Twitter bio, or your Pinterest profile. For B2Bs especially: If your company is on LinkedIn, make sure to fill out your Products & Services page as seen in Figure 5.17. It's the only way your clients and colleagues can get to the "Recommend" link.

Figure 5.17 The LinkedIn Products & Services page of Bosch Security Systems contains a Recommend link.

Review and Feedback Apps Facebook apps such as Smash It Social's Fan Reviews app (www.smashitsocial.com), UserVoice (www.uservoice.com), and Get Satisfaction for Facebook (https://getsatisfaction.com/corp/product/integrations/facebook/) publish reviews and customer feedback directly to your Facebook business page. See Figure 5.18 for a peek at the Fan Reviews app.

![Fan Reviews app interface showing Hal Soden, Jr. CPCU, AAI, CIC Facebook page with a "Write a review..." field and "Submit Review" button, "Powered by Fan Reviews"]

Figure 5.18 Fan Reviews app from Smash It Social

Give Them the Hook-Up If your business thrives on in-the-moment social media advocacy such as Foursquare tips or Facebook check-ins, consider offering free wifi on your premises to make these tasks easier for your customers. If you're thinking this only applies to coffee shops, think again. Free wifi can be provided in hotels, bars, book stores, salon waiting areas, doctors' offices, health clubs, theaters, schools, or just about anywhere else.

Reviews at the Social/Local/Mobile Intersection

How would reviews management and customer acquisition be different without social, locally aware, and mobile technology? Simpler, certainly. You would not have to worry about friends-of-friends seeing comments like this one:

Fortunately, this technology can also be used to expand your opportunities to find, attract, and engage customers. Let's take a look at some of the unique considerations of reviews at the intersection of Social, Local, and Mobile, or in marketing slang, SoLoMo.

The SoLoMo Prospect

Smartphone users are purchasers. An eMarketer Mobile commerce forecast estimated that in 2013 mobile shoppers would contribute roughly 15% of e-commerce sales in the US. They also consume reviews: According to the Adobe 2013 Mobile Consumer Survey, 41% of mobile users felt that customer ratings and reviews were the most important feature when purchasing on a mobile website or app, and Nielsen reported in its Q1 2013 Mobile Shopping Report that 46% of tablet users and 39% of smartphone users read reviews of recent or future purchases.

Continues

Reviews at the Social/Local/Mobile Intersection *(Continued)*

SoLoMo prospects include people who are both passively and actively consuming information about your business. Passively, they are bombarded with word-of-mouth, friend-aware advertising and location-aware offers. Actively, they may be seeking out offerings like yours on mobile apps, and they are often factoring review data into their decisions even if they only fired up an app to look for basic location information, as seen in these search results for <comics> on the Google Maps app:

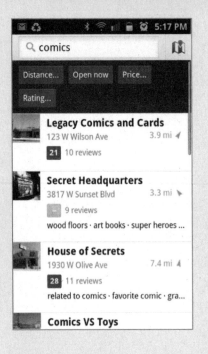

The SoLoMo Customer

For those who venture into your brick-and-mortar business, the mobile customer experience is often intertwined with the in-store shopping experience. Studies show that over 70% of smartphone owners use their phone while shopping, and retailers are eager to engage and convert mobile consumers.

Mobile devices are also unquestionably part of the post-purchase reviewing process. Nielsen reports that 20% of tablet users and 19% of smartphone users post comments on a purchase in social media.

Customers who broadcast their feedback from the SoLoMo space do it in myriad ways. They may upload sepia-toned Instagram photos of your hipsterrific marquee, or publish Facebook check-in commentary about the long lines or luscious rose bushes outside your establishment. Or, they may tap out reviews like this one.

Continues

Reviews at the Social/Local/Mobile Intersection *(Continued)*

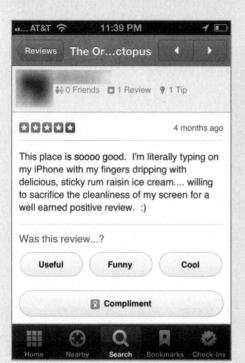

The Savvy Business and SoLoMo

According to Boston Retail Partners' 14th Annual POS Benchmarking Survey, more than one-third of retailers offer mobile tools for interacting with customers in-store, such as mobile coupons, specials, and personalized promotions. Here are some ways you can work the SoLoMo angle for your business:

- Design your mobile app or website so that reviews are easy to find.

- Think of ideas for providing a social experience for in-store shoppers, for example, by creating opportunities to share a purchase on social media or tap into discussions and tips on what they're looking for.

- Make offers available on your Facebook page or other social channels, and make sure that the offers you promote can be easily accessed and redeemed by mobile users.

- Consider testing mobile incentives offered by review sites, such as check-in offers or coupons.

- Focus your advertising on prospects that make geographic sense for your business. *Geo-fencing* is the practice of displaying ads only to viewers who are within a specified radius; look for this capability if you're placing mobile ads or promoted Tweets.

You do not need to wrangle an app developer or become a full-fledged social media marketer to engage your SoLoMo customers. Even if all you have is a printer, you can encourage customers to check in, as seen in this example.

Continues

128

Reviews at the Social/Local/Mobile Intersection *(Continued)*

Here are some resources to keep your finger on the SoLoMo pulse:

- The blog maintained by location analytics company Placed: `http://www.placed.com/blog/`

- News and insights from Greg Sterling, a local and mobile marketing expert: `http://screenwerk.com/`

- Mobile marketing industry news and opinions: `http://www.mobilemarketer.com/`

Just like your smartphone-toting prospective customers, SoLoMo marketing is constantly in motion. Mobile device adoption will continue to grow, and increasingly these devices are an integral part of how we live, learn, shop, and communicate. Make sure your marketing strategy keeps up the pace!

An Enabled Team of Advocates Many businesses and organizations have the opportunity to draw on a loyal group of advocates for help with online reviews. Schools and churches naturally fall into this category, but many nonprofits, destinations, and special-interest businesses can as well.

Here's an example of a team of advocates at work: A small private elementary school we know suffered a drop in enrollment after tough economic times. Hungry for new families, the volunteer-run marketing team considered expensive print advertising options. Instead, they decided on a two-pronged grassroots approach: First, they sent an email blast to current families requesting reviews on GreatSchools.net. The email explained the importance of reviews in helping families who research online, and it requested honest and detailed reviews of the school. A solid collection of new reviews resulted from this request. Best of all, this tactic could easily be repeated with new families each year. (GreatSchools.net did not appear to find the sudden influx of reviews suspicious; other review sites, particularly Google+ Local, TripAdvisor, and Yelp, might.)

Digging deeper, this school also began to monitor local neighborhood forums for advice requests. It's common for users of local forums and neighborhood-based social networks like Nextdoor to post requests for recommendations on local products and services, as seen in Figure 5.19.

> **Schools that foster creativity?**
> --
> Our 4 year old is entering Kindergarten next year and we are completely clueless about schools in the area. She is a really super creative kid who enjoys writing stories, doing art, making up her own songs and has a love for acting and performance. We'd love to find a school that fosters this and allows plenty of opportunity to flex her creative muscle.

Figure 5.19 This request for school recommendations provides an opportunity for parent-advocates to spread some positive information about their favorite school.

With a dedicated team keeping an eye on local neighborhood forums, this school is now much better represented in these conversations.

Word-of-mouth marketing finds its stride when businesses give customers a reason to spontaneously speak among themselves. There's a vibrant marketing subculture built around creating the "Wow!" moments, such as clever promotions, charitable activities, or out-of-the-ordinary customer service, that get people talking. For inspiration and ideas, visit www.womma.org or sign up for the excellent "Damn, I Wish I'd Thought of That" newsletter at www.wordofmouth.org.

Exercise: Compare Post-Transaction Emails

To get results and stay out of the trash folder, a post-interaction email must strike the perfect balance of brevity, clarity, and convenience. Here's an exercise for you: Read the following sample emails and give each of them a score of 0–3. Look for these characteristics:

- The email is personalized, pleasant, and brief. +1 point
- The email provides a convincing reason for recipients to create a review. +1 point
- The email makes it easy for the recipient to complete the review. +1 point

The first sample email is from online travel agent, Orbitz:

Welcome back from Gurnee.
How was your hotel?

Hello

We hope you enjoyed your stay at **Keylime Cove Resort Waterpark**, a 3-star hotel. Did you have a positive experience? Tell us about your hotel stay from 04/03/2013 to 04/05/2013 and receive <u>5% off your next hotel stay</u>. Your feedback helps us provide fellow travelers with a positive travel experience.

5% off
your next hotel reservation

Submit your hotel review

We give a 3 to this email. It's personalized and brief, and it gives a clear incentive to write a review.

Here's how TripAdvisor handled a review request for the same traveler:

How was Gurnee?

Did you take that trip you were thinking about?

If TripAdvisor reviews helped you plan a trip to Gurnee, now's your chance to return the favor and <u>add a review</u> of your own. Thanks!

HAVE YOUR SAY ›

Another 3 score! In fact, we like this one better than the Orbitz email. TripAdvisor is not only more succinct, it seems to understand the emotions that trigger a review. A desire to repay a debt can be even more compelling than a 5% discount.

The next example comes from Amazon merchant PetFusion.

Continues

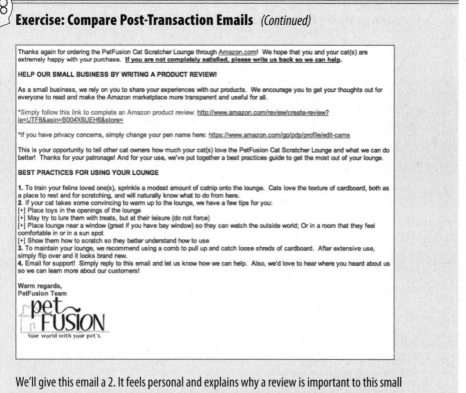

Thanks again for ordering the PetFusion Cat Scratcher Lounge through Amazon.com! We hope that you and your cat(s) are extremely happy with your purchase. **If you are not completely satisfied, please write us back so we can help.**

HELP OUR SMALL BUSINESS BY WRITING A PRODUCT REVIEW!

As a small business, we rely on you to share your experiences with our products. We encourage you to get your thoughts out for everyone to read and make the Amazon marketplace more transparent and useful for all.

*Simply follow this link to complete an Amazon product review: http://www.amazon.com/review/create-review?ie=UTF8&asin=B004X6UEH6&store=

*If you have privacy concerns, simply change your pen name here: https://www.amazon.com/gp/pdp/profile/edit-cams

This is your opportunity to tell other cat owners how much your cat(s) love the PetFusion Cat Scratcher Lounge and what we can do better! Thanks for your patronage! And for your use, we've put together a best practices guide to get the most out of your lounge.

BEST PRACTICES FOR USING YOUR LOUNGE

1. To train your feline loved one(s), sprinkle a modest amount of catnip onto the lounge. Cats love the texture of cardboard, both as a place to rest and for scratching, and will naturally know what to do from here.
2. If your cat takes some convincing to warm up to the lounge, we have a few tips for you:
[+] Place toys in the openings of the lounge
[+] May try to lure them with treats, but at their leisure (do not force)
[+] Place lounge near a window (great if you have bay window) so they can watch the outside world; Or in a room that they feel comfortable in or in a sun spot
[+] Show them how to scratch so they better understand how to use
3. To maintain your lounge, we recommend using a comb to pull up and catch loose shreds of cardboard. After extensive use, simply flip over and it looks brand new.
4. Email for support! Simply reply to this email and let us know how we can help. Also, we'd love to hear where you heard about us so we can learn more about our customers!

Warm regards,
PetFusion Team

We'll give this email a 2. It feels personal and explains why a review is important to this small business. But the email is too long, thanks to the product instructions that are tacked on at the end. We'd trim it after "Thanks for your patronage!" and keep the focus on the review.

Now let's look at a review request email from eBay:

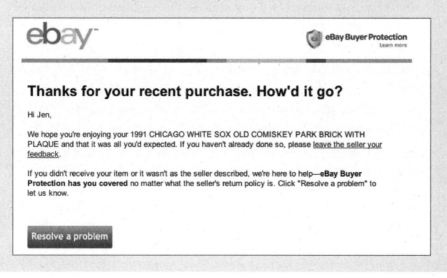

Continues

We'll give this email a 2. It's succinct and easy to understand, but neglects to tell us why the review would help. Also, notice that the review link is overshadowed by the "resolve a problem" link. This indicates to us that getting a review is a secondary goal for this email.

Our final example is a personal email request.

Hi Everyone!

Hope everything is well, and you are having a excellent new year!

I'm in the process of expanding my business and bringing in new customers, and I'm hoping you can take a few minutes to write a review for me on Google Maps or Yelp if you've been satisfied with my services..

I'm listed under ▓▓▓▓▓▓ and you can follow the links bellow to post a review...

Thank You very much for your time and your support!

▓▓▓▓

http://www.yelp.com/biz/▓▓▓▓▓▓▓▓▓▓▓▓▓▓

http://maps.google.com ▓▓▓▓▓▓▓

Also feel free to check out my website at ▓▓▓▓▓▓▓▓▓▓▓

This email gets a 1. It did a good job of making the case for customers to write a review. But here are a few things it got wrong:

- This email was copied to a large group. Mass mailings are not only impersonal; they also may increase the chances of reviews getting filtered out by the review site. A large number of reviews coming in at the same time will make some review sites suspicious.

- The email was sent ages after the service actually took place. An email like this should be sent when the work is fresh in the customer's mind.

- The email links to Yelp and Google+ profiles, but those work best for active Yelpers and Google+ users. Since this is a home services business, an Angie's List link could have been a good addition.

- The Google link doesn't point to the specific URL for the business. Always link directly to the page where people can write reviews. See Chapter 6 for more details about Google+ Local.

Now that you've scoped out a few other businesses' emails, turn the spotlight on yourself. If your business already has an outreach email like these, take a look at it and give it a 0–3 score now. Then show it to someone else and get their opinion as well. If this type of email is something you haven't yet developed, you've got a lot of examples at your fingertips; try sketching up your own version now!

Authenticity and Ethics

As you work to increase and improve your online reviews, it may not be obvious when you're crossing the line between proactive marketing and unacceptable techniques. Some tactics, if detected, can cause a review to be removed or result in public accusations that can tarnish your business's reputation. Read on for some guidance on avoiding common pitfalls.

Staying Outside the Spam Filter

Review spam algorithms level the playing field by removing false negative reviews and, more commonly, by removing false positive reviews from businesses that do not deserve them. But the filters are not just out to catch fakes. They also attempt to remove reviews that contain unacceptable advertising or promotion, or that were achieved via unacceptable methods, even if the reviews are real and written by actual customers.

When it works, a filter is great. Filtering out fake, misleading, or inappropriately promotional reviews benefits the consumer and enhances the credibility of the review venue. Review venues take a number of actions to identify and wipe out spam, including using software to perform behavioral analysis of reviewers, monitoring by quality control teams, responding to community flags and feedback, and even setting up sting operations to catch companies that attempt to hire writers for fake reviews.

The filtering methods are far from perfect, and the review venues are not pretending otherwise. Yelp and Google+ Local admit that legitimate reviews sometimes get caught in their filters. These venues don't actually claim to filter out *only* inappropriate reviews, either. Yelp uses words like "less trustworthy," and "real but suspicious" to describe some of the reviews that it filters, and as the algorithms change or an individual reviewer's behavior changes over time, some filtered reviews can be released from their filter purgatory to do all the things that liberated reviews do, such as be seen by the public and factor into a business's overall review star count.

In most cases, the practice of filtering reviews benefits the review venue and the consumer more than it does the business stakeholder, so you're more likely to encounter an overzealous review filter than a lax one. On its blog, Yelp states that a whopping 20% of reviews posted the site are filtered out.

Solicit Safely

Maybe, during the course of reading this book, you slapped your forehead and said, "I've been missing out on too many opportunities to get reviews; I'd better make up for lost time!" If so, we want you to be particularly careful when jump-starting review solicitation, because getting too many reviews in too short a time period can look suspicious. Here are some scenarios to consider.

See a Customer, Ask a Customer Our assessment: *Safe*

Create an environment in which everyone is encouraged to write a review as they encounter your offerings, with reminders on your menu, signs in your waiting room, post-purchase prompts, and so on. Any method that casts a net for all of your customers is more likely to cause the kind of review creation profile that appears natural to an algorithm.

Email Blast to Your Past Customers Our assessment: *Risky*

Sending out a single email to all of your past customers asking them to review you is risky—especially if you or your reviewers have just created a profile on a review site. This can backfire spectacularly on Yelp, with honest customers' glowing reviews getting filtered. It's a logical guess that a number of new reviews hitting at the same time from reviewers with a paltry reviewing history are going to raise some algorithmic eyebrows. Avoid this approach for Google+ Local, Yelp, and TripAdvisor. Less finicky review sites, like GreatSchools, Citysearch, and Insider Pages, or sites that validate reviewers, may not have a problem with it.

Using a Review-Collection Service That Makes Big Promises Our assessment: *Risky*

Be cautious about jumping on board with any company that promises a sudden and dramatic change in your online reputation, especially if their process is not completely clear to you. Some of these services may take steps that put your business at risk of being removed from review venues or make you look bad to potential customers. No reputation management service should ever pose as customers or place inauthentic favorable content on your own site or anywhere else. And Google frowns on some of the quick-and-dirty methods we've seen for rapidly building and promoting reviews on your own site, such as scraping content from other sites, abusing rich snippets, and stuffing keywords into the text.

Review-from-My-Computer Party Our assessment: *Don't bother*

If you were considering bringing your laptop to church one Sunday and asking all of your customers or acquaintances to use it to log into Yelp to review your barbershop, don't do it. The same goes for setting up a review station in your waiting area. This will stack you up with a list of reviews that all came from the same IP address—a sure red flag. Google+ Local, which is more tolerant of the practice of asking for reviews than Yelp, explicitly warns against the practice of collecting multiple reviews on a single device.

Avoid Manipulative Tactics

It's hard work getting new reviews, and we don't want your efforts to be wasted! We always try to keep things positive, but here is a rare list of "do nots." We warn because we care, and we hope you'll take these admonitions to heart.

Don't write reviews for your own business. Channel your self-promotional comments into more acceptable venues, such as public responses to reviews or private communications with reviewers.

Don't write text and provide it to your customers to use in their reviews. We know how tempting it is, especially for those of you with marketing flair, to want to craft perfect verbiage to help your online reputation. But as you learned in Chapter 3, consumers are looking for helpful reviews, not marketing copy. The review venue's quality control teams are reading the text and processing it intelligently, and so are your prospective customers! Don't underestimate them by prefabricating your own review text. If you must micro-manage your customers' reviews, toss out some possible talking points instead, for example, "We like to think we have the friendliest bartenders and the tastiest cocktails in Highland Park. Whatever you think, we hope you'll take a moment to review us."

Don't ask your customers to publish identical reviews in more than one place. This is against the terms of service for many review venues, some of which claim ownership of review text once it is posted to their site. Google+ Local has suggested that review duplication is one of the reasons it removes reviews from display.

Don't provide compensation for positive reviews or for modifying reviews. Paying for positive senti-ment is always a bad idea. Learn more about the compensation and the FTC guidelines in the section "Staying on the Right Side of the Law," later in this chapter.

Don't solicit reviews from e-commerce customers before they have received their order. This is not only an ethically questionable approach, but it's also likely to be fruitless. Verified-customer review venues can see both the order date and the review date for any transaction. Collecting reviews before the customer has had a chance to receive the shipment will get the reviews removed, and the review venue can take further actions, such as warn-ings or public notifications.

These activities are unethical and might be caught by review venues. Worse, by asking a customer to play along in any kind of review manipulation, you're taking the risk of lowering your current and potential future customers' opinion of your business.

Amazon—Tips for Authors

No discussion of customer reviews would be complete without a nod to Amazon.com, the world's larg-est Internet retailer and arguably the site that paved the way for the prominence of customer reviews online.

You don't need us to tell you that customer product reviews are displayed prominently throughout the Amazon shopping experience and that gaining a large number of mostly positive reviews is important for brands, manufacturers, and authors.

As authors ourselves, we've taken a relatively laissez-faire approach to encouraging Amazon reviews, sticking to requesting reviews via email anytime a reader sends us a question or compliment. Here's the gist of it:

"Would you be willing to post a review of our book on Amazon? We would love for you to share your opinion with others. Here's the link: [link goes here] Thanks!"

Amazon—Tips for Authors *(Continued)*

In addition to personally requesting reviews, here are some other tactics for authors to gain Amazon reviews:

- One of the more easily negotiable items in publishers' contracts is the number of free book copies that are sent to the author. We recommend maxing this number out (if they offer you 10, ask for 40!) and sending these books to people who you think will read and review them.

- Include an Amazon link anywhere you think a potential reviewer might see it, for example, on your website or blog, in your email signature, or as a feature in your email blasts.

- Services such as BookRooster allow authors to send out free review copies in exchange for the promise of reviews. If you go this route, or any other route that involves giving a free book away, be sure the reviewer discloses it. As Amazon states: "If you received a free product in exchange for your review, please clearly and conspicuously disclose that you received the product free of charge."

- Amazon lists its top 10,000 reviewers at www.amazon.com/review/top-reviewers. Many of these reviewers are amenable to receiving review copies of books and other products. Just be sure to read their profiles, where they often describe their interests:

> **Location:** South-Central, PA USA
>
> **E-mail:**
>
> **Web Page:**
>
> **In My Own Words:**
> Manufacturers/Publishers, please feel free to contact me about a review of your products. My main interests are health, gadgets, and video/photo related products and books (mostly Sci-Fi, Technology/Science, and history).

- Amazon's Meet Our Authors forum allows authors to shamelessly promote their books and request reviews:

  www.amazon.com/forum/meet%20our%20authors

- If you think Amazon has removed a review they shouldn't have, you can send an email to review-moderation@amazon.com and request an appeal.

For Amazon's author-specific help, including tips on working with customer reviews and managing editorial reviews, visit https://authorcentral.amazon.com.

Staying on the Right Side of the Law

If you take a few minutes to get the gist of a government document called the "Guides Concerning the Use of Endorsements and Testimonials in Advertising," you may come to a fuller understanding of the reasoning behind the cranky terms and conditions that exist on most review venues. The Federal Trade Commission (FTC) issued these guides to help advertisers stay in compliance with the Federal Trade Commission Act. The document is lousy with legalese, but the main ideas amount to common sense. Paraphrasing no doubt to the point of irresponsibility, we can boil the Guides down to the following main topics:

1. Endorsements must be truthful.

2. Advertisers must convey typical product experiences appropriately.

3. Advertiser–endorser relationships must be disclosed in some cases.

Don't take our word for it. (Seriously, don't. We're not lawyers.) You can read the full document here:

www.ftc.gov/os/2009/10/091005revisedendorsementguides.pdf

In 2009, the FTC updated these Guides for the first time in almost 30 years to explain the requirement for transparency on blogs and social media. One section in particular, which covers the relationship between advertisers and endorsers, caused a bit of hand-wringing for online advertisers and marketers. From the Guides,

When there exists a connection between the endorser and the seller of the advertised product that might materially affect the weight or credibility of the endorsement (i.e., the connection is not reasonably expected by the audience), such connection must be fully disclosed.

Questions swirl around this statement, including "How can I cram appropriate disclosure into a tweet?" and "What if the giveaway is just a dollar-off coupon? Does that need to be disclosed?" and "Does a check-in count as an endorsement?" You can use your noggin on this one. If you wouldn't want your potential customers knowing the truth behind how a review was generated, then you're probably running afoul of the Guides in some way. We can't venture into any legal advice, but here are some thoughts on commonsense honesty and disclosure as it pertains to the FTC's endorsement guidelines and online reviews:

What's at Stake? The FTC's Guides are not laws; they are interpretations of laws, written to help people understand and abide by the Federal Trade Commission Act. As such, the FTC cannot issue fines for noncompliance of the Guides, but the FTC has investigated, warned, and made complaints against companies that it believes to have violated the Federal Trade Commission Act, resulting in some expensive settlements for the offending businesses.

When to Disclose a Relationship If your business has a relationship with a reviewer in which you provide them with products or services with the expectation that they will provide a review, this relationship should be disclosed in the review. The FTC provides an example of a videogame company that sends a free game to a blogger known for reviewing videogames. In this case, the free game was sent with an expectation of receiving a review, so the blogger should "clearly and conspicuously" disclose in his review that he received the game for free. Similarly, if your restaurant gives away a free meal to a known restaurant critic, her review should contain a disclosure about the freebie. What about if your store gives away coupons or free samples to all of your walk-in customers? In that scenario, your store probably has no expectation of receiving reviews in exchange for the giveaways, and disclosure is therefore probably not necessary. On the other hand, the value of the free item matters, so if you give away a valuable free item, for example, a car, any resulting review should disclose the relationship.

How to Disclose As a business stakeholder, not an endorser or reviewer, you may be wondering why you need to care about the specifics of disclosure. Some of the most talked-about examples of FTC investigations and settlements involved retailers whose bloggers or affiliates failed to appropriately disclose their relationship with the retailer. When speaking about a $250,000 settlement involving a company called Legacy Learning Systems Inc., David Vladeck, director of the FTC's Bureau of Consumer Protection, said, "Advertisers using affiliate marketers to promote their products would be wise to put in place a reasonable monitoring program to verify that those affiliates follow the principles of truth in advertising."

There is no specific mandated method of disclosure, such as an approved paragraph, a badge, or a hashtag to use when disclosing an advertiser–endorser relationship. In its document ".com Disclosures: How to Make Effective Disclosures in Digital Advertising," the FTC says, "The ultimate test is not the size of the font or the location of the disclosure, although they are important considerations; the ultimate test is whether the information intended to be disclosed is actually conveyed to consumers." This document offers considerations, including proximity, placement, and language, for evaluating whether disclosures are clear and conspicuous. It also describes scenarios to avoid, for example, hiding disclosures away in a website's terms of use, or linking to disclosures using general language such as "details below."

To get interpretations and examples directly from the source, take a look at the FTC's helpful advice at

`http://www.ftc.gov/os/2013/03/130312dotcomdisclosures.pdf`

Complying with Terms of Service

Every review venue has its own terms and conditions that apply to participating businesses and reviewers. We advise you to find them and read them for any venue that you are targeting for your review gathering efforts. Understanding the particulars of the terms and conditions is the safest method of avoiding spam filters, warnings, public notices calling your business's ethics into question, or even being reported to the authorities. Many review venues have policies that mirror the FTC guidelines, requiring honest, uncompensated reviews. But other terms and conditions are not as intuitive. When in doubt, ask for assistance or clarification from the review venue's support staff. Table 5.1 provides links to rules and excerpts from popular review venues.

▶ **Table 5.1** Review site terms and conditions

Site	Rules and related pages	Notable quotation
TripAdvisor	**Review Moderation and Fraud Detection FAQ:** www.tripadvisor.com/vpages/ review_mod_fraud_detect.html **Guidelines for Traveler Reviews:** www.tripadvisor.com/help/ postingandediting **Management Response Guidelines:** www.tripadvisor.com/help/ management_response_guidelines	"Any attempt to mislead, influence or impersonate a traveler is considered fraudulent and will be subject to penalty."
ResellerRatings	**Trust & Ethics Policy** www.resellerratings.com/ trust-and-ethics	"We do not allow retailers to pay for positive reviews, or to solicit reviews from customers the same day the order is placed (a common tactic—asking a customer to write a review while taking their phone order). We receive tips about this activity daily and we remove affected reviews and warn the retailer— plus, our system automatically detects these same-day reviews."
Reevoo	**The Reevoo Manifesto:** www.reevoo.com/why- reevoo/the-reevoo-brand/ reevoo-manifesto **Terms and Conditions of Posting:** http://reviews.reevoo .com/review/terms_and_ conditions?locale=en-GB	"We do not tolerate anyone editing or removing negative reviews or showing only the reviews they like."

Continues

Site	Rules and related pages	Notable quotation
Google+ Local	Policies and Guidelines Regarding Removals of Google Places Reviews: `http://support.google .com/places/bin/answer .py?hl=en&answer=187622` Google Places Quality Guidelines: `http://support.google .com/places/bin/answer .py?hl=en&answer=107528`	"Don't use reviews for advertising or post the same or similar reviews across multiple places, don't post fake reviews intended to boost or lower ratings, and don't include links to other websites. For certain types of businesses that are prone to spam, we also reserve the right to prevent reviews from publicly appearing across Google."
Amazon	General Review Creation Guidelines: `www.amazon.com/gp/ community-help/ customer-reviews-guidelines` Customer Review Guidelines Frequently Asked Questions: `www.amazon.com/gp/help/cus- tomer/display .html?ie=UTF8&nodeId=201077870`	"We do not allow any compensation for a customer review other than a free copy of the product (provided up front). If we find evidence that a customer was paid for a review, we will remove it." Special warning for authors and artists: "If you have a direct or indirect financial interest in a product, or perceived to have a close personal relationship with its author or artist, we will likely remove your review."
Shopper Approved	Terms and Conditions: `www.shopperapproved.com/ terms.php`	"[A]ll ratings and reviews collected by Shopper Approved immediately become the sole property of Shopper Approved. In order to protect the integrity of the Shopper Approved brand for everyone, we cannot allow you or any other third party to host or display any ratings collected by Shopper Approved without our direct consent."
Booking.com	Terms and Conditions: `https://admin.bookings.org/ hotelreg/terms-and-conditions .html`	"Booking.com will not enter into any discussion, negotiation or correspondence with the Accommodation in respect of (the content of, or consequences of the publication or distribution of) the Guest reviews."

Continues

Site	Rules and related pages	Notable quotation
Shopzilla/BizRate	Merchant Ratings FAQ: `http://about.shopzilla.com/ store-ratings` Merchant Program Agreement: `http:// merchant.shopzilla.com/oa/ general/t_and_c.xpml`	"Eight of the fifteen quality ratings are determined at the point-of-sale or 'checkout.' These are collected by asking a store's customers to evaluate their purchase experiences immediately after completing the online transaction. The remaining 7 quality ratings are determined after the product is expected to have been delivered."
Yelp	Content Guidelines: `www.yelp.com/guidelines` Support Center - Common Questions: `https://biz.yelp.com/support/ common_questions`	"You can use the 'About This Business' tab to tell people a little something special about your business. Please keep it relevant: don't use this feature to attack your competitors, reviewers, or Yelp, and don't use it to seed keywords or post special offers or promotions—we'll remove them if we see them."
Bazaarvoice	Client Agreements: `www.bazaarvoice.com/legal/ clientagreements/#.UbKewCtgZW8` Bazaarvoice Express Terms and Conditions: `www.bazaarvoiceexpress.com/ expressminisite/ termsandconditions.jsp`	"You shall…require that any Product Review or portion thereof written on Your behalf (e.g., by contractor, employee, or third party with or without compensation) shall be identified by the Staff Reviews Badge through the Bazaarvoice Dashboard."
Angie's List	FAQ: Reviews and Your Listing: `http://support.business .angieslist.com/app/ answers/detail/a_id/105/~/ reviews-and-your-listing` Service Provider's Business Agreement: `http://business.angieslist.com/ visitor/useragreement.aspx`	"Keep in mind, Angie's List maintains a strict policy against self-reporting. Angie's List policy also prohibits businesses from submitting review forms on behalf of their customers—doing so is considered self-reporting."

Having trouble finding the rules for a site that's not listed in the table? Some venues list reviewer guidelines in their general website terms and conditions, whereas others have separate pages for ethics statements, business guidelines, and reviewer guidelines. If you can't find them easily, try going through the initial steps of composing a review, and you'll likely uncover links to the rules.

Yelp's Controversial Filter

Scroll down to the bottom of many Yelp profiles and you'll find a teeny, tiny link to the filtered reviews for that business. Clicking through often reveals a mix of positive and negative reviews. Sometimes, a business's Yelp filter contains a generous list of genuine reviews that have been filtered out.

Some business stakeholders believe something sinister is afoot, with one common accusation being that Yelp spitefully applies its filter, either reordering or refiltering reviews when a business refuses to buy advertising or stops paying for advertising.

Our own Ask the Experts Blog (www.yourseoplan.com/blog) contains a collection of angry chatter from commenters who believe that this practice is real:

- "It seems no matter what someone writes, if it is a positive review for us, YELP will not let it post. This is a[n] evil scheme and small business owners NEED TO UNITE and show politicians and this one company the power of many, we are the engine of the economy!"

- "I cannot believe how they should be in the business of destroying the core of America… Pay me or I will bring you down."

- "It's about hard-working small business owners being literally held hostage on the Yelp system."

We spoke with a Yelp account executive who weighed in on the issue. This employee, who wished to remain anonymous, has heard plenty of complaints and rumors about Yelp's sales tactics and filtering mechanism. He feels that there may sometimes be a connection between turning down Yelp advertising and an increase in filtered reviews, but not the kind of connection that the conspiracy theorists have in mind. His take: "After people get a Yelp sales call, they decide to go ask for a bunch of reviews. But they are solicited reviews, so they get filtered." He adds that Yelp's advertising department operates independently from the department that handles the review filter.

We're not Yelp insiders by any stretch of the imagination, but we don't think Yelp sics its filter on businesses that turn down its advertising advances. Lawsuits that made similar claims have gotten nowhere. But it does seem entirely possible that rogue Yelp salespeople have, at times, led businesses astray, either by making false claims or by walking the path of ambiguity, allowing businesses to retain a misconception that advertising on Yelp would be their ticket to review salvation. Yelp addresses some of these concerns in its Myths about Yelp page at www.yelp.com/myths. This page answers some common concerns head on and describes steps that Yelp takes to prevent its employees from gaming the system, for example, "Yelp salespeople don't have back-end administrative privileges that would allow them to alter the Yelp review database."

There is no customer support department for free listings at Yelp, and we think this contributes to a climate in which businesses tend to draw their own conclusions and rant publicly. Aggressive sales practices also raise the hackles of many business owners. Yelp could go a long way toward repairing its relations with businesses by offering more support to nonpaying businesses, a reconsideration process for filtered reviews, and mediation services for negative reviews.

Whether you consider yourself rule-bound or rebellious, it's important to know where the lines are drawn so that you can make informed decisions about your review solicitation efforts. We hope that understanding the potential traps and tripwires of your reviewscape will save you from headaches and lost reviews.

With the ideas you've gained from this chapter, you've planted the seeds of smart, sustainable review cultivation. Next up, we'll help you blossom into an online review expert as we examine some important review venues in detail.

Review Venues: Need-to-Know Tips for Your Action Plan

As you get to work improving and managing your online reviews, you'll want to learn everything you can about your top-priority review venues. We've selected six of the most important review sites and platforms to serve up details and insider tips to ease your way. These six represent a cross section of the online reviews space, sites, and products that matter to brick-and-mortars, e-commerce, brands, professionals, and service providers.

Yelp

Yelp is a popular review site for finding and reviewing businesses that have a physical presence or in-person interactions with their customers. Yelp is top-of-mind for many businesses; when we speak with local businesses about their online reviews, Yelp is usually the first site they mention. As of this writing, Yelp has a presence in over 20 countries, with over a million claimed business listings and 40,000 business advertisers. Yelp's traffic is enormous, with over 100 million monthly unique visitors, including more than 10 million mobile app users.

In early 2013 almost half of Yelp searches came from mobile devices. Mobile usage is key for Yelp's growth, and CEO Jeremy Stoppelman has called Yelp a "mobile first" company. Yelp's increasing interest in mobile consumers mirrors the explosive increase in mobile consumer activity. You should be increasingly interested in mobile consumer behavior too, so keep an eye out for future mobile developments on Yelp, like more robust mobile features for advertisers, and more ways to attract and engage mobile visitors.

If you skipped to this section of the book looking for a quick and easy way to get five-star reviews on Yelp, we'd like to gently redirect you to a more useful state of mind. As you're no doubt aware, Yelp is a source for acquiring new customers as much as it is a place to collect reviews. Therefore, the best Yelp strategy involves a holistic approach with the following goals:

- Maximize your opportunities for being found on Yelp.
- Make it easy for potential customers who find you on Yelp to become your actual customers.
- Build up a large body of reviews from real customers—with an honest mix of positive and not-so-positive feedback.

In this section, we'll talk mostly about the first two goals: getting a bigger and more effective presence on Yelp. As for gaining new reviews, we'll deliver some need-to-know insights, but you should also reference Chapters 1–5 of this book, which provide essential information about what kinds of reviews are the most effective, ethical ways to encourage new reviews that showcase your business's best qualities, and ways to minimize the chances of losing reviews to the filtering algorithm.

Claiming Your Listing

Because anyone can create a business listing on Yelp, you may already have a listing and not know it. Even if you don't plan to go nuts with Yelp visibility strategies, do claim your listing, because doing so gives you better control over what's displayed in your listing, and it's the only way to receive alerts and gain access to performance statistics.

There are a couple of ways to claim (or, in Yelp's terminology, *unlock*) your Yelp business listing. One way is to navigate to a business page and click on the "Unlock This Business Page" link, as seen in Figure 6.1.

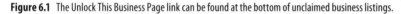

Bedford Stuyvesant YMCA

★★★☆ 48 reviews ⚌ Rating Details

Category: Gyms

1121 Bedford Ave
(between Quincy St & Monroe St)
Brooklyn, NY 11216
Neighborhood: Bedford Stuyvesant

(718) 789-1497
http://www.ymcanyc.org/index.php?i...

Nearest Transit Station: **Good for Kids:** Yes
Franklin Av (A, C)
Bedford - Nostrand Avs (G)
Franklin Av (S)
Hours:
Mon-Fri 6 am - 11 pm
Sat-Sun 8 am - 8 pm

✎ Edit Business Info   ★🏢 Work Here? Unlock This Business Page   ⚙ First to Review   Clare B.

Figure 6.1 The Unlock This Business Page link can be found at the bottom of unclaimed business listings.

Another way is to go to https://biz.yelp.com and click "Create your free account now." You'll be asked to search for your business. Once you find the listing you want to claim, click the Unlock button. If your business doesn't show up, Yelp provides you with a link to add a new business.

Here are some tips on getting the most out of your claimed listing:

Claim listings for all of your locations. Businesses with multiple addresses should make sure that each location is represented by a claimed listing on Yelp. Here are a few possible ways to handle this:

Free Manually claim or create a listing for each location, and manage them separately on Yelp.

Small Monthly Fee Yext, a business listing management company, offers a service called Yelp PowerListings (www.yext.com/yelp) that claims and helps maintain listings for businesses with up to four locations.

Rolled into a Yelp Advertising Campaign Yelp provides bulk management services for a fee. Start here: www.yelp.com/advertise.

Fill in your listing completely. Your visibility in Yelp's search results is partly affected by the information you enter into your business listing, including the categories you select for your business and the descriptive text that you write about your business. As long as you're careful to write descriptive, accurate text that is not keyword-stuffed, it's advisable to fill in everything as completely as possible. If you can do so without stretching the truth, use all three of the category labels available to you.

Figure 6.2 shows an example of Yelp's search for the query <consignment shops>. Notice the Open Now check box? A business without hours information in its listing can't show up for searchers who check that box. Likewise, a consignment shop that sells women's clothing must have the category "Women's Clothing" associated with its listing in order to be seen by searchers who click that box.

Price	Features	Category
☐ $	☐ Offering a Deal	☐ Used, Vintage & Consignment
☐ $$	☐ Open Now 1:03 PM	☐ Women's Clothing
☐ $$$	☐ Dogs Allowed	☐ Thrift Stores
☐ $$$$	☐ Accepts Credit Cards	☐ Community Service/Non-Profit
	More Features	More Categories

Figure 6.2 Yelp's search filters are different depending on the search query.

If you're managing a Yelp page for a restaurant, provide a link to your up-to-date menu. Although your menu won't give you more visibility in Yelp Search, it may be quite helpful in making customers out of the Yelpers who arrive on your business page. If you don't have an easy way to upload or update your menu, SinglePlatform (www .singleplatform.com) and Locu (www.locu.com) can help, with services ranging from free to cheap. Yelp and OpenTable play nicely together, so visitors can make a reservation directly from Yelp for restaurants that use OpenTable.

Photos are also important. Yelp reports that site visitors spend two and a half times as long looking at profiles with photos than those without. And your Yelp photos matter outside of Yelp.com, too. They are shown in your Apple Maps business listing and feed into Bing's local listings. Why be satisfied with a couple of low-res, low-quality images? Hiring a photographer to create a small collection of excellent images that show off your business can be a low-cost way to step up your business listing and stand out from your competition.

Sometimes, portions of your Yelp profile can get "locked," meaning that Yelp prevents you from making edits. This frustrating scenario can happen even if you've claimed your listing, and even if you have a legitimate reason for wanting to make edits. This is not a penalty, but it is a pain and can take a long time to resolve. See "Troubleshooting and Support" later in this section for ways to pursue a remedy.

Choose categories strategically. Your categories are not set in stone when you claim your business listing. Do your own Yelp R&D by searching for keywords that you care about. For example, let's say your business is a bakery. If you search Yelp for "bakery," what categories show up in the search results? If you see "sandwiches" or "coffee & tea," consider whether these categories should be added to your business listing. See Figure 6.3 for an example of these categories in Yelp Search. Next, navigate to the business pages of your competitors, or similar businesses in other cities, and see if there are any good ideas to glean. For example, if you manage the Yelp listing for a synagogue, a quick check of other houses of worship may inspire you to add the category "Venues & Event Spaces" to your business listing.

bakery Glendale, AZ					Showing 1-10 of 252
Browse Category: Bakeries					
Hide Filters -					
Sort By	**Cities**	**Distance**	**Price**	**Features**	**Category**
Best Match	☐ Glendale	Bird's-eye View	☐ $	☐ Offering a Deal	☐ Bakeries
Highest Rated	☐ Phoenix	Driving (5 mi.)	☐ $$	☐ Open Now 8:42 PM	☐ Food
Most Reviewed	☐ Peoria	Biking (2 mi.)	☐ $$$	☐ Take-out	☐ Restaurants
	☐ Avondale	Walking (1 mi.)	☐ $$$$	☐ Good for Kids	☐ Sandwiches
	More Cities	Within 4 blocks		More Features	More Categories

Figure 6.3   Yelp's search filters can give you ideas for choosing categories for your business listing.

Use keywords. Incorporating keywords into the descriptive text in your Yelp listing may help you in a couple ways. When people search Yelp using keywords that match what you've included in your business listing, there's a small chance that your business will get a little boost in Yelp search results. We don't want to inflate this; it really is a *small* chance and a *little* boost. The text in your reviews is a bigger factor, but assuming you are doing things ethically and according to Yelp's policies, you do not have any influence on the word choice of your reviewers. See the sidebar "Optimize Your Listings with Keywords" for tips and tactics for keyword optimization.

To be sure, just because you claim your listing doesn't mean that the public can't edit it. Any Yelp user can click on the "edit this business" link, upload a photo of their plate of linguini, or answer Yelp's survey questions as they write reviews. After intervention by Yelp's human-powered or algorithmic moderation tools, there is a chance that this user-submitted information will be incorporated into your business listing. And you won't be able to edit every element of your listing. Objective information such as whether a business accepts credit cards or is wheelchair accessible can be entered by the business owner, whereas subjective information such as price level can be entered only by reviewers.

Optimize Your Listings with Keywords

Throughout this chapter, we remind you to fill in your review site profiles completely and include descriptive keywords in your text. This is important because the words that are present on your profiles—whether in your business title, description, categories, or user-generated reviews—can influence whether your listing shows up when people search either within the review site or on search engines like Google.

For SEOs like us, it's second nature to include keywords in any copy that we write for the Web. For you, the business stakeholder in the trenches, it may be a challenge to craft text to match the words that are popular with searchers. So we'll keep our advice simple: Describe your offerings specifically and thoroughly, using words that your target audience would use to describe you. Be complete, but also mention the obvious. Don't stop at saying you sell "cupcakes" when you also offer "cupcake towers" and "cupcake delivery." If you're a plumber, it's not TMI to mention that you work on "drains," "faucets," and "toilets." If you're a mortgage broker, list the type of loans you specialize in, such as "FHA loans," "VA loans," and so on.

Here are some quick ways to get ideas on keywords that might be popular with searchers:

- Try typing words that describe your offerings into Yelp's search box, and see what shows up in the list of keyword suggestions. As an example, here are Yelp's keyword suggestions related to knitting:

- You can try the same thing on Google: Start typing words that relate to your business into the search box and see what keywords Google suggests. Here are Google's suggestions for the keyword <knitting>.

Continues

Optimize Your Listings with Keywords *(Continued)*

```
knitting                                    🎤   [🔍]
knitting patterns
knitting stitches
knitting factory
knitting help
Press Enter to search.
```

- Overachievers can log into their AdWords account and mine search volume data from the Google AdWords Keyword Planner.

A word of caution: Don't cross the line from optimization to spam. Using excessive repetition, representing your business with a false, keyword-stuffed name, or adding inaccurate or misleading keywords will backfire with potential customers and review sites, which have algorithms to detect this sort of thing. And always make sure you understand the content guidelines of the review site you're working on.

Your prime directive is to use accurate, compelling, and well written messaging to represent your business. After that, sprinkle a few keywords into the mix, and you've probably done all the optimizing you need.

Filtering and Reviewer Verification

In Chapter 5, "How to Get More Reviews," we introduced you to Yelp's review filter, which aggressively yanks reviews that it suspects have been solicited by businesses, or are false, misleading, or otherwise suspicious. According to Yelp, about 20% of reviews are filtered.

Perhaps you're already acquainted with Yelp's review filter, but if not, here's how to see filtered reviews. On any business page, scroll to the bottom of the list of reviews. If any reviews are filtered, you will see a link like the one here:

1 to 40 of 107 (22 Filtered) | Page: 1 2 3

In this example, clicking on "22 Filtered" takes you to a page showing the filtered reviews for this business. You may see some reviews that seem legitimate, like the one shown in Figure 6.4.

✪✪✪✪✪ *10/4/2012*

I am in Chicago again and decided to stay at the Four Seasons Chicago .

Nice size rooms and great bedding. everything has a nice clean modern look.
they have a great location right in the middle of all the shopping and i actually have a lake view this time.

Seems like the internet is a bit outdated and very slow, that's a bit of a disappointment but I can just run across the street
to Starbucks (up the block a bit) and get online.

Its a great place to stay in the perfect location.

Flag this review

Figure 6.4 This legitimate-looking review was filtered by Yelp.

Yelp does not publicly share information about what causes reviews to be filtered, saying, "We intentionally make the filter difficult to reverse engineer—otherwise, we would be overrun by reviews written by people hoping to game the system." Yelp also acknowledges that some real reviews get filtered out, as many businesses are painfully aware.

Getting a review filtered doesn't cause any penalty for your business, but it represents a waste of your efforts in encouraging reviews and hides away a good review that should be out there in public helping your business. The ratings in your filtered reviews are not factored into your overall star average.

We think Yelp's advice bears repeating: Rather than trying to get more of your customers to write Yelp reviews, *get more Yelpers to become your customers*. The Yelp reviews that are least likely to get filtered are the ones from people who routinely write reviews on Yelp. Reviews from Yelpers with Elite status are on the most solid ground. Here are some ways you can deal with the Yelp filter:

- Focus on getting more visibility in Yelp, through free, paid, and community promotions discussed in this section. This will make more Yelpers see you, and as more Yelpers become your customers, more of them will review your business.

- Become an active Yelper yourself, and respond to your Yelp reviews. Additionally, rumor has it that interacting with your reviewers, for example, by adding them as friends or marking their reviews as "helpful" or "funny," may help keep their reviews out of the filter; however, when we spoke with Yelp they indicated that this was not a good idea. Whether or not this technique works, it smacks of manipulation, so don't overdo it.

- Filtered reviews can be unfiltered. If a customer tells you that their review for your business was filtered, you can advise them to continue writing reviews for other local businesses, download and use the Yelp mobile app, connect their Yelp and Facebook accounts, and generally be an active Yelper. This might help their reviews pop out into public view.

- Let your customers know you're on Yelp, with signs in your establishment, printed icons on your invoices and receipts, links on your website and in your emails, and as part of your day-to-day conversations with customers. Yelpers are often happy to share their knowledge with others and use their kind words to reward your business for great service. Maybe all they need is a little reminder.

- Encourage customers to check in at your business using the Yelp app. Yelp may have a stance against asking for reviews, but there is no such prohibition against asking for check-ins. Even better, Yelp follows up directly with customers after they check in and asks for reviews. You can get official print-ready check-in reminders from Yelp at:

   www.flickr.com/photos/yelp/sets/72157623054478330

- To create special promotions that incentivize check-ins, unlock your Yelp profile and click on "Check-in Offers." See "Promotion and Advertising Opportunities" later in this chapter for more details on check-in offers.

If Yelp's filter makes you want to give up and stop thinking about Yelp altogether, you wouldn't be the first business to feel that way. But think of it this way: If your potential customers are using Yelp, Yelp deserves *your* attention, too.

Troubleshooting and Support

Maybe you've finally carved out 15 minutes from your extremely busy day to work on improving your Yelp presence and monitoring your online reputation. During this time, you become aware of something that makes your blood pressure rise, like a flagrantly bogus negative review, a duplicate listing, or a locked field when you try to edit your business page. Naturally you'll want Yelp to help you sort through these issues. When you're looking for assistance from Yelp, keep a few key points in mind:

Yelp does not arbitrate disputes. If you feel you are the victim of false or misleading reviews on Yelp, you are officially on your own. There is also no official channel for disputing Yelp's review filtering decisions.

Claiming your business listing does not give you special access to Yelp support staff. Some nonpaying business owners who have contacted Yelp for support report quick responses; others, not so much.

The only way to gain guaranteed access to a Yelp support ear is to purchase advertising. This is not a cure-all, though. No amount of money can buy you total control of your listing. The teams in charge of advertising are separate from the teams in charge of content at Yelp. Don't expect that purchasing an advertising campaign will help you modify existing bad reviews. According to Yelp's FAQ, "You can't pay us to remove or reorder your bad reviews—it's just that simple."

Now that your expectations are appropriately in line, here are support options available to nonadvertisers:

The Ability to Flag a Review Every review on Yelp has a "Flag this review" link as seen in Figure 6.5. When you flag a review, you have the option of leaving a note explaining the issue. This option shouldn't be employed for every negative review, just ones that are fraudulent or otherwise violate Yelp's content guidelines, which you can find at www.yelp.com/guidelines.

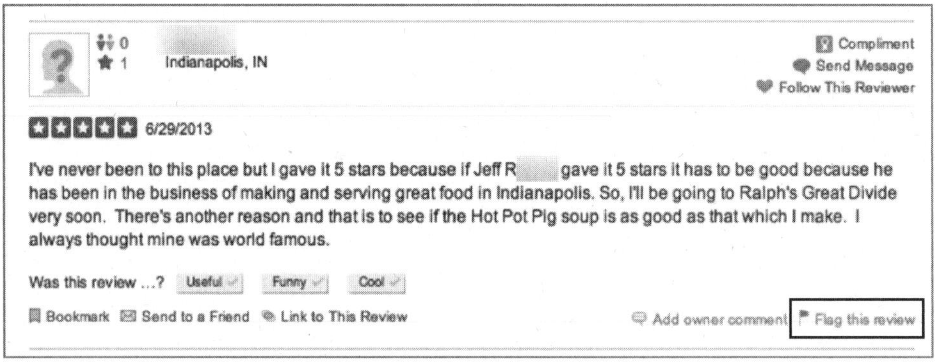

> 0
> 1   Indianapolis, IN
>
> Compliment
> Send Message
> Follow This Reviewer
>
> ★★★★★ 6/29/2013
>
> I've never been to this place but I gave it 5 stars because if Jeff R____ gave it 5 stars it has to be good because he has been in the business of making and serving great food in Indianapolis. So, I'll be going to Ralph's Great Divide very soon. There's another reason and that is to see if the Hot Pot Pig soup is as good as that which I make. I always thought mine was world famous.
>
> Was this review …? Useful ✓   Funny ✓   Cool ✓
>
> 🔖 Bookmark   ✉ Send to a Friend   🔗 Link to This Review   💬 Add owner comment   ⚑ Flag this review

Figure 6.5 Businesses can flag reviews that appear suspicious or violate Yelp's rules.

Flagging reviews is a one-way conversation: Yelp does not reply to flags, and you will not be notified of Yelp's resolution, if any occurs.

Business Support Center The business support center at https://biz.yelp.com/support contains FAQs, tips, videos, and a Yelp for Business blog.

Contact Form A contact form is available at www.yelp.com/contact that lets business owners request assistance on topics such as questionable content, missing reviews, or duplicate listings. You'll get this not exactly encouraging response.

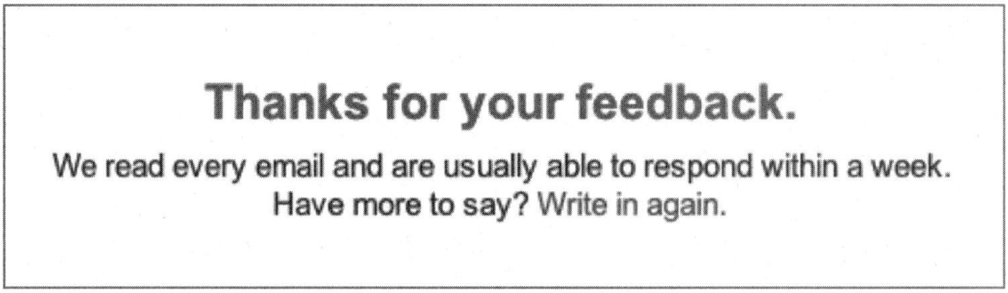

Thanks for your feedback.

We read every email and are usually able to respond within a week. Have more to say? Write in again.

Forums Plenty of business owners ask questions, many of which are tinged with the sweat of desperation and excessive capitalization, on Yelp's forums. A surprising number of questions on the forum receive responses from Yelp's Community Managers, employees who act as liaisons to the local Yelp community and its business members. To find the forum for your area, go to www.yelp.com/talk, or click on the "Talk" tab from any page on the Yelp site. If you find that you're looking at a forum for the wrong city, just click "More Cities" at the top of the page and you'll be on the right path.

Town Hall Events Want to discuss ways to improve your Yelp presence with actual Yelp reps? You can, if you are lucky enough to snag a spot in one of Yelp's town hall events taking place in select cities across the US and Canada. These events, which fill up quickly, typically include a talk by a Yelp representative, a panel of knowledgeable local business owners, and a chance to network with local businesses and your local Yelp community manager. If you're interested in attending, find your community manager as described in "Yelp Events and Elite Events," and let them know that you'd like to be on the invitation list for any Town Hall events that come to your area.

Communicating with Reviewers

Hoping for a little virtual chin-wag with a Yelp reviewer? You have two options: public comments and private messages. You can get to both of these options by logging into your claimed listing and navigating to a review.

> *You may message 5 more customers today, and your business may make up to 3 more public comments.*
>
> [Send Private Message]   [Add Public Comment]

The standard guidelines about refraining from profanity, personal attacks, and other ignominious interactions apply to owner comments and messages. But there is one special rule for business owners, presumably intended to keep things civil: Before you send a message or post a comment, you must upload a photo of yourself to your business listing. According to Yelp, "photos should clearly show your face (no sunglasses please) and not include too many people."

You can comment publicly on any of your reviews, including filtered ones. As shown in Figure 6.6, your comment will appear directly below the review that you replied to.

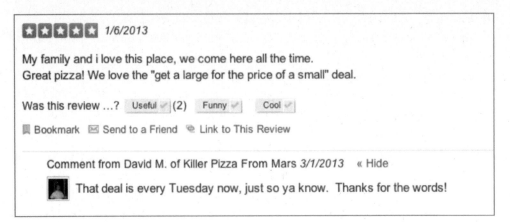

Figure 6.6 Owner comment on Yelp

Yelp advises business owners to use private messages to thank Yelpers for their positive reviews (according to Yelp, doing this publicly can be "overbearing") and also recommends reaching out privately to resolve issues before posting public comments. Reviewers have the option to turn off private messaging or block users who have sent them private messages.

Read more about responding to reviews from Yelp at:

`https://biz.yelp.com/support/responding_to_reviews`

We'll discuss best practices for responding to reviews in Chapter 7, "Navigating Negative Reviews."

Promotion and Advertising Opportunities

Given the frustrations of Yelp's filter and the site's official stance against businesses asking for reviews, you may find it more effective to work on increasing your business's visibility in Yelp, rather than working directly on increasing your reviews. Yelp has a growing menu of advertising options. Some are self-serve and are built on a commission model, whereas others require the assistance of a representative and function on a pay-per-impression model.

Yelp Deals, Gift Certificates, and Check-in Offers

Tales of pushy Yelp salespeople are rampant among the business owners we spoke with, and complaints about Yelp advertising are posted all over the Web. This makes some business owners reluctant to experiment with paid options for improving their visibility on Yelp. Yelp Deals, gift certificates, and check-in offers are promotions that you can set up yourself, without the commitment and expense of a Yelp Ads campaign.

Check-in Offers To dip your toe into social/local/mobile promotion, create a Yelp check-in offer. These are promotions that can be redeemed only if your customer uses the Yelp app's check-in feature at your location, as seen here.

2. Warehouse Suit Sale ◄ 15 mi

$

★★★★★ 38 Reviews

333 W Alondra Blvd, Harbor Gateway

Men's Clothing

Check-in Offer: $15 off alterations on suit purchase.

The obvious benefit of using a check-in offer is that it creates an incentive for customers to announce publicly that they patronize your business. One less obvious but equally delightful benefit is that Yelp follows up with Yelpers who have checked in to a location to ask for a review, as shown in Figure 6.7. This Yelp-driven review solicitation is an exciting feature, considering Yelp actively tries to suppress reviews that businesses request from customers.

Your Next Review Awaits

Cypress Park Branch Library ✕

★★★★★

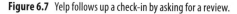 1 check-in here

Start your review...

Figure 6.7 Yelp follows up a check-in by asking for a review.

Set up your offer by logging in to your claimed profile and clicking "Check-in Offers." Check-in offers display to users who view your business listing in Yelp Search or the Yelp mobile app. Because Yelp check-in offers are featured on the Yelp mobile app when a user clicks "Nearby," these deals may be especially appealing if you know you have customers who use Yelp, or your business tends to attract the serendipitous, I-was-in-the-neighborhood-and-thought-I'd-give-this-place-a-try kind of customer. See Figure 6.8.

Deals and Gift Certificates Yelp Deals is a pay-per-action form of advertising that may be attractive to businesses that want to gain more exposure on Yelp, or test whether the Yelp audience will convert. To create a Yelp Deal, you advertise a discounted offering (for example, you offer a price of $75 for $125 in services). Customers complete the transaction on Yelp, and bring proof of purchase to be redeemed at your location. See Figure 6.9 for an example of a Yelp Deal.

Figure 6.8 Check-in offers are featured prominently on the Yelp mobile app.

To set up a Yelp Deal, log in to your claimed profile and click on "Deals & Gift Certificates." You set the price and the service offered, and Yelp retains a portion of the purchase price for every Deal sold. Just like with check-in offers, Yelp follows up with customers who have redeemed a Yelp Deal to ask for a review.

Yelp gift certificates function similarly to Yelp Deals, with the primary difference being that gift certificates are purchased for their face value (for example, $125 for $125 in services).

Businesses with active Yelp Deals have a number of visibility advantages, including a special category in Yelp Search for businesses offering Yelp Deals (you saw this in Figure 6.8), a "Deals" button on the Yelp mobile app home screen, and an attention-grabbing icon and deal description next to your business listing in Yelp Search (see Figure 6.10).

$30 for 2 Tickets to a Ghost and Vampire Tour (reg $40) at French Quarter Phantoms

Yelp Deals

Buy Now for $30

Reg. Price	Discount	Savings
$40	**25%**	**$10**

Limited quantities available

Like 1   **Tweet** 0

What You Get

- Valid for two persons only — children 7 years old and younger are free with parents

- Tour runs everyday at 6pm and 8pm and meets at Flanagan's Pub

- Ghost & Vampire tour guests also receive Buy One, Get One Free Hurricane drinks the hour prior to each tour with proof of tour purchase

Important Restrictions

- By phone reservation only, call (504) 666-8300 with your Deal voucher code

Additional Restrictions

Promotion lasts for 1 year from date of purchase. After that period, your voucher is redeemable for the amount you paid. Only 1 Voucher can be purchased and redeemed per person. Only 1 Voucher may be purchased as a gift for another. Must be used in a single visit. Must make reservation at least 24 hours in advance. Not to be combined with other vouchers, coupons or discounts. Subject to the General Terms.

Figure 6.9 Yelp Deal for $10 off a $40 service

2. George Parks Roofing & Painting 34.7 mi

★★★★☆ 25 Reviews
1048 Irvine Ave, Newport Beach
Painters, Roofing
$155 for $200 Deal

Figure 6.10 Yelp Deal prominently displayed in Yelp's mobile search results

If you create a Deal, gift certificate, or check-in offer, make sure to communicate with your staff so that they are prepared to handle the logistics. Reviewers can be vicious when expected promotions are not honored, as seen here:

> ★☆☆☆☆ 2/21/2013   🚗 Purchased a Yelp Deal
>
> DO NOT BUY THE YELP DEAL OF 20-for-10 BECAUSE THE ESTABLISHMENT FINDS EVERY EXCUSE TO NOT HONOR THAT.

Yelp Ads

Yelp's advertising options are described at www.yelp.com/advertise. There is a wide range of offerings; businesses with multiple locations or a national presence have more options available to them than small businesses. Let's take a look at a few core advertising options.

Advertise on Yelp Search Yelp advertisers get premium placement, displaying above Yelp's search results for your geographical area. Factors that affect your ad's visibility include

Budget Working with an ad rep, you set a per-month cost that is based on the number of guaranteed ad impressions you'll receive.

Competition Your ads are rotated with other advertisers' ads in your category. Only one ad is shown at a time.

Location Your ads are shown only to people searching for businesses in your service area.

Text in Your Business Listing and Positive Reviews On Yelp, businesses do not sponsor a list of keywords that they wish to be found for, as Google AdWords advertisers do. However, the text used to describe your business (particularly Specialties text) and the text in your reviews may affect whether and how your ad displays for certain searches. In the ad, Yelp may display review text from positive reviews, aggregate review stars if you have a large enough volume of reviews and a high star count, or an excerpt of your business description text. For this reason, it's a great idea to craft your business listing text like an ad so that you have the most compelling advertising presence possible. Here's an example of text from the Specialties section of a business listing that makes for a compelling ad:

Yelp Ad

Color Fx Inc
Printing Services

Sun Valley
11050 Randall St
Sun Valley, CA 91352
(818) 767-7671

ColorFX Printing offers complete Trade & Retail Printing Services Nationwide. We offer exceptional pricing and service to our trade partners with quality that is second to none. Offer Business...

Advertise on Related Businesses In the physical world, you may not have the chutzpah to plant your sign in front of your competitor's front door, but in the virtual world, Yelp can set you up with a similarly slick move. As an advertiser, your Yelp ads will be displayed on the business pages of nearby businesses in your category (see Figure 6.11). As with visibility for your Yelp Search ads, competitor ad placement is based on budget and other factors, so your ads will not be on display one hundred percent of the time.

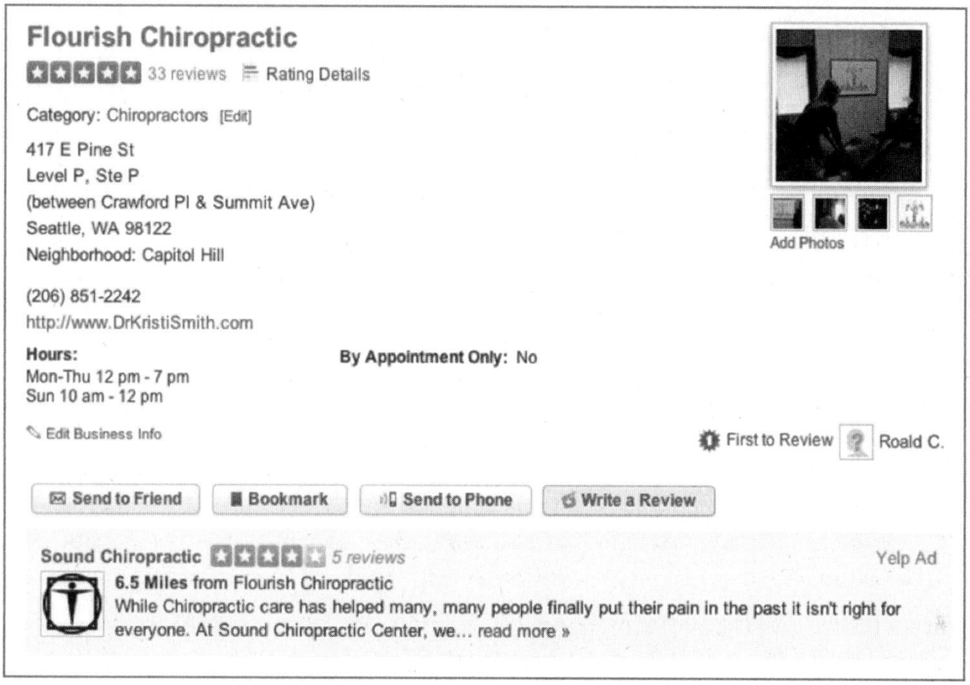

Figure 6.11 An ad for Sound Chiropractic displays on the business page for Flourish Chiropractic.

Removal of Competitor Ads You probably don't enjoy seeing competitor ads on your own Yelp business page. Paying for advertising will sweep them away.

Call to Action Button Yelp's Call to Action button allows a business to add links from its Yelp listing directly to desired transactions on its own website. Calls to action include "Schedule Appointment," "Book Now," and "Get Quote."

Photo Slideshow and Professionally Produced Video You may have plenty of customer-uploaded photos on your Yelp page, but you don't control their content, or the order in which they appear. Yelp advertisers have a workaround here: They can feature their own large images front and center on their business listing and can organize them into slideshows. If you enter into a longer-term advertising contract, you can opt to have Yelp's video production partner create a short, professional video for your company. You can buy the rights to the video for a few hundred dollars.

A Yelp Success Story

For some businesses that provide sensitive or confidential services, getting reviews can be difficult. Take Armando Cosio, owner-operator of La Cucaracha Pest Control Services in Los Angeles. Armando remembers one restaurant owner who asked, "Can you guys send a truck with no markings, park down the street, and hide the patch on your uniform?" While some clients may be shy about admitting to using pest control services, others are more than happy to leave reviews, and in fact Armando considers himself something of a Yelp success story.

After getting his first few reviews organically on Yelp, Armando was approached by a Yelp ad sales representative about starting an advertising campaign. But thinking back to an expensive, fruitless advertising campaign on another directory site, Armando says, "I was really hesitant to advertise. They had to make me an offer I couldn't refuse." Yelp offered Armando an introductory month-to-month arrangement, which he eventually accepted.

"It started out slow, but I did get a few calls that I wasn't getting before." And the phone kept ringing. "My slow season is January through April. Traditionally January and February are super slow. The first February with Yelp advertising was my busiest month compared to the previous year. It escalated from there, and eventually I hired three more people." Armando believes that Yelp advertising and the accumulation of reviews over time were major factors in the growth of his business.

Armando's reviews sometimes get caught in the steel trap of Yelp's filter. Armando recalls, "When I first started getting reviews, I did a job out on the beach in Santa Monica. It was a beehive, and I had to rent a 50-foot ladder, park on the street, and hike to the site, climb 50 feet up in a bee suit, spray the bees…I worked hard at this!" His appreciative, happily bee-free client wrote a great Yelp review, but it never saw the light of day. "I get a positive review that I didn't ask for, and it gets filtered," Armando says.

Armando's success may not be representative of the average Yelp advertiser. For one thing, he believes that in his line of work, reviews have a direct and significant effect on the number of calls he gets. He observes that positive reviews drive new customers whereas negative reviews can "cool down the phone a bit." Additionally, Armando's Yelp advertising rates are affordable and his Yelp rep worked with him to select introductory contract terms that he was comfortable with. And at the time Armando started his advertising campaign many of his competitors weren't on Yelp, which allowed him to pull ahead quickly in the race for reviews.

Although there's no guarantee that you'll ride your Yelp stars to success, there is a good chance that if you make an effort to use Yelp more fully by claiming your business listing, monitoring Yelp-related customer activity, and doing what you can to encourage reviews, you'll be getting out ahead of your competitors.

How much does Yelp advertising cost for a typical small business? That answer depends on the category your business advertises in and the number of ad impressions you buy, but expect to be quoted anywhere from a few hundred to a few thousand dollars per month. One source at Yelp told us that the most expensive categories are real estate and home services such as plumbers and other contractors, whereas restaurants tend to pay less. Unlike Yelp Deals, gift certificates, and check-in offers, Yelp ads are not self-service, so you'll need to work with an advertising representative to get your campaign underway. Reps are likely to push potential advertisers toward longer-term contracts, but shorter-term contracts are available.

Yelp Events and Elite Events

With persistence and no small amount of luck, you may be able to feature your business in special offline community events. Yelp Events are open to the entire community. See a Yelp Event invitation in Figure 6.12.

Figure 6.12 An invitation for Cuppa Yelp, a public Yelp Event featuring local coffee houses

In contrast, Elite events are open to Yelp Elite reviewers only. As you learned in Chapter 3, "Understanding Reviewers and Reviews," Yelp Elite reviewers are a select group of prolific Yelpers who are invited to attend special Yelp parties where they can bask in the company of other Yelp royalty and sample offerings from featured businesses.

The key to participating in events is to get the attention of a Yelp Community Manager. Community Managers are Yelp employees who perform many duties, including organizing local events, in their role as liaisons to their local communities.

Find your local community manager by visiting www.yelp.com/elite. You should be redirected to your local Yelp page. Scroll down to the bottom of the page for a link to message your community manager. If you're redirected to the wrong page, just click on the link in the upper right (for example, "Not in Rotterdam?") to choose another city. You'll find a "Send Message" link on the community manager's profile page, as seen in Figure 6.13.

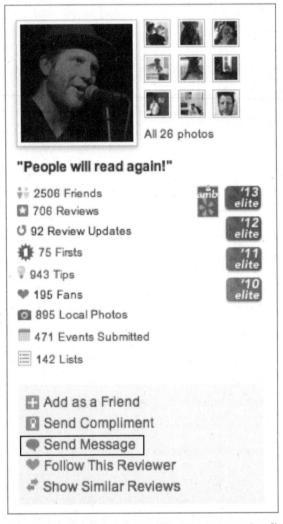

Figure 6.13 The Send Message link on a Yelp community manager's profile page

Participating in Yelp-sponsored events does not come with any guarantees of sales, new reviews, or even views of your business listing. Yelp event pages are not prominent on the site and don't show up in Yelp's search results. Yelp's PR department tells us, "These events are not advertising opportunities for small businesses. [Small businesses] do not pay Yelp to host them. They are simply opportunities to expose their business to members of an active and engaged community." With Yelp-sponsored events, the path to gaining new reviews is indirect. Participating in events gives you exposure to a particularly attractive set of potential new customers—the kind who engage with Yelp in your local community—and the potential word-of-mouth marketing that they bring to the picture.

Showing Off Your Reviews

Showing off your Yelp reviews can benefit your business in multiple ways. First, it provides social proof, a badge of credibility to broadcast your great reviews to anyone who is researching your business. Second, a well-placed reminder that you're maintaining an active presence on Yelp might encourage existing customers to leave a review of their own.

Businesses that are proud of their Yelp listing can spread the good news both online and off.

On Your Website Log in to your business account and click "review badges" to see options for badges and buttons that are easy to add to your website. These come in multiple designs, including buttons that dynamically display your review count. A couple of examples are shown in Figure 6.14.

Figure 6.14 Yelp review badges

If you want to customize your website's link to Yelp, for example, with excerpts of your reviews or callouts of your deals or promotions, Yelp offers an API for developers to build tickers or other widgets. View the requirements here:

    www.yelp.com/developers/getting_started/display_requirements

There are also WordPress plug-ins to show Yelp reviews on your site, which can be found here:

    http://wordpress.org/plugins/tags/yelp

In Your Establishment Showing off your reviews in the offline world is at its most visible with the ubiquitous "People Love Us on Yelp" window clings, which Yelp mails out to qualifying businesses. Although these decals cannot be purchased, rumor has it local community managers are able to hand them out. See the earlier section "Yelp Events and Elite Events" to learn how to connect with your community manager.

Feeling creative? Yelp makes an assortment of promotional graphics, including buttons and printables, available for business owners for free at

www.flickr.com/photos/yelp/sets/72157623054478330

Monitor and Measure

Many of the business owners we talk to use less-than-scientific measures to gauge the effectiveness of Yelp. This is largely because Yelp businesses are mostly brick-and-mortar establishments, and it's quite difficult to identify a connection between a view to your Yelp page and a customer walking through your door. Showing up at your location, or punching numbers into a phone to call you are examples of offline conversions, and they are notoriously difficult to track. Here are some ways to monitor what you can and dial down the guesswork:

Email Alerts Yelp has several email notification options, including the option to receive an email every time you get a new review. You can associate just one email address with each claimed Yelp listing. For this reason, it may be best to create a dedicated email address that you use just for Yelp. This will make it easier to hand over monitoring tasks to a staff member if the business owner is too busy to keep up.

Revenue Estimator Tool If you've claimed your Yelp listing, you have access to Yelp's free revenue estimator tool (see Figure 6.15). This tool, which assigns a monetary value to Yelp visitor actions, may be a helpful way for you to measure how valuable Yelp is for delivering you business. Or it may be a heavy-handed way for Yelp to try to justify the costs of advertising on Yelp to increase visibility. Yelp inserts an estimated revenue-per-customer-lead figure, but you can plug in a different number if you prefer.

We are huge advocates of using data to inform your business, but we suggest you fold a little skepticism into the use of this tool, as it has the potential to paint a too-rosy picture. The tool lists a number of actions that it calls Customer Leads. These range from actions in which Yelp is a clear referral source (clicks to your website from Yelp.com, or calls made from the mobile site or app to your business) to actions in which Yelp is involved, but not necessarily the driver of the customer/business interaction (mobile check-ins, photo uploads). All of these so-called Customer Leads are assigned the same dollar amount by the tool.

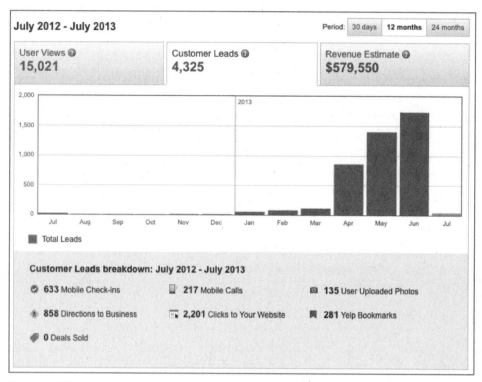

Figure 6.15 Yelp's revenue estimator tool shows data for a local business.

Web Analytics If you've set up Google Analytics or another web analytics tool, you can use it to measure how many visitors enter your site from your Yelp profile. A large percentage of the people who discover your business on Yelp won't click through to your website, but checking your analytics data will give you some insights about those who do.

Check-in Offers When a customer redeems a Yelp check-in offer, it's clear that Yelp was involved in the customer experience. But did the customer come to you because of the check-in offer, or did they come to you first and then notice the check-in offer on their phone? You may not know unless you ask, and let's face it, you probably won't ask. Causality aside, knowing that customers use your check-in offer is good information, because it establishes Yelp as a tool for engaging your customers. Plus, since Yelp will reach out to encourage Yelpers to write reviews after a check-in, you may be able to connect the dots between Yelp check-ins and new reviews.

In-Yelp Transactions There's no real way to know whether Yelp's advanced promotional options will benefit your business unless you give them a try, but one thing is clear: They're trackable. Yelp Deals, Gift Certificates, and Calls to Action are all ways in which the becoming-a-customer part of the customer relationship happens directly on Yelp, thus turning a mysterious offline conversion into a measurable online conversion.

Is Yelp Advertising Worth It?

After hearing a lot of negative rumors, we've been surprised by the high level of satisfaction we've heard from business owners who pay for Yelp Ads. If you're in the habit of slamming down the phone when you get a Yelp sales call, we suggest you give it another look, maintaining a healthy balance between open-mindedness and skepticism.

We'll start with the good: The 2013 study "Unlocking the Digital-Marketing Potential of Small Businesses" by the Boston Consulting Group (which was partially funded by Yelp) surveyed approximately 4,800 small businesses and found that free listings on Yelp generated increases in annual revenues of $8,000 on average. Sweet—that's $8,000 in free money with no expenditures! Advertising resulted in more gains: Businesses who advertised on Yelp reported an average $23,000 revenue increase.

Now, let's throw in some skepticism: Yelp says the average advertiser spends $4,200 per year for Yelp ads. That means the advertising really only brought in $23,000 minus $4,200 (what they spent on ads) minus $8,000 (what they'd get for free), or about $11,000 in extra revenue.

Some business categories may see bigger returns than others. In this study, Arts and Entertainment reaped the highest financial returns and Beauty and Spas had the lowest. Two categories, Restaurants and Event Planning, show a very small difference between nonadvertiser and advertiser revenue.

It seems to us that if you're in these low-return categories, your free or lower-cost promotion options at Yelp should be tested before shelling out the bigger bucks. See the chart on page 3 of the report to find your own business category:

www.yelp.typepad.com/files/boston-consulting-group-study.pdf

Google+ Local

We all know Google's importance, which is reinforced by some seriously impressive numbers: Google is the world's dominant search engine, with an estimated *100 billion searches* per month globally in 2012 and roughly two-thirds of the search market share within the United States.

A healthy portion of the billions of daily Google searches feature Google+ Local results like those shown in Figure 6.16. At least 40% of all Google searches have a local intent, meaning the searcher is interested in seeing results from a specific geographic location. Not surprisingly, mobile searches tend to be more locally oriented than desktop searches.

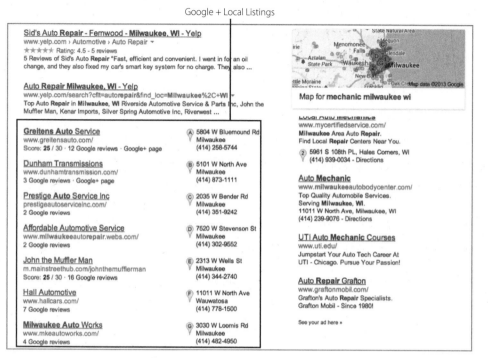

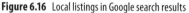

Figure 6.16 Local listings in Google search results

Google may also display local listings in a carousel at the top of search results, as seen in Figure 6.17.

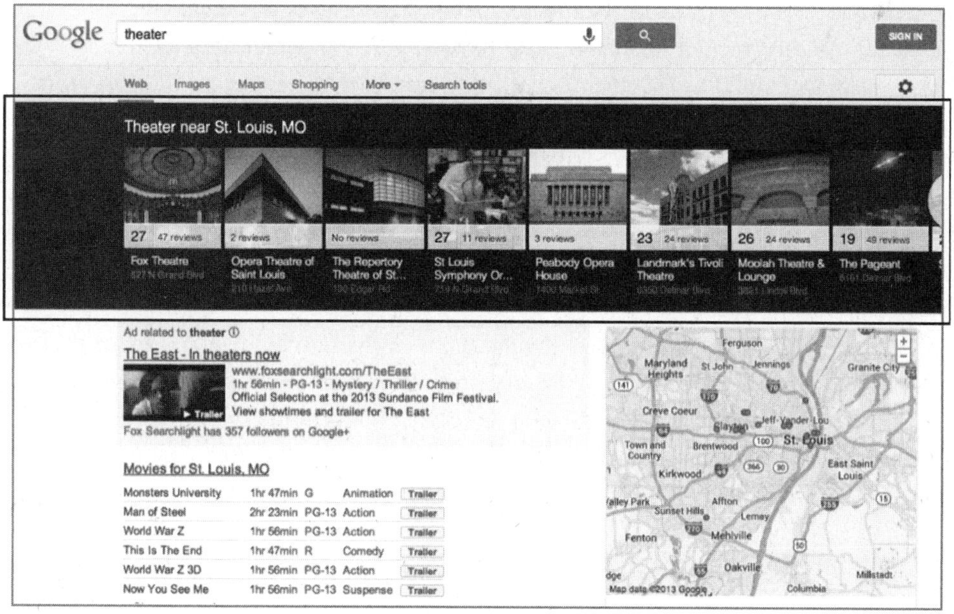

Figure 6.17 Local listings get a prominent position in this Google search result.

Other review sites fret about Google+ Local's unfair advantage in search results, but that very advantage is what makes Google+ Local so important to you. If you have a local business—either with a brick-and-mortar presence or serving local clients at their locations—it's hard to imagine a reason not to care about your Google+ Local presence.

Sorting Out Google's Services

The names of Google's various services can leave you as confused as a chameleon in a bag of Skittles. Here's a quick reference to keep them sorted out:

Google A search site, also known as a search engine. Google results are compiled from a combination of sources inside Google, which include its index of websites as well as a separate Google + Local index, advertising listings, and others.

Google Maps (Formerly Google Local) A mapping service that is embedded within Google and that powers other sites and apps as well. Google often displays Google Maps results within its main web search results.

Google+ A social network that is integrated with Google search; it's often called a "social layer" that is overlaid on the Google search experience. People can set up profiles on Google+ and use these profiles to interact with other people and with businesses. Google+ interactions can show up in search results and can affect the search experience for Google+ users. Just like Facebook, Google+ has both personal profiles and business pages. A page created for a local business is called a local Google+ page.

Google+ Local Google+ Local (sometimes called Google Places or Google Places for Business) is a directory of businesses that have in-person contact with customers. Local business listings in Google+ Local contain information such as address, store hours, photos and videos, and reviews from Google+ users. Google uses this directory to populate its Google Maps results. For businesses with multiple locations, each business location has a separate listing in Google+ Local. The *Google+ Local listing* for a business is not the same as a *local Google+ page* for that business; however, the two can be merged, once a business owner verifies them. Figure 6.18 shows a typical Google+ Local listing.

If this remains about as clear as mud, here's a tip: Start with claiming or creating your Google+ Local page as described later in this section, and don't worry too much about all the names and definitions. Google is likely to reshuffle the deck soon enough, anyway.

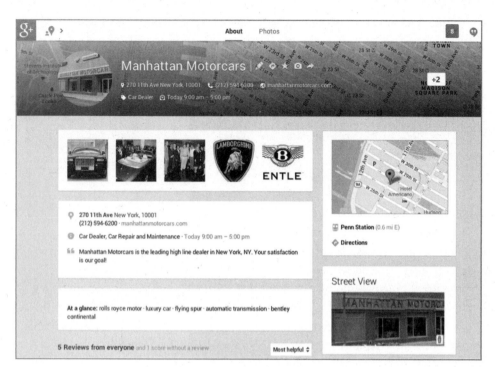

Figure 6.18 This Google+ Local listing includes business info, photos, and reviews.

Who Sees Google+ Local Listings?

Visitors are likely to see Google+ Local listings when they're researching businesses in their area. Searches that have a local intent in Google's eyes include words that can be used to describe local businesses, such as these:

- <pizza>
- <chiropractor>
- <bicycle>

Or they can be phrases that identify a city or local region, such as these:

- <atlanta pizza>
- <30325 chiropractor>
- <rockport ma bicycle>

States, provinces, and country names when added to a search term, for example, <california lawyer>, do not generally trigger Google+ Local business results.

Google can also display a business's Google+ Local listing in results for branded searches like these:

- <embassy suites hotel austin>
- <sun lighting> [the name of a local mom & pop business]

Looking more closely at the Google+ Local listings that are displayed in results, we see several options for the searcher to take steps toward becoming your customer:

Links to business website

Links to Google Maps results

Links to Google+ Local listing

Shows a preview of Google+ Local list

Google packs a lot of possibility into this little listing! The searcher can click on any of the available links, or they might just read the phone number or location and stop there, mission accomplished.

Figure 6.19 shows the type of result that a searcher may encounter when they already know the name of the business they're researching, in this example <sun lighting>, a local store in Tucson, Arizona. Maybe they're out of the house, using Google Maps on their smartphone to find an address. Or they're checking online reviews for a business before making a final purchase decision.

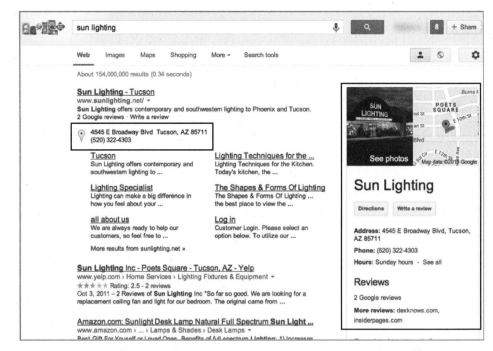

Figure 6.19 This Google result for <sun lighting> includes links to read and write reviews on the Google+ Local listing.

Google provides multiple opportunities for searchers who encounter your business listing to leave reviews:

- They can click on the "Write a review" link or button from Google's search results as seen in Figure 6.19.

- They can click on the "Write a review" link or the pencil icon on your Google+ Local page.

- They can click on "Rate & review this place" using the Google+ Local mobile app, as seen in Figure 6.20.

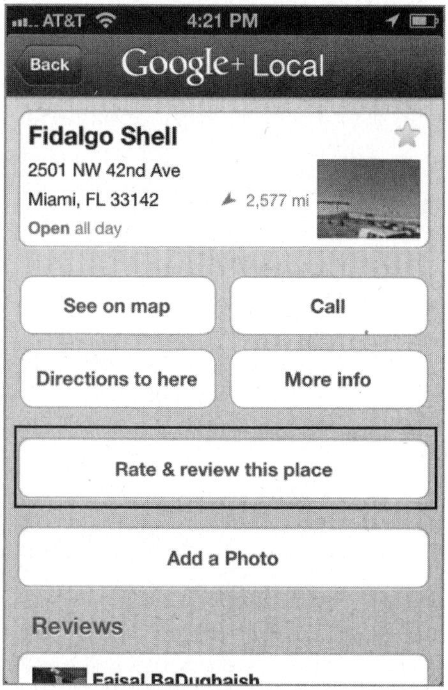

Figure 6.20 Users can use the Google+ Local app to write reviews.

Claiming Your Listing

Claiming your Google+ Local listing is important because it allows you to manage and update your business information, view analytics about visitors and actions on your page, and respond to reviews. Google walks you through the steps to create or claim a Google+ Local business listing here: http://places.google.com. You'll need a Google account and a way to verify that you are an authorized representative of the business.

Before you get started, set aside five minutes to read Google's Quality Guidelines, here:

https://support.google.com/places/answer/107528

Anatomy of a Google+ Local Page

Here are the review-related features for a typical Google+ Local listing:

Visitors can click the pencil icon to write a review

Anyone can submit an edit for Google's consideration, which is one reason it's important to keep an eye on your listing.

"Scores" are old ratings that did not include a text description. New reviews always include text.

Click here to claim your listing.

Click here to report a problem such as an incorrect business location.

Reviews from people in the viewer's social circle will display most prominently on this list.

Google links to other review sources on the web.

Visitors can click here to write a review.

Don't mess around with trying to game the system—you don't want your listing floating around in penalty limbo when it could be working for your business. Here are a few pointers on setting up or claiming a listing:

Set up or claim the profile with a Google account that you'll be maintaining. Google allows only one verified business owner, so it's important to choose a reliable account for this role. Don't let a temporary intern or your helpful cousin set up ownership using their Google account. You might want to create an email address just for this purpose so that management can be easily transferred later, if necessary.

Use the legal full name of your business. It's best if the name of your Google+ business listing matches the name displayed on your website and other review sites exactly. It is against Google's Terms of Service to stuff keywords into your business name; however, professionals can include titles, such as "Joe Brown, MD."

You are not permitted to use a P.O. box... Google wishes to show your listing only at its true physical location, so P.O. boxes are out.

...but suite numbers are okay. It's not unusual for multiple businesses to share the same street address with different suite numbers, and Google allows this, as long as the businesses are genuinely separate. Google also allows separate listings for distinct departments or practitioners within a business—for example, university departments or real estate agents—but only when they are public-facing and separately contactable.

Have a unique address and phone. Sharing a phone number with another business can confuse Google. Also, many businesses have reported bugs in Google's system, causing it to merge listings for separate companies that share a street address. It's best to use a distinct street address and phone number that no other business has.

You do not have to make your address visible to the public. Many businesses do not want their address shown on Google for various reasons, including privacy concerns or zoning restrictions. And if you travel to your customers rather than serving them at your business location, Google requires you to hide your address. In this case, select "My business has service areas..." as seen here:

Fill in every available field. The more complete your listing is, the more search visibility it will have. You're allowed to include up to 10 different categories; surely there are a few that fit your business. And the description field has room for several paragraphs. Why skimp here? A hearty description gives visitors more to chew on and may help your listing's ranks.

Getting reviews on Google+ Local is one of many factors that can help your listing rank higher in Google's search results. We'll throw a few more ranking tips your way in "Ways to Increase Your Visibility," later in this section.

Filtering and Reviewer Verification

Many business owners grumble that getting reviews on Google+ Local is difficult and the process is fraught with bugs, glitches, and confusion. A major reason businesses find it hard to get Google+ Local review is this: In order to write a review on Google+ Local, a person must have a Google+ account. This is not the same as a Gmail account. Although Google will be happy to remind you that it has over 100 million active monthly users, many of those users probably don't even know they have Google+ accounts. Google's incessant retooling of its services and branding is a hindrance to awareness and adoption. In our conversations with businesses and customers, we noticed that most people seem to be completely lost when it comes to Google+ Local.

Because of this confusion, to get reviews on Google+ Local you may need to walk your customers through the process of setting up or accessing their Google+ accounts. It's not difficult; anyone with a Gmail account can easily upgrade to a Google+ account, starting with a click on "+You" in Google's top navigation:

Folks who don't yet have a Google+ account will get a prompt to sign up if they try to write a review. Google does not allow anonymous reviews, and the system will reject users who try to sign up for a Google+ account with names that Google does not think are real. (Don't be thrown off if you see reviews that appear anonymous, with the title "From a Google User." Those are artifacts from the old days when only a Gmail account was required.)

Once your reviewers have passed the barrier of having a Google+ account, they face another obstacle: Google's review filtering. In Google's words, "Sometimes our algorithms may flag and remove legitimate reviews in our effort to combat abuse." Many business owners feel this is an extreme understatement, with a large number of genuine reviews getting unfairly caught up in the spam net.

There is a lot of speculation about what makes Google remove a Google+ Local review. Here are some examples that Google has stated publicly:

Reviews Containing a URL In a help forum, a Google representative wrote "reviews with URLs in them are automatically marked as spam. No URLs, please!"

Copycat Reviews Plagiarism or duplication from another site (such as Yelp), or for more than one business location can result in removal. Also, each person may write only one review per business.

Reviews with Inappropriate Content Unacceptable content ranges from spammy advertising to hate speech. For a full list, see this page:

www.google.com/+/policy/content.html

Reviews That Aren't Actually about the Business If a reviewer describes general concerns, for example, the political causes behind the price of gasoline instead of the practices of a particular gas station, or accidentally writes about a different business than the one represented in the Google+ profile, that is grounds for removal.

Reviews That Were Paid for or Represent a Conflict of Interest Google is looking for any indicators of fraud or incentive for positive reviews. Because Google prefers a natural pattern of review creation, it advises against setting up a kiosk at a business location "for the sole purpose of soliciting reviews." Reviews by business owners or employees are also not allowed, but businesses can write reviews for other businesses.

Reviews Marked as Private by the Reviewer Any review can be pulled out of circulation by its original creator.

Read Google's official write-up here:

https://support.google.com/places/answer/187622

Truth is, even a business that's doing everything right can run afoul of Google's filtering algorithm and have its reviews removed. In addition to the guidelines that come directly from Google, industry analysts have made the following suggestions for keeping your customers' reviews outside of Google's filter:

- Make it a habit to request reviews. As Local SEO expert (and this book's technical editor) Phil Rozek writes, "Asking for a review should be like handing out your business card," something you do without thinking, a continuous and regular part of your business practice. Don't play catch-up by sending out a review solicitation email blast to all of your past customers.

- Some industry experts suspect Google looks at the way people navigate to your Google+ Local page when they write a review and may filter reviews if the reviewer followed a link to your Google+ Local page from an email message. We don't think this is anything to worry about, but keep an eye on Google's content guidelines so that you'll be in the know if this rumor is substantiated.

- Some online sources report that reviews have a better chance of "sticking" on Google+ Local when they are created in the Google+ Local app on a mobile device. Despite this speculation, we suggest that you not try to control how your customers write their reviews, what they write, or what devices they use. Let them do whatever comes naturally for them. Emphasize your desire for their honest review—good or bad. The best way to appear natural is to actually *be* natural.

- Don't stuff keywords or locations into your listing unnaturally. Many sources have noticed that businesses with repeated keywords in their profile descriptions ("We are an insurance company specializing in insurance, insurance, and insurance"), keywords or locations sneaked into business titles ("Jones Auto Insurance of Salt Lake"—unless that is the business's legal name), or categories that contain location or keywords ("Utah car insurance, Salt Lake City insurance") seem to have more problems with their reviews being filtered.

- Some industries have reported a more strenuous filter from Google+ Local, specifically HVAC and home services, dentists, locksmiths, and auto dealers. It's possible that Google has clamped down on these industries due to a history of abuse and spam. If you're in one of these industries, be patient and prepared for an extra challenge.

Losing reviews on Google+ Local is no fun! As one business owner told us: "Google lost 30 really great reviews that we worked very hard to get. Starting all over is a pain in the butt." On the bright side, filtered reviews do sometimes come back as Google adjusts its algorithm. If the reviews are genuine, there's a chance they'll be released from the filter eventually.

Communicating with Reviewers

Google+ Local allows verified businesses to publicly respond to reviews. To do this, just click "Respond" next to the review after logging into your business profile, as seen in Figure 6.21. Your response will display publicly on the page.

Responding to reviewers on Google+ Local is just the tip of the social iceberg that is Google+. Businesses can find myriad opportunities for connecting with customers and with other businesses on the social network, including live conversations (called Hangouts), community forums, and reviewing other businesses. If you're ready to start your Google+ journey, Google has graciously compiled a list of resources for you here:

www.google.com/+/business/resources.html

Figure 6.21 Businesses can publicly respond to reviews on Google+ Local.

Troubleshooting and Support

Google+ Local surely wins the prize among review venues for having the largest number of flustered business users. Here are some common concerns that relate to reviews, along with possible paths to resolution:

"I need to change my address, but I don't want to lose all my reviews." If you move or your address changes, be sure to update your Google+ Local listing. Google will usually migrate reviews from the old to the new location. There are some exceptions, according to Google, "for businesses heavily tied to their locations, like hotels, golf courses, or scenic attractions." If all goes well, you'll simply need to verify your new address and your reviews will follow along. Be sure to update your address everywhere that you can think of. If your old address remains on other sites around the Web (for example, on business directories such as Localeze [www.neustarlocaleze.biz] or on your own website), Google+ Local might get confused about your real location and retain a listing at the old address. If you move locations and your reviews don't migrate, don't panic—the reviews should still exist deep inside Google. Contact Google as described in the sidebar "Asking Google for Help" and let them know the problem.

"Google made a listing with the wrong information on it—where did it come from?" Of course you need to claim your listing and correct the information, but you should also find and fix the sources of any incorrect info about your business to prevent further confusion. Google draws from many sources to compile its Google+ Local database. Some prominent local business directories include Localeze, Acxiom (https:// mybusinesslistingmanager.myacxiom.com/), and Express Update (http://www .expressupdate.com). Search for your business at these directories and correct your listing if needed. One handy tool for checking your listings for errors and inconsistencies is GetListed.org.

"My reviews all say 'from a Google user' instead of names." As you learned in Chapter 3, reviews that come from a credible source may be perceived as more trustworthy than anonymous reviews. Reviewers may need to republish old Google reviews to allow the display of their real names. If you are able to connect with your past reviewers, ask them to click on Local within Google+, then "Publish your reviews," as seen here:

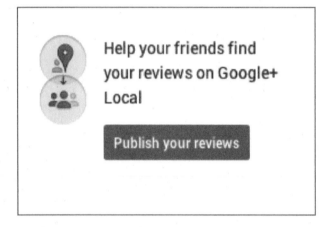

"My reviews keep disappearing and never stick." Some businesses struggle because the review filter seems to watch them like a hungry hawk. If your authentic reviews keep getting snatched up, start by making absolutely sure you're following the Quality Guidelines for Google+ Local and our recommendations in this chapter. Getting rid of anything spammy or keyword-stuffed in your listing can't hurt and may just help. It's possible that Google is filtering your reviews because of unnatural timing; be sure to ask for reviews consistently and avoid spikes of activity or long periods of inactivity. If you've done everything you can to make your listing and review-encouragement process squeaky clean, try communicating with Google as described in "Asking Google for Help."

"I can't respond to reviews." If you can't respond to reviews, it might be because Google thinks your account is not the primary owner for the business, or there might be duplicate listings you don't know about. As a quick way to regain control, try making a null edit: Click "Edit" then "Save" without making any edits. This may bring your account back into primary owner status temporarily. If you have duplicate listings for the same address, it's a good idea to choose a single listing to be the primary one (make sure it's the one with reviews and marked as "Active" in Google) and delete the others. You may need to log into every Google account you can think of, or contact Google support, to get access to the duplicates. Don't give up too quickly! Google doesn't make it easy to wrangle all of your business listings together, but clearing out duplicates will help eliminate lots of bugs and glitches that can otherwise haunt you.

The list of possible issues on Google+ Local is long; we've focused only on those relating to reviews. If you've got other problems with your listing, try a visit to Google's helpful online troubleshooting tool:

`https://support.google.com/places/troubleshooter/3125936`

Asking Google for Help

We think you'll be pleasantly surprised by the amount of support that Google offers to local business owners. A good place to start is on the forums, at `https://productforums.google.com`. Google employees often reply to requests for help here, or you may find someone else dealing with the same problem as you.

You can address a multitude of common problems by visiting the support page at `https://support.google.com/places`. Find and address your problem by choosing an option under "Fix," or click the Contact Us button to be directed to Google's call center or email support.

From your verified listing, the "Report a Problem" link on your Google+ Local listing takes you to a form where you can seek to correct inaccurate information on your listing:

Continues

Asking Google for Help *(Continued)*

Fill in as much detail as possible on the form, and be sure to include your email address so that Google can keep you posted on the status of your requested update.

Finally, if you see a review that includes hateful or inappropriate speech, is off-topic, contains advertising or spam, or has a conflict of interest, you can flag it for review by clicking on the small flag at the bottom right of the review:

A **Google User** reviewed a year ago
Overall **Excellent**
Straightfroward. I never get the feeling that I am being ripped off. Willing to work with me.

Increasing Your Visibility

Of course you want your Google+ Local listing in front of as many people as possible! Google describes its local ranking algorithm as being based on "relevance, distance, and prominence." Here's how these factors affect your ranks when a local search is performed:

Relevance Among other things, keywords are a factor here. When a person searches with local intent keywords, Google looks to see if their search term matches words in your website, the categories you've assigned to your local listing, and more.

Distance Google does its best to match the geographically closest results to the location being searched.

Prominence How well known or prominent is your business? Google may answer this based on the number and quality of your reviews, the overall authority of the website associated with your listing, and the number and quality of other sites containing your business's name, address, and phone number (these mentions are called *local citations*).

We'll discuss Google's local search algorithm in more detail in Chapter 8, "Showing Off and Being Found." The effort involved in getting good local ranks, called *local SEO*, is a marketing specialty unto itself. We recommend that any local business exert itself to get at least a basic level of local SEO in place for its website and Google+ Local listing. Here's a great place to start learning about local SEO:

```
http://searchengineland.com/library/local-search
```

In addition to local SEO, there are some other opportunities to increase your presence in Google's local results.

Google AdWords Express AdWords Express is a simplified version of Google's mammoth ad platform, AdWords. Created for local businesses, AdWords Express allows you to specify a radius and display ads in Google results, using a simple, self-explanatory interface. Figure 6.22 shows an example of an AdWords Express ad in action.

Ads ⓘ

24/7 Locksmith washington DC
Experienced & Skilled Professionals
Satisfaction Guaranteed-Free Quote!
www.mr-locksmith-dc.com/
1250 Connecticut avenue N.W., Suite 200,
Washington

Figure 6.22 AdWords Express ads display your business information to searchers in your area.

AdWords Express listings will display only in the advertising areas of Google result pages—not in organic search results or the local business results.

Google Offers Businesses can post discounts and specials, called Google Offers, either as a percentage off or as a dollar discount. These discounts show up in locations throughout the Google empire: in Google Maps results, on the business's Google+ Local page, integrated into the Google+ social experience, and in the Google Offers and Wallet apps. Figure 6.23 shows an example of Local Offers in the Google Offers app.

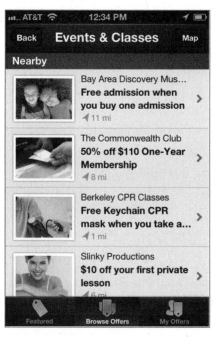

Figure 6.23 Google+ Local Offers can help Google+ users discover local businesses. The Events & Classes category in the Google Offers app is shown here.

Google+ users can also subscribe to receive emails containing Local Offers, as seen here:

Don't miss out! Subscribe to get Oakland / East Bay offers straight to your inbox. Subscribe

Watch out for possible misfires, such as this Google Offer that displays alongside a negative review:

Offers

Barnes & Noble Booksellers El Cerrito

"I found employees to be extremely rude and snooty"

Save $120 on NOOK

The Google Offer is essentially a coupon that customers can download for free from Google and then redeem in person at the business. Google does not charge a fee for businesses to create offers, and the business can limit the number of offers that are redeemed, so your financial outlay doesn't need to be huge to test this feature. If you're in the habit of handing out coupons in the offline world, why not match them online with Google Offers?

Closing the Loop

Time is a precious commodity for a local business, so it's important for you to gauge the value of your efforts on Google+ Local.

Google+ Local offers some numbers (Google calls this *Insights*) to help you measure how your listing is doing:

- Impressions—the number of times your listing was displayed in Google results
- The number of clicks for more info on Maps
- The number of clicks for driving directions
- The number of clicks to your website (this can also be tracked in Google Analytics)

These numbers give you an idea of how much action your local listing is getting, but they can't fully measure the effect your listing—and reviews—are having.

TripAdvisor

TripAdvisor calls itself the world's largest travel site, and who are we to argue? With over 100 million reviews and 200 million unique global visitors a month (a big portion—75%—are outside the United States), the site officially qualifies as enormous.

Although best known for its hotel reviews, TripAdvisor also includes reviews for attractions and destinations such as amusement parks and museums, as well as restaurants and tour operators. Figure 6.24 shows typical TripAdvisor reviews.

97 reviews from our community — Write a Review

Traveler rating

Excellent	50
Very good	22
Average	10
Poor	13
Terrible	2

Trip type

Family reviews (14)
Couples reviews (52)
Solo travel reviews (3)
Business reviews (15)
Friends reviews (6)

See which rooms travelers prefer - 16 traveler tips

97 reviews sorted by Date ▼ Rating   English first ↕

"Interesting Place"
⊙⊙⊙⊙○ Reviewed June 18, 2013

Tulsa, Oklahoma
Top Contributor
★ 92 reviews
26 hotel reviews
Reviews in 21 cities
61 helpful votes

We were looking for a place to stay near relatives living in Orlando, this was within a mile or two of them. We chose a Wellborn Suite. On older apartment building, staying fairly true to an Art Deco style. When we checked in we were told by the clerk that our room, 311, was his favorite. It was on the...

More ▼

Was this review helpful? Yes   Problem with this review?

"Helpful Tips for Courtyard at Lake Lucerne"
⊙⊙⊙⊙○ Reviewed June 15, 2013

Tampa, Florida
Top Contributor
★ 97 reviews
24 hotel reviews
Reviews in 20 cities
61 helpful votes

Some may argue with my rating of a 4 as being too high but I feel that it's fair. Here are some helpful tips to make the most of your stay 1) This is not a Marriott property. The "courtyard" in the name is because they have an actual outdoor courtyard that is filled with plants and charming places to...

More ▼

Was this review helpful? Yes ‹ 2   Problem with this review?

See 10 more reviews by  for Orlando

Figure 6.24 Hotel reviews on TripAdvisor

TripAdvisor is most commonly used by people searching for lodging when they are planning a trip, but it is also used by travelers who are already at their destination and looking for places to go and things to do. TripAdvisor for Mobile includes a "Near Me Now" function to help travelers find businesses in their immediate vicinity. TripAdvisor reports that 31 million people have downloaded its mobile apps, which include TripAdvisor for Mobile, City Guides, and SeatGuru. TripAdvisor reviews get a broader audience due to their integration into Bing local results, as shown here:

Swiss Lodge Motel
bing.com/local

1 2800 E Colorado Blvd, Pasadena · (626) 449-1122
Directions · 2 star hotel · ★★★★★ 7 TripAdvisor reviews

Claiming Your Listing

Claiming your TripAdvisor listing is simple and free and gives you many helpful capabilities such as these:

- Manage your listing, including contact information, photos and videos, and business details.
- Get alerts when new reviews are posted.
- Respond to reviews.
- Use free marketing tools such as widgets for your website.
- View impression data and demographics for visitors to your TripAdvisor listing.

To claim your listing, scroll down the bottom of the listing page and click on "Manage your Listing," as seen here:

Owners: What's your side of the story?

If you own or manage Quinn's Family Restaurant, register now for free tools to enhance your listing, attract new reviews, and respond to reviewers.

Manage your listing

On the registration screen, be sure to select the checkbox to receive emails when your establishment gets new reviews.

If your business does not yet have a listing on TripAdvisor, you can create a new one. Read what kind of businesses can be listed, and get started with submitting your listing here:

www.tripadvisor.com/GetListedNew

All TripAdvisor businesses that have claimed a listing can set up email alerts and view a basic snapshot of activity on their profile, including recent reviews, overall review activity, and reviewer photo uploads. Paying subscribers unlock access to more information, including competitor metrics and market trends. Details about the available information can be found here:

http://www.tripadvisor.com/TripAdvisorInsights/introducing-property-dashboard-and-snapshot-unleash-power-analytics

Once your listing is claimed, fill it out completely, including high-quality photos. There is no limit to the number of photos that a business owner can upload, so go crazy on this one! As TripAdvisor Chief Marketing Officer Barbara Messing told us, "Pictures are very powerful, regardless of language."

Filtering and Reviewer Verification

TripAdvisor allows anyone to write reviews and does not require verification that the reviewer is an actual customer. Many hoteliers have complained over the years that this makes the site susceptible to fraud. To fight fake reviews, the site employs a filtering system to identify fraudulent patterns and a large team of moderators to examine questionable content. It is also on the lookout for businesses that cross the line from *encouraging* reviews (an acceptable practice) to *incentivizing* reviews (which goes against the terms of service). Messing describes some activities that go over the line: "Incentives and rewards, raffles, discounts are absolute no-nos. If we hear that a hotel says you'll get an upgrade for writing a review; that is a *big* no-no."

If your business gets a review that is fraudulent or otherwise violates TripAdvisor's guidelines (for example, it contains inappropriate language or off-topic or irrelevant comments, or it does not describe the traveler's own experience), be sure to log in and flag it by clicking "Problem with this review" as seen here:

"Pricey but worth it!"

◎◎◎◎○ Reviewed June 22, 2013 NEW 📄 via mobile

Located on the first floor of the Epic hotel on Biscayne Blvd, Zuma does not fail to immediately allure you through it's textured wood door opened by not you but by a friendly doorman. As soon as you walk inside, you enter a noisy bar and dining room. Make reservations and unless you want to not hear the person next...

More ▼

Was this review helpful? Yes   Problem with this review?

TripAdvisor promises to investigate every review that is reported via this method.

Communicating with Reviewers

TripAdvisor encourages businesses to respond publicly to both positive and negative reviews and claims that management responses tend to create a favorable impression for prospective customers. In its advice to business owners, TripAdvisor cites a 2012 PhoCusWright survey in which over half of the respondents said that "seeing a management response generally makes them more likely to book (versus a comparable hotel that did not respond to travelers)."

Once your business is verified, you can respond publicly to any of your reviews from within your TripAdvisor Management Center. Read TripAdvisor's management response guidelines here:

www.tripadvisor.com/help/management_rse_guidelines

to help ensure that your response will make it past the moderators and into public view. You'll find links to management response tips and best practices on that page as well.

TripAdvisor discourages private responses; its stance is that the site is a public forum and resolving a customer's issues and concerns should be public as well. Businesses wishing to engage in a private conversation with a reviewer can include contact information in a public management response and encourage the reviewer to reach out privately. An example of this approach is shown in Figure 6.25.

FOManagerHC, Manager at Hotel Commonwealth, responded to this review

July 2, 2013

Dear

Thank you very much for your kind review about our hotel and staff. We are very proud of the service we are able to provide. We are able to turn the water pressure down in the shower. Please contact me at your earliest convenience and I can add this note to your profile.

Best,

Shane McWeeny
Director of Operations
Smcweeny@hotelcommonwealth.com

Figure 6.25 This management response contains an email address and a request for the customer to make contact.

You can send a private message to reviewers, although this is not TripAdvisor's preference. To do this, hover your mouse over a reviewer's name, and you will see a pop-up with information about the reviewer, as shown in Figure 6.26. Click on the "Send a message" link to communicate directly with the reviewer.

Depending on the circumstances, sending a private message to a reviewer can verge on creepy, so you should limit this approach if you use it at all. And never use this method to contact a reviewer if you're in an emotional state as a result of a negative review. Read up on response guidelines in Chapter 7.

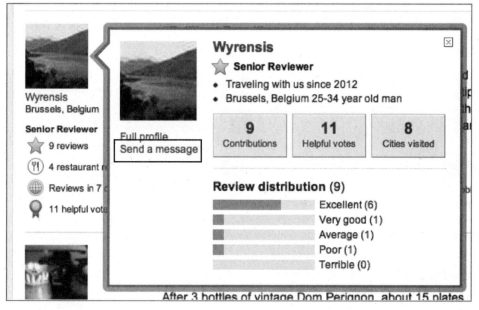

Figure 6.26 Although TripAdvisor doesn't encourage this, businesses can contact reviewers by clicking "Send a message."

TripAdvisor does not offer any arbitration services to help businesses resolve negative reviews, and reviewers are not able to change their reviews after posting (although they can add photos at any time). So a negative review is likely to stay in place, assuming it doesn't violate any rules. However, the business always has the last word in public conversations. After a business responds to a review, there is no way for the reviewer to post a counter-response.

Increasing Your Visibility

Listings that are favored by TripAdvisor's ranking algorithm can get a huge boost in visibility. Take a look at the TripAdvisor page for Miami in Figure 6.27. Out of 2,935 restaurants and 320 attractions, only three from each category are sitting pretty on this page.

Messing told us there are no great mysteries to the TripAdvisor ranks: "It's pretty straightforward. Recency, frequency and ratings are the drivers." A steady stream of positive reviews can keep a business in top listings, even if its total number of reviews is smaller than its competitors' total. To keep both recency and frequency high, a business should encourage reviews from all of its customers.

Top-rated restaurants and attractions

Restaurants

Bombay Darbar
⊙⊙⊙⊙⊙ 55 Reviews

neMesis Urban Bistro
⊙⊙⊙⊙⊙ 52 Reviews

Zuma
⊙⊙⊙⊙⊙ 424 Reviews

Browse all 2,935 restaurants

Attractions

Zoological Wildlife Foundation
⊙⊙⊙⊙⊙ 66 Reviews

Vizcaya Museum and Gardens
⊙⊙⊙⊙⊙ 962 Reviews

Arcade Odyssey
⊙⊙⊙⊙⊙ 29 Reviews

Browse all 320 attractions

Figure 6.27 TripAdvisor's Miami page features a small number of top-rated restaurants and attractions.

Review Gathering Tools

In Chapter 5, you learned that TripAdvisor offers business tools for encouraging reviews. These are not to be missed! Here they are in a bit more detail:

Review Express Email Tools and Templates TripAdvisor's Review Express tool allows businesses to easily generate reminder emails encouraging reviews from customers—up to 1,000 at a time. You saw a screenshot of a sample Review Express email in Chapter 5. Although Review Express emails are created within the TripAdvisor Management Center, the email's return address is your own. You can customize the email text, or use TripAdvisor's prefabricated text, which is available in 23 languages. Tips for using Review Express can be found here:

> http://cdn.tripadvisor.com/pdfs/email/OP_ReviewExpressTips_US.pdf

Printed Reminders TripAdvisor offers free business card–sized reminders that can be customized and handed out to customers and guests. See Figure 6.28 for an example.

Printed flyers are also available for download in many languages.

Review Forms for Your Website With these simple widgets, your website visitors can start writing their TripAdvisor reviews directly on your site. You can see an example in Figure 6.29.

In your business account, click on the Get More Reviews link to see all of these tools, and keep an eye on the management center to see when TripAdvisor throws new opportunities into the mix.

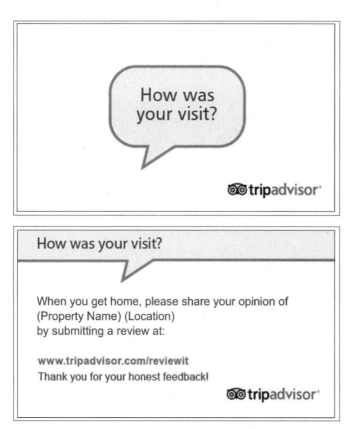

Figure 6.28 TripAdvisor reminder cards help encourage reviews.

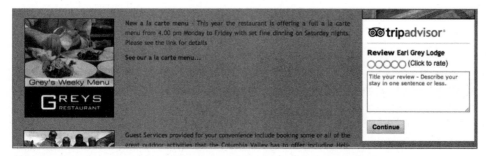

Figure 6.29 The Earl Grey Lodge includes a TripAdvisor review form on its website to encourage guest reviews.

Driving Visitors between TripAdvisor and Your Website

TripAdvisor is not a booking site, so it's important to provide a path from TripAdvisor to your website so that visitors can book their stay. It can also be beneficial to deliver visitors from your website to TripAdvisor, particularly if your TripAdvisor profile is a more compelling and up-to-date presence than your own site. Here are ways to build those bridges:

TripAdvisor Link Widgets   TripAdvisor link widgets range from tiny logos, like this one…

…to snazzy scrolling animations showing excerpts from your reviews:

These widgets all link to your business's TripAdvisor page, so you should only include them on your site if you think a visit to TripAdvisor is going to encourage a sale for your business.

 Business Listings   TripAdvisor's enhanced listings, the generically named Business Listings, start at a few hundred dollars a year and include advanced reporting and the ability to create special offers and announcements. There's one feature that is hard to resist: TripAdvisor adds your contact information and links to your website at the top of your TripAdvisor page. Get started here:

    www.tripadvisor.com/BusinessListings

See Figure 6.30 for a look at Business Listings features.

Figure 6.30 Links to the hotel website, hotel packages, the phone number, and offers and announcements are all available to businesses that pay for a Business Listings subscription.

If you pay for a Business Listings subscription, you'll also have the opportunity to create special offers, which can improve your visibility regardless of your TripAdvisor ranking.

Support

There's no shortage of help and advice if you're hoping to get the most out of your TripAdvisor presence:

- For help with claiming or managing your listing, start at `www.tripadvisor.com/Owners`.

- Get news, tips, and free resources from TripAdvisor Insights, at `http://www.tripadvisor.com/TripAdvisorInsights`.

- If TripAdvisor comes to your town, you can sign up for free half-day seminars called Master Classes. Keep an eye on the schedule at `www.tripadvisormasterclass.com`.

- A library of free on-demand webinars is available at `http://www.brainshark.com/public/tripadvisor`.

Angie's List

Angie's List collects and displays customer reviews for over 700 categories of local service professionals on its website, `www.angieslist.com`. Consumers pay a membership fee to gain access to reviews of businesses in their local area. Although there are many different types of businesses on Angie's List, the site specializes in "high cost of failure" services—ones that tend to cost more and have a high impact on customers' lives—such as roofing, home remodeling, and health care. Angie's List ratings are doled out report-card style, with grades from A to F.

Many businesses we speak with don't have Angie's List top-of-mind, perhaps because the site is less visible in the search engines than Yelp and Google+ Local. However, there are compelling reasons to make your way to your Angie's List business page and make sure it's representing you in the best light. It's a large and growing review venue. Angie's List had over two million paid members in 2013 and reports that its typical member household has a yearly income of at least $100,000. Another reason to give Angie's List a try is that it's more attentive to the needs and concerns of businesses than most review sites, with robust support services to help you resolve issues and market your business to targeted members. And finally, it's possible that there's more opportunity or cause for concern than you realize hidden behind that customer login. Because the site requires a paid membership to see ratings and reviews, you may have missed important sentiment about your company when you were identifying your top priority venues in Chapter 4, "Monitoring and Learning from Your Reviews."

In an effort to demonstrate its focus on accountability and reliability, Angie's List hires international auditing firm BPA Worldwide to conduct annual audits of its reviews and internal procedures. In June 2013, Angie's List reported that it was "certified again as a fair, impartial, and trustworthy resource."

See Figure 6.31 for an example of a review on Angie's List.

Review Date: February 12, 2013

Company Name:

Categories: Carpet Sales/Installation/Repair
Flooring Sales/Installation/Repair

Services Performed: Yes
* More Weight is given to a review where work has been completed.

Approximate date of service February 01, 2013
(or last contact):

                    Hire Again: Yes

Approximate Cost: $3,900.00

Home Build Year: 1981

Concerns? Please tell us!

PAGE OF
happiness NOMINEE

Overall	A
Price	A
Quality	A
Responsiveness	A
Punctuality	A
Professionalism	A

View This
Member's Profile

View Member
Review Histogram

View all Reviews
by this Member

Description Of Work:
replaced all of the carpeting in our entire home. This included three bedrooms, four closets (two walk-ins), an upstairs hallway, stairs and family room. They ripped up the old carpet and padding, replaced worn out tack strips and laid new padding, carpet.

Member Comments:
The entire process, from beginning to end, was fantastic. Greg came to our home with an array of samples and listened to what we wanted to accomplish. He gave us an estimate before leaving that evening and never tried to oversell us. He was very knowledgeable and we immediately wanted to go with them. For due diligence, we received two other quotes, both of which were much higher, included high-pressure tactics and, in one case, we were left looking at rolled up carpet in a warehouse to try and choose from.
Naturally, we went with and they were able to schedule the work for the very next weekend. They completed all of the work in one day and the new carpeting looks great! They cleaned up everything before leaving and vacuumed the entire home. I will absolutely go with for all of my flooring needs in the future and recommend them 100%!

Figure 6.31 A review on Angie's List

Claiming Your Listing

Listings on Angie's List are free for businesses. To see if you already have a listing, or to create a new one, start at `https://business.angieslist.com`.

Even if you don't seek out Angie's List, your business can have a listing on the site and be reviewed by a customer. If this happens, you may receive an email letting you know that you've been reviewed, as shown here:

Once you claim your profile, fill it out completely, and be sure to include your service area zip code, which is an important factor in your visibility. Keeping your profile spiffy and up-to-date will not only provide useful information for Angie's List members and differentiate you from your competitors, but will also serve you well should your listing be displayed in Google search results. Even though Angie's List is a members-only site, it exposes business profiles to the search engines. These public profiles display business info but hide all of your reviews and ratings. See Figure 6.32 for an example of a public page that can be accessed by nonmembers.

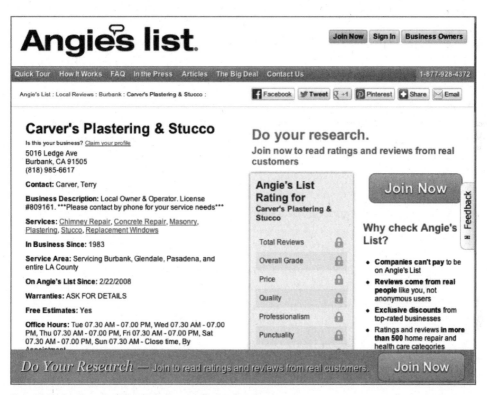

Figure 6.32 Searchers can click to this business profile page from Google.

Another great reason to make sure your listing is filled out and accurate is the Text2Me feature. Using this feature, Angie's List members can send your business contact information to their phones in just a couple of clicks, which is a nice little prod down the path to becoming your customer. Figure 6.33 shows the Text2Me link on a business page.

Businesses with claimed listings can receive alerts when new reviews are posted and see a snapshot of their overall ratings as well as their ratings on a category-by-category basis. Claiming your listing will also give you access to the site's abundant support features, described in "Troubleshooting and Support" later in this section.

Figure 6.33 The Text2Me feature on an Angie's List business listing

Filtering and Reviewer Verification

Your customers do not need to pay for Angie's List membership to leave you a review. Anyone, even nonmembers, can leave reviews on Angie's List. Reviews left by nonmembers are visible on your business page, but only their comments, not their grades, are displayed. Grades from nonmembers are not factored into your overall ratings, but they will be added in if the reviewer later becomes a member.

There are no anonymous reviews on Angie's List. All reviewers must submit their full name and contact information along with their review. Reviewers are reminded that their full name and address information may be shared with the business being reviewed.

Angie's List does not require an actual purchase or completion of services to take place in order for a customer to post a review. Any sort of interaction with a business can be reviewed, so it's possible that your company could be graded based on your quoting process, a sales call, or even a cancelled appointment.

Communicating with Reviewers

To respond to a review, just log in to your claimed listing and compose your response. All business responses go through a moderation process, in which Angie's List staffers ensure that the text is appropriate—and we suspect they've saved more than a few businesses from posting an imprudent response to a negative review. You can edit your response after you post it, but you'll need to contact Angie's List for help to do that.

Angie's List provides complaint resolution services for its members, which no doubt helps customers feel empowered and may create some trepidation for businesses. A customer can initiate a complaint, and if it meets certain eligibility requirements, Angie's List staff will assist the customer in requesting resolution such as repairs or refunds. If you are contacted by the complaint resolution department, it is wise to pay attention and respond, because a satisfactory outcome for the customer can result in the removal of a negative review, and an unsatisfactory outcome can cause your reputation concerns to magnify. There are three possible outcomes for the complaint resolution process:

Resolved In this case, the customer accepts your resolution, and the negative review will be removed.

Stalemate This may be the outcome if, for example, the customer does not accept the resolution you offer, or if you respond to the complaint but decline to fulfill the member's request. In this case, the negative review stays visible on your listing.

Penalty Box Your business may be placed in the Penalty Box if you fail to respond to a complaint, if you don't fulfill your promises to resolve the problem, or if you don't use the proper channels to respond. Companies placed in the Penalty Box can be removed from visibility in category and keyword searches on angieslist.com and can suffer more shaming with a call-out in the Angie's List monthly magazine.

The customer has the final say as to whether the situation is resolved.

Increasing Your Visibility

Your profile is all filled out, your business page is ready for its debut, and your ratings and reviews are available for viewing by Angie's List members in your service area. Now, it's time to boost those views! Here are some options for getting in front of more members.

Review Gathering Tools

Your presence on Angie's List depends largely on your reviews there. The site's ranking algorithm favors companies with higher overall ratings, higher numbers of recent reviews, and higher numbers of total reviews. And one of the criteria for advertising on Angie's List is that you must have at least two reviews.

In Chapter 5 you learned best practices for encouraging reviews. Here are some of the ways that Angie's List helps you in your review solicitation efforts:

Fetch Review Retrieval Program In this free program, you share your customer list with Angie's List. Their staff will identify any of your customers who are also Angie's List members and reach out to those folks to ask for a review.

Printed Forms and Reminders You can print out free ready-to-mail review forms and hand them to your customers when you complete a service. The data department at Angie's List makes sure that reviews submitted by mail find a home on your online business listing. Find the forms at

http://business.angieslist.com/pdfs/ALBCRptForm.pdf

or

http://business.angieslist.com/pdfs/ALBCHlthRptForm.pdf

if you are a health care provider.

For a small fee, you can also order customized tear pads, business cards, and stickers to help remind your customers to leave you reviews.

Review Badges and Custom Links Log in to your Angie's List business page and click on Custom Review Link to get a widget that links directly to a customized review form on AngiesList.com. See Figure 6.34 for an example of this widget in place on a business website.

Figure 6.34 The review link widget on a business website

Advertising

Angie's List has a diverse advertising menu that includes keyword-based advertising, deals and discounts, print magazine ads, and call center promotions. We think the most approachable form of advertising is a discounted offer called the Big Deal, which you are eligible to try if your business has an A or B rating and at least two current reviews.

Businesses offering Big Deals gain additional exposure on the site. Big Deals are featured in Angie's List search, and they get top billing on the home screen of the mobile app, as shown in Figure 6.35.

Businesses that have "achieved and maintained a superior service rating" on Angie's List and are based in select cities are eligible for the Super Service Award, which comes with additional advertising options. According to Angie's List, less than 5% of its companies meet the Super Service Award criteria.

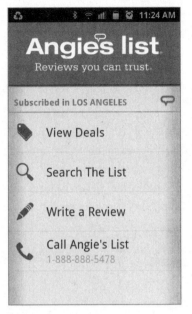

Figure 6.35 Big Deals are featured prominently on the Angie's List mobile app home screen.

Troubleshooting and Support

For an online review site, Angie's List offers a refreshing amount of business support, including a surprising amount of the nondigital, real-person variety.

Call Center We don't know of any other review site that heavily promotes the use of a call center, both for members and businesses. A real person can assist you with some concerns, for example, if you receive a review from someone claiming to be your customer who was not. Call 1-866-843-5478.

Online Support Find FAQs and a contact form at http://support.business.angieslist.com, or log in for context-sensitive help text as you manage your business listing.

Removal Options Like most review sites, Angie's List will not remove a business listing once it has been added to the site. Unlike many review sites, Angie's List will remove your visibility from category and keyword searches if you request it, so that you can only be found if someone searches for your exact company name or phone number.

Angie's List claims neutrality and will not attempt to determine whether a review is true or false. As we described earlier in this section, removal of negative reviews is possible when a customer initiates a complaint resolution process and the issue is resolved to the customer's satisfaction.

These support options are available to all businesses that claim a listing—not just advertisers—so be sure to take advantage of them if you have any concerns about your Angie's List presence.

ResellerRatings

ResellerRatings is a platform that collects reviews of online stores from verified buyers and displays them on its site, www.resellerratings.com. ResellerRatings is a solid product that can drive a lot of new reviews for online merchants, but to be perfectly honest with you, there's just one reason we recommend it to our clients, and that's Google integration. Reviews from ResellerRatings are fed into the aggregated Seller Ratings in Google Shopping, which translates into a nice serving of visibility for your reviews in Google. See an example in Figure 6.36.

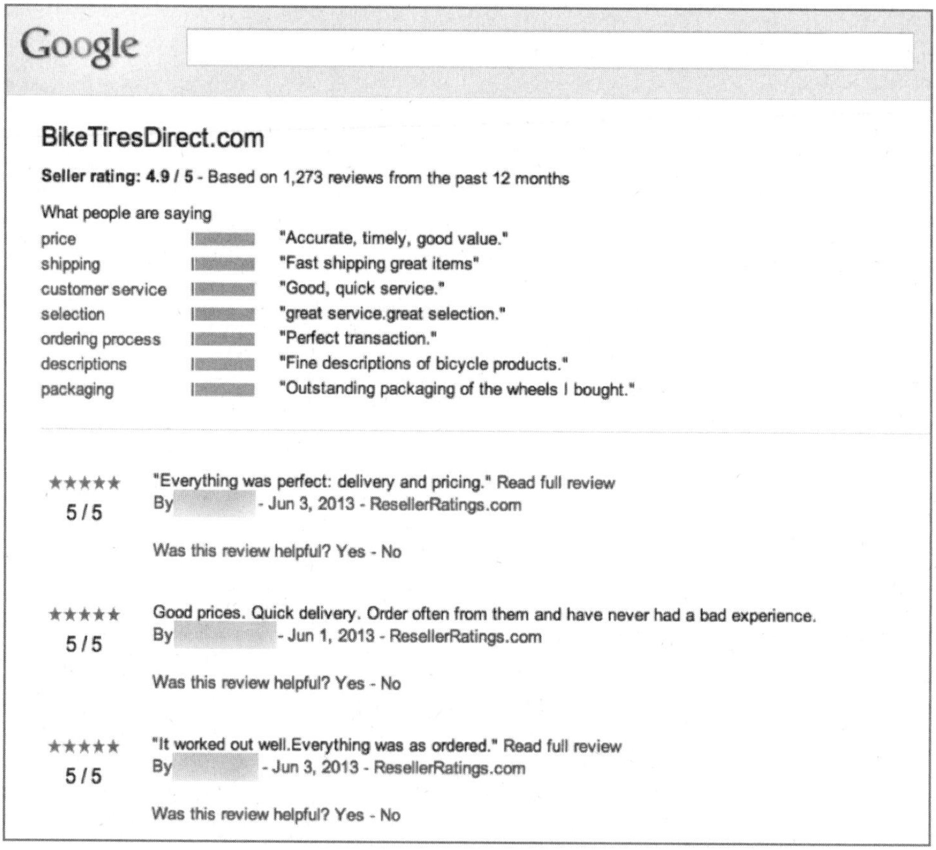

Google

BikeTiresDirect.com

Seller rating: 4.9 / 5 - Based on 1,273 reviews from the past 12 months

What people are saying

price	▮▮▮▮	"Accurate, timely, good value."
shipping	▮▮▮▮	"Fast shipping great items"
customer service	▮▮▮▮	"Good, quick service."
selection	▮▮▮▮	"great service.great selection."
ordering process	▮▮▮▮	"Perfect transaction."
descriptions	▮▮▮▮	"Fine descriptions of bicycle products."
packaging	▮▮▮▮	"Outstanding packaging of the wheels I bought."

★★★★★
5 / 5
"Everything was perfect: delivery and pricing." Read full review
By ▓▓▓▓ - Jun 3, 2013 - ResellerRatings.com

Was this review helpful? Yes - No

★★★★★
5 / 5
Good prices. Quick delivery. Order often from them and have never had a bad experience.
By ▓▓▓▓ - Jun 1, 2013 - ResellerRatings.com

Was this review helpful? Yes - No

★★★★★
5 / 5
"It worked out well.Everything was as ordered." Read full review
By ▓▓▓▓ - Jun 3, 2013 - ResellerRatings.com

Was this review helpful? Yes - No

Figure 6.36 Google displays ResellerRatings reviews in this Google Shopping page for a bicycle tire retailer.

Reviews aggregated on Google Shopping matter a whole lot to online sellers because getting reviews here is the only way to get stars to display in AdWords text ads, like the one in Figure 6.37. According to Google, ads displaying these stars (which it calls Seller Rating Extensions) have a 17% higher click-through rate than they would without the stars.

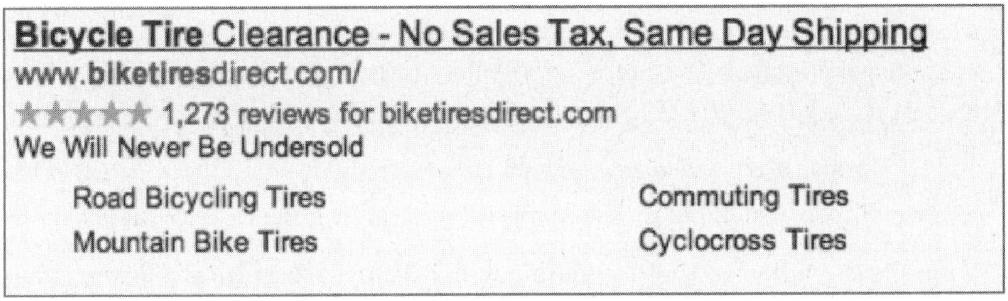

Bicycle Tire Clearance - No Sales Tax, Same Day Shipping
www.biketiresdirect.com/
★★★★★ 1,273 reviews for biketiresdirect.com
We Will Never Be Undersold

Road Bicycling Tires   Commuting Tires
Mountain Bike Tires   Cyclocross Tires

Figure 6.37 Stars in AdWords text ads are pulled from ratings compiled by Google Shopping.

In brief, here's how the pieces must fit together to get your ResellerRatings reviews into Google Shopping and AdWords:

- Your store must have a listing on ResellerRatings, but the listing does not need to be claimed.

- You must sponsor AdWords advertisements using the same domain name as your ResellerRatings profile.

- Although it is not a requirement, the most common approach to getting AdWords stars includes running Product Listing Ads in Google Shopping; this is a paid advertising service. To get visibility for your store here, upload your product information with a Google Merchant Account, and manage your ads with a Google AdWords account. Google walks you through setup here:

  https://support.google.com/adwords/answer/2454022

- If you do not run Product Listing Ads, it is still possible for your seller ratings to feed into AdWords, based on Google's ability to match your store name and domain name between ResellerRatings and AdWords.

- Text ads are managed separately from product listing ads in Google AdWords. Getting stars in your AdWords text ads happens automatically if your business accumulates 30 or more seller ratings and an average star rating of 4 stars or higher in Google Shopping. You can opt out here:

  https://services.google.com/fb/forms/SellerRatingExtensions

Are there other ways to get reviews that feed into AdWords? Sure there are. But most of the other sources of reviews are shopping comparison sites, such as

PriceGrabber and Bizrate, or Google Wallet, and not every business wants to get into those relationships.

Claiming Your Listing

There's no free way to claim your listing; you must enter into a paid relationship with ResellerRatings. The monthly fees range from $99 to thousands of dollars, depending on factors such as revenue and the size of the business.

As a paying customer, you receive the following from ResellerRatings:

- A simple, automated process for ResellerRatings to gather customer reviews
- Customizable alerts when new reviews come in
- The ability to respond to reviews publicly or privately using ResellerRatings tools

Businesses without a paid relationship with ResellerRatings are at a distinct disadvantage on www.resellerratings.com. For one, ResellerRatings displays a disturbing red alert on the profile page for a free business listing, as seen in Figure 6.38.

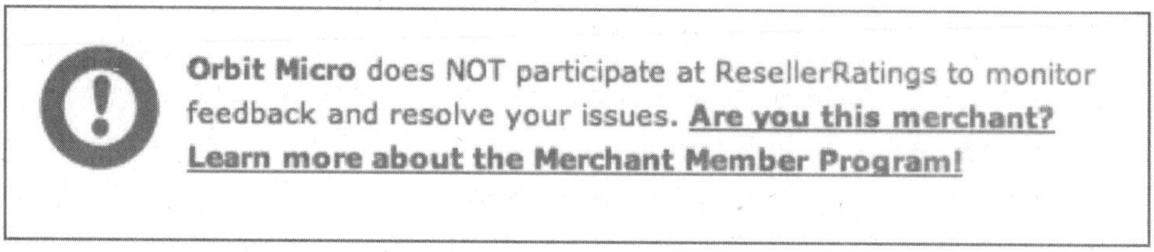

Orbit Micro does NOT participate at ResellerRatings to monitor feedback and resolve your issues. **Are you this merchant? Learn more about the Merchant Member Program!**

Figure 6.38 ResellerRatings shows an alarming red alert on profiles of businesses that do not have a paying relationship.

Second, ResellerRatings filters reviews of businesses that solicit reviews from customers without having a paid relationship with ResellerRatings. As Figure 6.39 shows, reviewers have a role in reporting rogue solicitations.

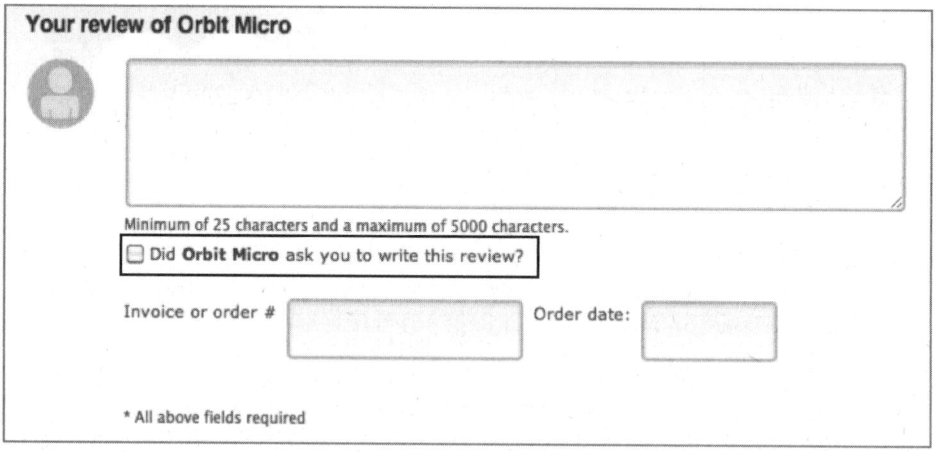

Your review of Orbit Micro

Minimum of 25 characters and a maximum of 5000 characters.

☐ Did **Orbit Micro** ask you to write this review?

Invoice or order #   Order date:

* All above fields required

Figure 6.39 If you ask for reviews without a paid account, ResellerRatings will remove them.

According to ResellerRatings, the practice of removing these reviews is a form of quality control, intended to prevent unscrupulous businesses from paying for or coercing reviews.

Gathering Reviews

The core of the ResellerRatings offering is its review-gathering service. The typical setup process is simple for online merchants:

- You place a piece of code on the "Thank You" page of your store.

- After a purchase, a pop-up window asks customers to opt in to receive a survey that will arrive by email after a specified amount of time has passed. See Figure 6.40 for an example of the pop-up window.

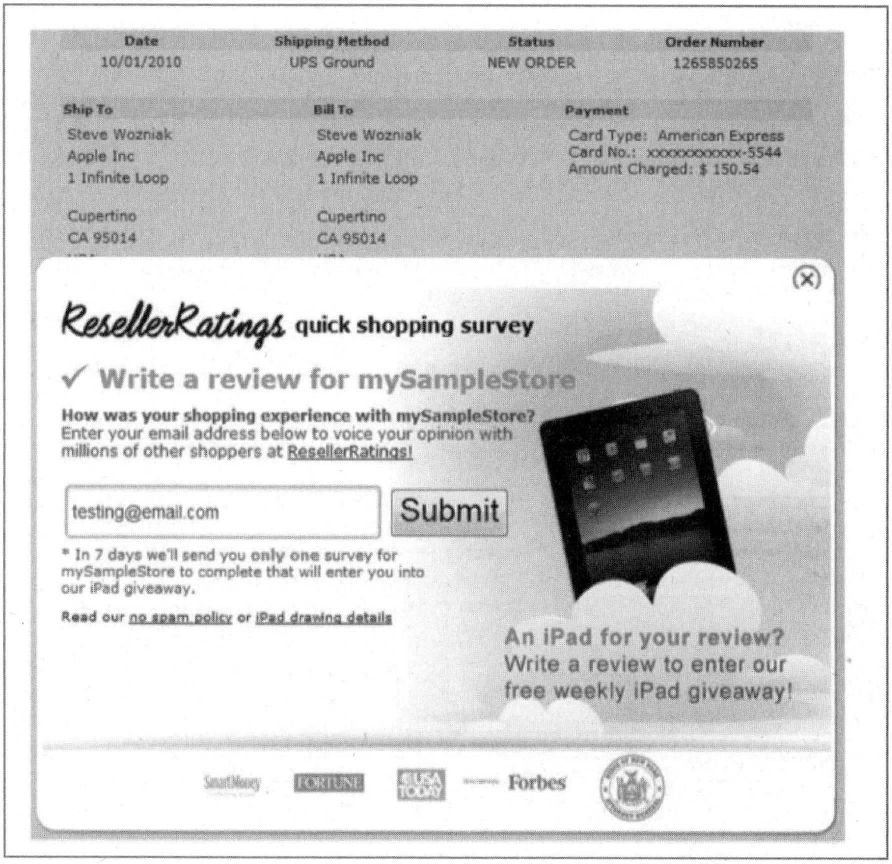

Figure 6.40 After a purchase, ResellerRatings asks customers to opt in to receive a survey by email.

- The code can be configured to allow your website to prepopulate the pop-up with the customer's email address and order number. This makes it easier for a customer to opt in because they do not have to enter their email address, and it also gives you the opportunity to trace individual reviewers to the transactions they made.

- Seven days later, ResellerRatings reaches out to the customer to request a review.

ResellerRatings reports a review completion rate of about 1% for customers who have to enter their own email address and up to 3% for customers who get the prepopulated pop-up. As a paying merchant, you can customize the length of time that ResellerRatings waits before requesting a review and choose which products do and do not display the ResellerRatings pop-ups. If you're using other channels, such as Bizrate, to sell products and generate reviews, you can prevent the ResellerRatings pop-up from showing to customers who use those channels.

Managing Your Reviews

The ResellerRatings dashboard allows paying merchants to read and respond to reviews, flag reviews that you think are fraudulent, and set up alerts. Here are some things you should know about ResellerRatings review management features:

Communicating with Reviewers One of the most business-friendly features of ResellerRatings is the 48-hour grace period it offers between the time a review is created and the time it is published on the site. If you have signed up for alerts, you will receive a notification like the one shown in Figure 6.41 whenever a new review is written.

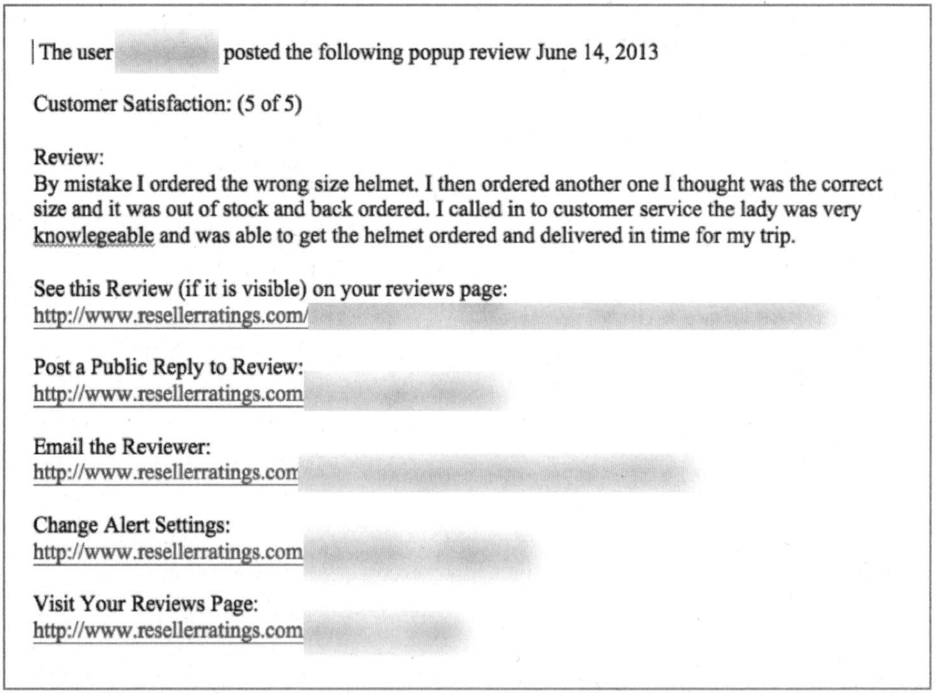

| The user ▮▮▮▮▮ posted the following popup review June 14, 2013

Customer Satisfaction: (5 of 5)

Review:
By mistake I ordered the wrong size helmet. I then ordered another one I thought was the correct size and it was out of stock and back ordered. I called in to customer service the lady was very knowlegeable and was able to get the helmet ordered and delivered in time for my trip.

See this Review (if it is visible) on your reviews page:
http://www.resellerratings.com/

Post a Public Reply to Review:
http://www.resellerratings.com

Email the Reviewer:
http://www.resellerratings.com

Change Alert Settings:
http://www.resellerratings.com

Visit Your Reviews Page:
http://www.resellerratings.com

Figure 6.41 Email alerts like this one arrive in your inbox 48 hours before the review is published.

The "Email the Reviewer" link and the 48-hour grace period make it simple for a business to reach out to unhappy reviewers to resolve problems before the review goes live. Though it's obvious on a gut level that most businesses will be doing this in hopes of getting a bad review changed, ResellerRatings requires businesses to sign an agreement promising that they will not ask reviewers to change or delete their reviews.

Flagging Reviews Paying merchants can flag reviews that seem fraudulent or that contain inappropriate language or the name of an employee. If ResellerRatings cannot verify that the reviewer is an actual purchaser, the review will be removed. For inappropriate content, ResellerRatings will follow up with the reviewer to clean up the review or remove it.

Reviews on Google Shopping Although ResellerRatings feeds your reviews to Google, there is no Google integration in the reporting dashboard. Many business owners struggle to remain calm while waiting for their ResellerRatings reviews to feed into their Google Shopping and AdWords ads. It can take several weeks for the reviews to carry over to Google, and ResellerRatings does not control this timing. Sit tight and you can be sure that eventually your reviews will get where you want them to be.

Reviewer Verification Reviewers' identities are not displayed to the public, but every review on ResellerRatings is from a verified customer. The majority of reviews are posted in response to the opt-in post-transaction communication we just described, but it's also possible for a reviewer to visit www.resellerratings.com spontaneously and post a review. In this case, ResellerRatings requires that the reviewer submit proof of purchase in the form of an order number and order date.

You'll notice we said *paying merchants.* These features are only available to businesses that have claimed their listing, for a fee. There is no way to flag or respond to reviews on ResellerRatings unless you enter into a paid relationship.

Bazaarvoice

As the infrastructure that powers product reviews on major retailer sites, including big names like Macy's, Best Buy, and Costco, Bazaarvoice hosts over 400 billion "authentic conversations" (aka customer reviews, questions, and responses) as of this writing. Bazaarvoice also serves smaller retailers, manufacturers, and the financial and travel sectors. Figure 6.42 shows a typical Bazaarvoice review integration on a Costco.com product page.

There's a strong bottom-line motivation for online merchants to include customer reviews on their sites. According to Bazaarvoice, e-commerce sites see a sales lift ranging from 30% to 200% when customer content is added to the site, and that doesn't require solely positive reviews. As Neville Letzeritch, Bazaarvoice Executive Vice President of Products, told us, "Purely negative feedback definitely won't drive sales, but a blend of positive and negative feedback shows authenticity."

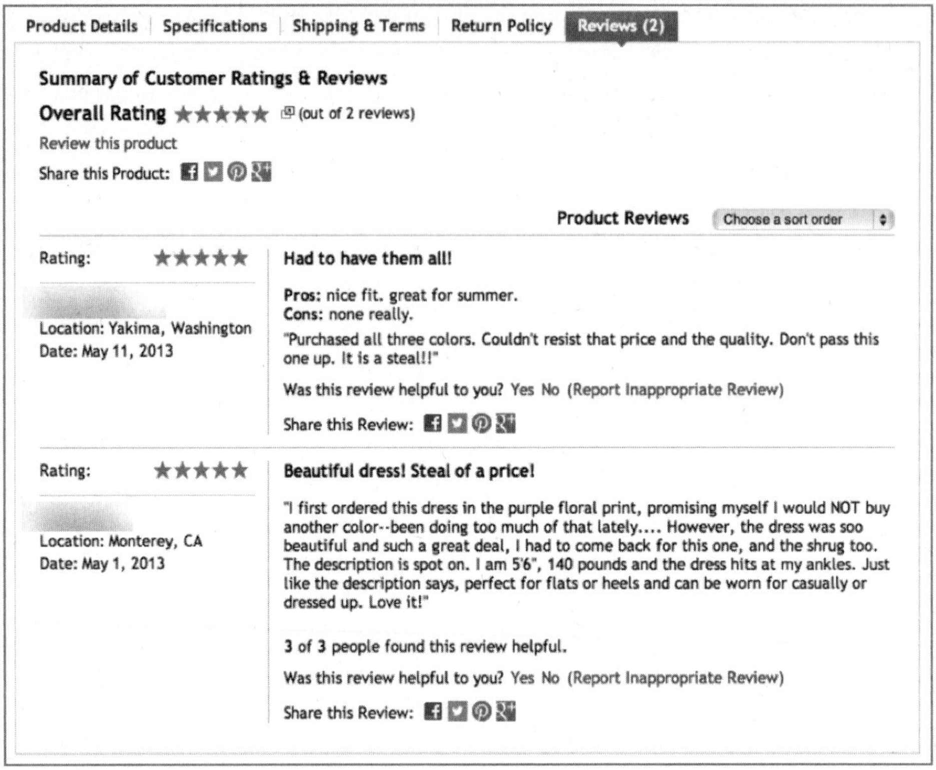

Product Details | **Specifications** | **Shipping & Terms** | **Return Policy** | **Reviews (2)**

Summary of Customer Ratings & Reviews

Overall Rating ★★★★★ ▣ (out of 2 reviews)

Review this product

Share this Product:

Product Reviews ⬚ Choose a sort order ⬚

Rating: ★★★★★ | **Had to have them all!**

Location: Yakima, Washington
Date: May 11, 2013

Pros: nice fit. great for summer.
Cons: none really.

"Purchased all three colors. Couldn't resist that price and the quality. Don't pass this one up. It is a steal!!"

Was this review helpful to you? Yes No (Report Inappropriate Review)

Share this Review:

Rating: ★★★★★ | **Beautiful dress! Steal of a price!**

Location: Monterey, CA
Date: May 1, 2013

"I first ordered this dress in the purple floral print, promising myself I would NOT buy another color--been doing too much of that lately.... However, the dress was soo beautiful and such a great deal, I had to come back for this one, and the shrug too. The description is spot on. I am 5'6", 140 pounds and the dress hits at my ankles. Just like the description says, perfect for flats or heels and can be worn for casually or dressed up. Love it!"

3 of 3 people found this review helpful.

Was this review helpful to you? Yes No (Report Inappropriate Review)

Share this Review:

Figure 6.42 These reviews, seen on Costco's website, are hosted by Bazaarvoice.

Collecting and Displaying Customer Feedback

Whereas all of the other review platforms in this chapter host reviews on their own online properties, Bazaarvoice places your reviews on your own site.

Bazaarvoice is not just a review platform; you could use Bazaarvoice to implement sophisticated consumer environments that combine elements of review collection, social media, and integrated marketing. We'll focus on its core review services:

Ratings and Reviews for E-commerce Sites The heart of Bazaarvoice's offering, called Bazaarvoice Conversations, allows brands and retailers to gather customer ratings and reviews on their websites, monitor and respond to reviews, and learn from reviews with sophisticated metrics and alerts. The tool can also provide ways for your customers to interact beyond just writing text reviews, such as answering questions about a product, uploading a review video, or telling a story about an experience with your brand.

Questions and Answers Potential customers can ask questions about a product and get a response from the community.

Review Dashboard for Brands Bazaarvoice serves manufacturers and brands with a dashboard that allows brands to see and respond to reviews of their products on retailer sites across the Web. Reviews can also be syndicated from a brand site to retailer sites. For example, a review of diapers on Pampers.com can be syndicated out to Walgreens .com, Walmart.com, and Diapers.com.

Small to medium-sized businesses looking for a simple tool to solicit, collect, and display customer reviews on their own site can use Bazaarvoice Express (formerly Power Reviews Express) to get an affordable, pared-down version of the Conversations tool. Find it at `www.bazaarvoiceexpress.com`. Figure 6.43 shows an implementation of Bazaarvoice Express on Roku.com.

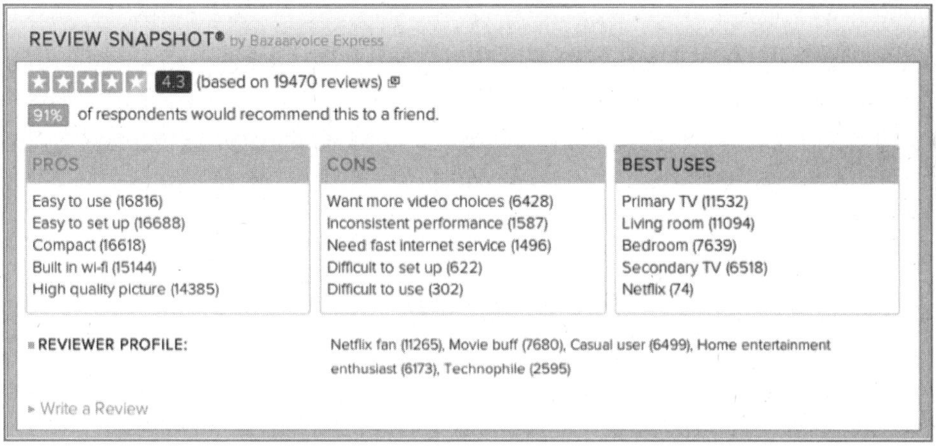

Figure 6.43 Bazaarvoice Express on Roku.com

Here are some basics for you to know about setting up and using Bazaarvoice:

Implementation Bazaarvoice implementation is simple in its essence: You put Bazaarvoice code widgets on your product page, and Bazaarvoice populates your page with product reviews and review submittal tools, and additional social features if desired. Bazaarvoice has pre-built deployments for many common platforms, including Demandware, Magento, and eBay Enterprise, that can make the integration process a snap. If your e-commerce setup is complex or homemade, you may be in for a more involved process.

Review Gathering Using Bazaarvoice's customizable post-transaction emails, you get the best of both worlds: You rely on Bazaarvoice technology to fire off review requests to customers, but you control the content of these emails with your own branding and customized messaging. Bazaarvoice offers email templates to get you started. According to Bazaarvoice, their customizable review request emails have a review completion rate of almost 7%.

Reviewer Verification Bazaarvoice requires authentication of reviewers. Merchants have the option of setting up authentication with either a login or an email address and can decide whether they want to require that the reviewer is a customer. A login requirement tends to be more cumbersome for the reviewer and may reduce the review completion rate, so retailers looking to maximize the number of reviews may want to implement the email validation option.

SEO Factors

Many businesses cite search engine optimization as a major reason they have chosen to include user-generated content such as customer reviews on their websites. Bazaarvoice does a good job of making sure the reviews your customers post on your site will be readable by search engines. Its Smart SEO module makes more of the customer review content search-engine-readable, but even without the module, a number of your reviews will be readable.

Bazaarvoice also configures your product reviews with metadata that help your pages get rich snippets in Google search results, like the stars and aggregate review information shown in Figure 6.44.

Ariat Boots | FREE SHIPPING! - Sheplers
www.sheplers.com/ariat-boots.html ▾
★★★★☆ Rating: 4.7 - 490 reviews
The fit wasgreat. Ihave a semi **wide foot** but it was perfect. January 9, 2013. Rated 5 out of 5 by luvaz247 Great **boots**! **Boots** look great, are quite **comfortable** for ...

Figure 6.44 Bazaarvoice reviews are displayed in Google's search results with rich snippets (stars and aggregate rating information).

Based on our experience as SEO consultants, we don't think customer reviews are a magic bullet for search engine rankings, but adding them can't hurt and it might help. We recommend making the decision to add reviews based on documented sales advantages and considering any rankings boost as icing on the cake.

Moderating and Responding

The Bazaarvoice business dashboard lets you see reviews, accept or reject reviews, respond to customers, and route issues to other members of your team. Manufacturers and brands can see and respond to reviews of their products on Bazaarvoice's network of retailer sites across the Web. See Figure 6.45 for a peek at the Bazaarvoice review response interface.

Product (blanket)
Category Miscellaneous

Reviewer Rejected ChrisOnTheOcean
lwbcy2zrl80
Location Palm Coast, FL
Badge

✓ Approved

Submitted: 02/21/12 14:19:20 CST

Featured: ○ No ◉ Yes

Moderator Codes:

☐ CR   ☐ CS   ☐ FL
☐ IMG   ☐ IU   ☐ LI
☐ NVS   ☐ PD   ☐ PF
☐ PS   ☐ SI   ☐ SPM
☐ URL

Client Codes:
☑ ABC   ☐ FRD   ☑ RBC
☐ REMOD

Photos ⓪   Videos ⓪   Comments ⓪ ⓪ ⓪   Responses ①

★★★★☆

Would recommend this
product

Useful blanket with room for improvement   22072688

Gender Male

Howdoyoutypicallyuseourproducts ForFun

My 9 year old loves how it keeps her dry & warm when she's playing outside on wet ground...
My only negative is the detachable band to help maintain the roll. I have promptly "misplaced"
mine & I wish it could have instead been attached to the blanket like sleeping bag loops.

Client Responses

Thank you for reaching out.

Response By
Sam

Department
Customer Support

Edit this Response   Delete this Response

Add Response

No Comments Submitted

Client Notes
03/01/12 03:47:30 CST
(Marie.Boulandet@BVoice.onmicrosoft.com)
Removed by client
03/20/12 08:01:53 CDT (demo) Removed by
client
05/03/12 16:21:06 CDT (jhix) Routed to
shipping for response
05/15/12 13:41:30 CDT (jhix) Awaiting
Customer Service response
10/09/12 08:38:36 CDT (mboulandet)
J'accepte car vlavla via
10/09/12 08:38:53 CDT (mboulandet)
https://workbench-
c1.bazaarvoice.com/portal/app?
service=page/ReviewManagementTool#
05/22/13 06:37:34 CDT (demo) vggjg

Additional Notes:

Save   Cancel

209
■
BAZAARVOICE

Figure 6.45 Interface for responding to a review on Bazaarvoice

Bazaarvoice staff screens reviews and moderates them based on criteria that you specify. This may involve removing inappropriate language, references to competitors, libel, or other bothersome banter. You can also log in to your dashboard to accept or reject reviews. Although there is an element of "your site, your rules" at play here, controls are in place. Bazaarvoice monitors for excessive rejection of reviews, and it may intervene if it feels that a business is abusing this capability. Of course, if you've been paying attention to the previous chapters in this book, you know it isn't helpful or advisable to scrub out negative sentiment and honest feedback from your customers, so you probably won't overuse the Reject button.

Alerts and Intelligence

Using Bazaarvoice's intelligence dashboard, there are about a zillion ways you can view, organize, and visualize reviews to gain insights into market opportunities, customer concerns, and meaningful patterns. This data could open the door to insights that will inform your marketing, product development, and customer service efforts. Or it could overwhelm you.

One way to keep your monitoring on track is to use Bazaarvoice's alerts, which are impressive in their customizability. You can receive regular alerts to stay aware of top-rated products, reviews that were rejected by moderators, and changes in a product's average star rating. You can also create your own rules for triggering as-it-happens alerts. Figure 6.46 shows examples of custom alerts for reviews with shipping issues and 1-star reviews.

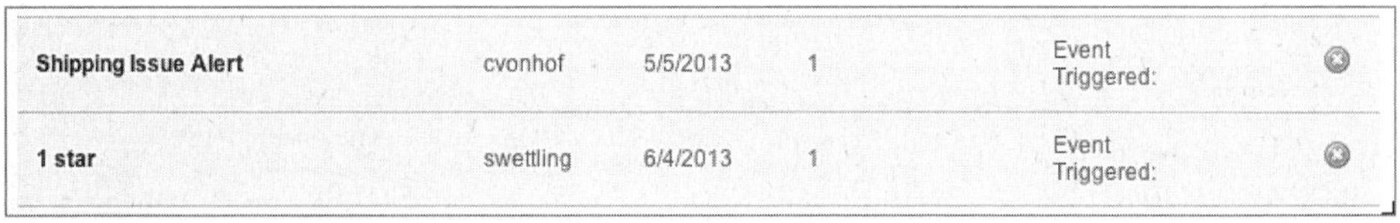

Shipping Issue Alert	cvonhof	5/5/2013	1	Event Triggered:
1 star	swettling	6/4/2013	1	Event Triggered:

Figure 6.46 Custom alerts created in Bazaarvoice

Another way to manage all this information is with visualization. See Figure 6.47 for Bazaarvoice's word cloud visualization feature in action.

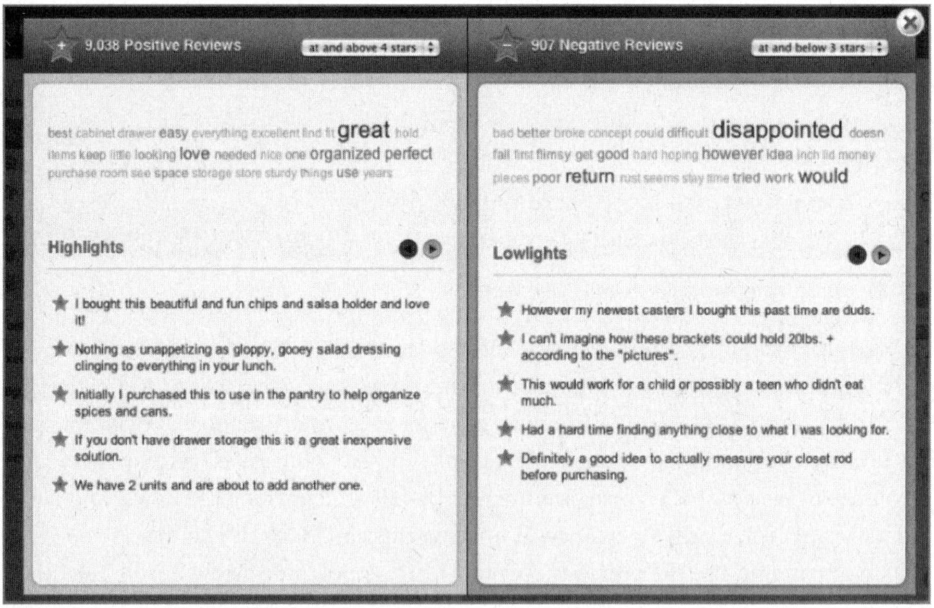

Figure 6.47 Bazaarvoice's word cloud review visualization

Like any analytics tool, the Bazaarvoice intelligence dashboard is only as good as the people using it. Bazaarvoice staff will help you configure the tool and define your processes to use it wisely, but ultimately it's up to you to make the most of its capabilities.

Whether your business is brick-and-mortar or e-commerce, local or national, sole proprietor or staffed by thousands, we hope this chapter has provided workable insights for improving your presence in the online reviewscape. Now, as you hope for the best, it's time to prepare for the worst; join us in the next chapter to learn all about negative reviews.

Navigating Negative Reviews

When a bad review enters your life, you may find little comfort in the studies and statistics showing that negative reviews are sometimes helpful to your business. You may not be particularly swayed by arguments about the intelligence and depth of judgment of your prospective customers who read those negative reviews. You just want it to disappear.

Bad reviews happen, even to exemplary businesses. Although you should have no illusions about preventing every possible negative review or removing those that have made it into the public eye, you can minimize damage by adopting a calm, thoughtful attitude and employing the strategies discussed in this chapter.

7

In this chapter:
Discouraging negative reviews
Responding to negative reviews
Redress and removal

If there's anything that captures the attention of businesses, it's negative online reviews. As one business manager told us, "I'm getting stomachaches and losing sleep over these reviews." An in-person criticism or dispute usually has few witnesses and disappears into thin air within minutes. In contrast, a thrashing on a prominent online review site can be seen by thousands and haunt a business for years to come.

At the other end of the spectrum from the business that dwells on its negative reviews, some businesses react to online disapproval by tuning out reviews altogether. We recommend a healthy middle ground. Your most important action relating to negative reviews is to pay attention to them and value the feedback they can bring. We set you on the road to learning from your reviews in Chapter 4, "Monitoring and Learning from Your Reviews," and we hope you took that advice to heart. Here, find strategies for minimizing negative reviews and responding to those you do receive.

Discouraging Negative Reviews

Of course we love 'em, but customers can be perplexing sometimes. When we encountered our first one-star review several years ago (by a reviewer who stated that he *never even read our book!*), our editor told us simply but not unkindly, "There'll always be chuckleheads out there."

Sometimes it's just that simple. In this world, there are a number of people who are impossible to please, unreasonable, impenetrable in their chuckleheadedness. Other times, the problem lies with you or your team. An error is committed, or a corporate culture is too broken to address problems or meet expectations, and customer satisfaction goes out the window. And in between those extremes there are endless scenarios playing out between customers and businesses, some of which will result in negative reviews.

Most of the time, negative reviews are written by reasonable people. In Chapter 3, "Understanding Reviewers and Reviews," we acquainted you with some of the triggers that can result in a customer leaving a negative review, and we're guessing you can identify with all of them, whether as a business owner or through your own experiences as a customer. These triggers include a particularly bad customer experience, an experience that did not align with the expectations that the customer held prior to the purchase, a lack of other communication channels to express dissatisfaction, and problems that go unresolved even after the customer seeks a fix.

There is a difference between companies that accrue a few stinging reviews in a predominantly positive collection and companies that are actually doing an awful job. If your company repeatedly fails to meet the expectations of your customers, you don't have a *review* problem, you have a *business* problem, and fixing that needs to be your first priority.

But you're reading this book for advice, not scolding, so let's move on with some tips for discouraging bad reviews.

Check In With Customers

In Chapter 5, "How to Get More Reviews," we discussed the multitude of ways you can encourage customers to write reviews for your business. But don't miss out on the usefulness of customer feedback outside of the review venues and during all points of the customer interaction. If you connect with your customers regularly to understand how they feel about what you do for them, you may find opportunities to correct existing problems for dissatisfied customers, improve the experience for future customers, and eliminate conditions that can generate negative reviews.

Take every opportunity. You can ask your customers "How's it going?" at any time during the service life cycle. Comment cards, feedback links on your website, or a friendly owner-to-customer chat are some ways to give your customers the chance to do you the favor of telling you directly how you can improve your business and avoid negative reviews. One small business we know was advised by a consultant to pose this question to its customers in-person at the completion of services: "If you were going to rate us on Yelp today, would you give us five stars?" See Figure 7.1 for an example of an email that Care.com sends soon after a customer begins using the service.

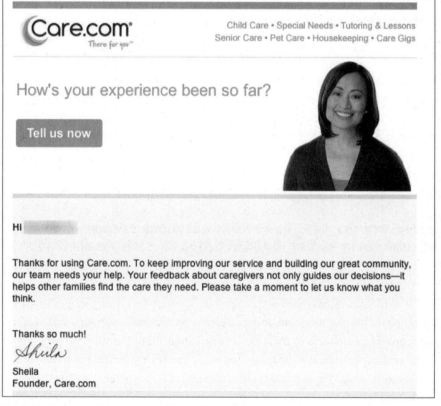

Figure 7.1 Care.com sends this email to recently signed customers.

Integrate feedback into your postsale process. Online reviews expert Mike Blumenthal told us he thinks all businesses should get in the habit of following up with customers after the sale to catch and correct any snafus that might have occurred without their knowledge. Mike says, "You need to follow up with every customer. This is the best opportunity to prevent the negative review. From my standpoint the sale isn't done until that piece is done."

Use internal surveys first. If you're in serious self-improvement mode, it may be better to direct your requests toward getting customers to complete surveys instead of writing online reviews. We spoke with Rick Berry, founder of Demandforce, who strongly encourages businesses to use internal customer satisfaction surveys before they put efforts into requesting reviews. He told us, "I highly recommend any business start off with internal surveys. The best way to improve your reputation is to ask your customers for feedback and make those changes. That's the cure. You can have plenty of medicine to treat the symptoms, but that's the cure."

Energetically checking in with your customers is a good way to prevent an annoyed customer from evolving into an angry ex-customer who may even kick off an online reputation crisis.

Provide Nonreview Paths for Common Complaints

Are there certain points in your customer's experience where there is a higher risk of dissatisfaction? If you anticipate these potential pain points and provide a direct path to communicate with your customer service, you may stave off a public negative review. One no-brainer is to make sure that your transactional emails—the ones that explain that an order was received or a shipment is on the way—provide a link for comments or support, as seen in this example from Sports Chalet:

Thank you for shopping with us!
Sport Chalet

Please feel free to contact us **with any questions or comments.**
You can also call us toll free at **888.801.9162** for questions about your order.

Any time you ask for a review, it makes sense to remind customers that you're listening and provide an alternate path for them to lodge complaints. Figure 7.2 shows a page created by a landscaping service using the review-gathering tool Grade.us. This tool, available at https://about.grade.us/, lets businesses build a simple web page asking customers to write reviews, and it can include a Contact Us link to give dissatisfied customers the opportunity to straighten out any problems before reviewing.

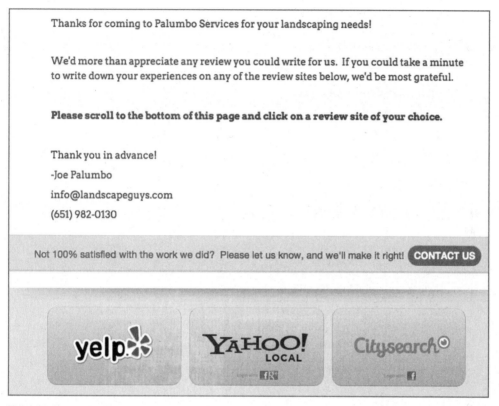

Thanks for coming to Palumbo Services for your landscaping needs!

We'd more than appreciate any review you could write for us. If you could take a minute to write down your experiences on any of the review sites below, we'd be most grateful.

Please scroll to the bottom of this page and click on a review site of your choice.

Thank you in advance!

-Joe Palumbo

info@landscapeguys.com

(651) 982-0130

Not 100% satisfied with the work we did? Please let us know, and we'll make it right! CONTACT US

Figure 7.2 This review-gathering page generated by the Grade.us tool includes a Contact Us link for dissatisfied customers.

Set Realistic Expectations

Sometimes, elements outside of your control can draw negative reviews. These may be temporary but unavoidable inconveniences such as renovation construction for a brick-and-mortar business or shipping or manufacturing delays for an online merchant. Or it may be a question of some customers being a better fit than others: Perhaps there's something about your business or product that most customers like but that rubs some people the wrong way. Use whatever channels of communication you can to make sure that customers won't be surprised when they encounter the temporary inconvenience or the love-it-or-hate-it factor that you're not willing or able to change. In the following example, a restaurant uses its OpenTable confirmation message to prepare customers for the fact that they may not have a choice of indoor or outdoor seating.

Here's another example: Knowing that holiday shipping is a common source of consumer stress and bad reviews, many online retailers state their ordering deadlines up front for holiday delivery. Macys.com gets this right; its holiday shipping deadlines can be seen here: www.macys.com/hdayShipping.jsp. If you know you're having temporary shipping delays or other flaws in service, let customers know via every possible communication channel.

You can also gently manage customer expectations with carefully crafted responses to negative reviews. A manager response stating "We're sorry that we were not able to provide you with a refund of the deposit" or "We're sorry that we cannot offer a delivery window of less than four hours" will help future customers know what to expect from your business. Read on for guidance on response-writing later in this chapter.

Broadcast Your Willingness to Listen and to Correct Issues

Some experts believe that if you send the message that you listen to your customers, they will be more likely to sidestep writing a negative review and instead contact your business directly. Here are some ways to communicate that your business is all ears:

- Respond publicly to your reviews, especially the negative ones. One review industry insider suggested to us that public responses to *all* reviews can reduce the number of negative reviews—or at least make them less vicious. Perhaps this is because it's easier for a reviewer to lash out at a faceless business than at a listening, human representative.

- Make it easy to find your contact information and social media channels on all customer correspondences.

- Add a prominent feedback link on your website.

- If you've made improvements to your business based on customer feedback, mention it in your email newsletter or website. See Figure 7.3 for an example. You can even post a notice on the wall of your brick-and-mortar establishment.

Figure 7.3 On its website, the Children's Museum of Denver announces changes based on customer feedback.

- Don't leave your social media commenters hanging! Read and respond to tweets, YouTube comments, and Facebook posts to your page.

Create a Process for Learning from Negative Feedback

We've met plenty of business owners who receive negative feedback, feel bad, and stop there. But it's easier on your psyche, maybe even empowering, if you have a plan for parsing out the actionable information and talking through this information with staffers who can make a change. For some businesses, customer reviews are not just report cards—they are welcome opportunities for learning. Read your reviews with an eye toward identifying useful insights and finding meaningful patterns. You don't have to slavishly make a change over every bit of customer sentiment, but be as objective as you can and look for ideas that deserve attention. Constructive criticism can be found in both angry rants and glowing reviews.

Make it a process, not just a reaction. Think about how you can create a repeatable system for using customer feedback to improve your business. Can you make time during your regular staff meetings or send out a regular email with review highlights? If you integrate these discussions into your standard internal communications, you won't only be hashing through the negative reviews; you'll also have an opportunity to give your staff a pat on the back when positive feedback comes your way.

Introduce accountability. Whether or not you have a formal customer relationship management process, you can treat reviews like trouble tickets that can be opened, closed, and routed to an appropriate staffer to address the problem or follow up with the reviewer. Determine who on your staff should assign the issues, what type of feedback should be routed to which staffers, and how you'll know when the ticket is resolved, for example, when the reviewer receives a response, or when a fixable issue is corrected.

Chapter 4 provides more information on how to improve your business with feedback from your online reviews.

The Tragedy of a Five-Star Product with One-Star Customer Service

Even excellent products can get poor reviews if customer service is not up to par.

Peg Robin owns Robin's Way, a small business selling pricey custom-made gifts (name and business details have been changed). Customers adore her creations and give extremely positive feedback on the quality of her work. Business is seasonal: Robin's Way brings in about 80% of its yearly revenue in the months between October and January, and during these busy months, Peg is stretched to the limit—and beyond.

A few years ago, the business's online reputation took some major hits. Peg confesses that customer service suffered around the holidays: "I didn't have time to do everything, so I focused on getting orders out the door. I convinced myself that a good enough product would make up for a late delivery." With Peg focusing on production, emails went unanswered. Making matters worse, the dropped emails were often from the most difficult and demanding customers, who were also the most likely to complain online: "When I look through my inbox, some of the emails look like they're going to take a long time to answer. If people are getting prickly, as busy as I am, I just push those emails away!"

Continues

The Tragedy of a Five-Star Product with One-Star Customer Service *(Continued)*

Some customers began to complain publicly on the business's Facebook page when they were not able to get a response via email, and these complaints multiplied with "me too" replies. Peg knew she had to make a change when an unhappy customer wrote a blog post: "He compared my work to a competitor's. Even though he admitted my products were better, he gave me an F on customer service and recommended the other business!" Peg realized that no matter how good her products were, by the time they arrived on her customers' doorsteps, the damage was already done.

Peg's challenges illustrate some universal truths of businesses with poor customer service:

- The high quality of your offering is not enough to overcome your service problems.

- Ignoring complaints does not make them go away. Rather, it can intensify the problem.

- Customers will post reviews whether or not you are looking, so you may as well monitor them so that you can fix problems before they snowball into a reputation concern or a significant loss of potential revenue.

Peg realized that she needed to make a change, so she forced herself to accept the hard truths delivered from multiple channels of customer feedback. Not surprisingly, she found that most complaints were about poor communication and a long wait for delivery. Peg listened, thought hard, and made some changes:

- She raised her prices and reduced the number of orders she takes in the busy season. "I shut off my online store whenever my backlog gets too high. I get fewer orders, but the revenue is the same, and the average customer wait time is reduced by about two weeks."

- With time freed up by a reduced production load, Peg can make sure every email is answered in a timely manner—especially those from the demanding customers she used to avoid.

- Peg sends emails proactively to every customer, keeping them posted on their order status and giving them the opportunity to get in touch. She didn't have the funds to upgrade her site's basic e-commerce setup, so she sends these emails manually. Keeping communication channels open means people no longer feel the need to seek redress on Facebook.

Now, a few seasons later, the negative posts on Facebook are a long scroll downscreen, and current feedback is positive. Best of all, after living in fear of online reviews for years, Peg is ready for the next step: reaching out and asking all of her customers to review the business online.

Responding to Negative Reviews

Responding to negative reviews is an important part of your review management process. Done right, your response will show that you're listening and you care about your customers' opinions and satisfaction. It will give you the opportunity to set the record straight, clear up confusion, humanize your business, and demonstrate your competent handling of a tough situation. It may even allow you to sway the opinion of an unhappy customer. In 2013, Wakefield Research on responses to product reviews found that "[s]hopper intent to purchase doubles when seeing a brand's response to a negative review versus a negative review by itself." But done incorrectly, a review response can do more damage to your business than the original review ever could.

As an aid in your efforts to get your responses right, we'll start you off with this mantra, adapted from advice given us by Mike Blumenthal:

I am not writing this just for the reviewer. Above all, I'm writing for everyone else who will see this review.

We believe this simple touchstone is the key to making your review responses the best they can be. Write it on a sticky note if you must, but don't lose sight of it as you go.

Before You Respond

You've been hit with a negative review, which feels—as Yelp describes it—"like a punch in the gut." You may be hurt and feeling an urge to retaliate. Before you strap on your brass knuckles, read these guidelines to make sure your response is a help and not a harm.

Take it slow. Every review venue representative that we talked to about negative reviews offered the opinion that business owners should take some time to get into a calm state of mind before responding to reviews. Many specifically suggested waiting until the next day. It's natural to want to respond rapidly to a negative review, especially one that is unfair or factually incorrect. But writing a response in the heat of the moment would be a mistake.

If you respond while you are angry or emotional, your writing is likely to be defensive or aggressive and not portray your business in the best possible light. Take a breath, take a walk, and remember your mantra: Your intended audience is potential customers who will see this review. As a rule of thumb, if the thought of saying "Thank you for your feedback" makes you sick to your stomach, you're not ready to respond.

Know the rules. Review venues have various rules and guidelines for review responses that you should follow. For example, TripAdvisor will not post a response containing personal insults, promotional materials, or ALL CAPS, among other offenses. ResellerRatings has a strict policy against asking a reviewer to change their rating. Google requires you to comply with the same content guidelines as reviewers do, restricting nudity, hate speech, impersonation, and more, and also advises business responders to "Be Nice." We hope we don't need to tell you that profanity is strictly *verboten*! Find more rules, along with other tips and suggestions here:

Google+ Local:

https://support.google.com/places/answer/184271

Yelp:

https://biz.yelp.com/support/responding_to_reviews

TripAdvisor:

www.tripadvisor.com/pages/management_response.html

Angie's List:

http://support.business.angieslist.com/app/answers/detail/a_id/111/~/
responding-to-reviews-on-angies-list

Bazaarvoice:

http://blog.bazaarvoice.com/2013/06/05/spin-gold-from-poor-reviews-
responding-to-feedback-wins-new-customers/

Decide who replies. Who in your organization is the best suited to respond to a negative review? This may not be an emotionally invested small business owner, but it also probably shouldn't be an intern who can't speak for the business. Your responder should be someone with authority over the issues and concerns your reviewers are writing about— and a temperament that will allow them to keep a cool head. You may even want to require more than one person to sign off on responses or bring in outside writing help to craft your response. One business we spoke with had an exemplary process for writing responses. A manager with responsibility for on-the-ground operations handled both positive and negative review responses on a daily basis, putting his head together with his boss for any tricky or potentially controversial questions.

Get the access you need. To respond to a review, you'll need to claim your business listing or set up the applicable merchant account. Some sites require more than this: As you learned in Chapter 6, "Review Venues: Need-to-Know Tips for Your Action Plan," Yelp requires a clear personal photo in the business owner's profile.

Know when not to respond. Reviews that cross the line from criticism to incoherence may not require a response. If a review uses inappropriate language or is threatening, spammy, delusional, or personally insulting, you might be able to have it removed, as described later in this chapter. If you suspect a review is fake, you should flag it and wait a few days before responding—and check the criteria in the section "Redress and Removal," later in this chapter, to see if any of them fit. On Yelp in particular, it's not uncommon for reviews to be filtered several days after they are posted. If you choose to respond to a review that you think is fake, read on for tips on building your review response.

Posts on complaint sites such as Pissed Consumer and Ripoff Report may require special handling. Internet attorney Kenton Hutcherson suggested to us that businesses should not post responses or rebuttals on these sites. According to Kenton, writing a business response generates more links to the page and adds content to it, which may increase its search engine presence. And your response could trigger additional complaints, fueling the flames of negativity.

Public and Private Responses

As a general rule, negative business reviews on sites that matter to you should get a public response. Leaving a negative review publicly unanswered inherently gives the last word to your detractor.

Some review venues allow business owners to choose whether to reply to a review publicly or privately. Many businesses, given the opportunity, will first reach out privately and try to resolve the problem directly with the reviewer. It's an effective tactic. The 2011 Retailer Consumer Report by Harris Interactive found that of negative reviewers who were contacted by the business, over a third deleted their original negative review, another third posted a positive review, and 18% became loyal customers. We've heard the same thing from several businesses: Reviewers will sometimes change or even remove their review after the business reaches out with a polite apology and an effort to make things right.

The decision to respond privately should be made on a case-by-case basis. We think an initial private response is appropriate when all of the following criteria apply:

- You believe that the review is real.

- Based on your assessment of the reviewer's attitude and tone, he or she does not appear extremely angry or vengeful toward your business. Some reviewers are just looking to unload their bushel of hate and are clearly not good candidates for any kind of dialogue. For them, it's best to stick to a level-headed public-facing response.

- You think there's a chance that you can clear up the problem, either with a straight-up apology, an explanation, or some form of restitution.

- The review venue allows it.

Private responses may also be the better option for healthcare practitioners whose public response is limited due to confidentiality considerations. But you should never divulge any potentially sensitive information in your response.

It may seem that your mantra, "*I am not writing this just for the reviewer. Above all, I'm writing for everyone else who will see this review,*" doesn't apply to private responses, but in fact, it does. Anything you write to a reviewer can be cut and pasted into a public forum, so you need to keep future potential customers in mind for every aspect of these conversations. Be prepared to see your words quoted back to you, as in this example:

EDITED TO ADD:
[____] responded to my review by saying that "[__] G" didn't pay and didn't buy products on a particular day in August. Guys, there are a LOT of [__]Gs in the world!! She is not referring to me. I was not in the salon on the day she is referring to. [_____], I hope you're not going to give the cold shoulder to the wrong [__]G! This one won't be back.

Recovering from Bad Reviews: Advice from a Yelp Staffer

We asked Morgan Remmers, Yelp's Manager of Local Business Outreach, how a business can recover from a glut of negative reviews. She told us about a process that she likes to share with business owners. "I've seen this work for businesses," she says.

The prerequisite for this approach is to absorb the criticism with an open mind, which is advice that is echoed by many review industry insiders we've spoken with. In Morgan's scenario, before getting started on reputation repair, you should not be in a state of denial but rather "You have acknowledged and accepted that this is consistently being said about you."

After that, it's a two-step process.

The first step is to identify the common themes that you find in your negative reviews and respond publicly to a few representative complaints. "There's usually two or three consistent gripes," says Morgan. "Identify three to five reviews that are addressing different gripes, and respond to those handful of reviews publicly." What makes a good response? Keep it professional. "Articulate in the best, most diplomatic way possible how you are going to change for the better."

Explaining that you understand there's a problem and describing what is being done to address it may help you mend fences with your disgruntled customer, and it also sends a message to anyone landing on your business page that your business listens to its customers. Morgan adds, "It also doesn't hurt to private message consumers who have similar sentiments."

The second step is to take a look at how you can improve your business page on Yelp. Morgan says, "Make sure that [you] aren't shying away from plugging in the content that you can—accolades, business information, Yelp Deals, check-in offers." According to Morgan, this is the time to think about "opening yourself to any opportunity to get more consumers in the door." Morgan suggests Yelp Deals as an attractive option. "When a business has a rating that is so-so, that Yelp Deal might make a consumer give them the benefit of the doubt."

Thinking about new customer acquisition along with reputation control makes a lot of sense to us. You can't control the customer reviews on your Yelp listing, but by making sure that your business listing represents you in the best light, you're controlling the information that you can and sending signals that you're a trusted, credible, and appealing business to counterbalance some of the negative sentiment. These principles are not just true for Yelp; they can be applied to any review venue that gives you some control over the content of your business listing.

Building Your Response

The best business responses to negative reviews tend to contain the same ingredients. Here are some important dos and don'ts to keep in mind when you write your public or private response:

- Thank the reviewer for their feedback. Do not allow a response to be posted without the words "Thank you" in it!

- Identify your role in the business. For maximum credibility, it's best to identify yourself by name. Ideally, the person responding should have direct authority over the issues the negative review brings up.

- When the reviewer has a valid complaint about a misstep made by your company, apologize directly for the problem they suffered. Be mindful of how you express apologies: The passively worded "We apologize that the wrong item was shipped in your order" can come off as guarded and insincere. For a more believable and constructive apology, name the problem and accept responsibility, as in, "We're sorry we messed up your order." If this feels difficult, you can ease into this apology by describing your ideal scenario first, for example: "We strive to make every service call on time, and I am so sorry to hear that we did not meet our goal." For complaints that express an opinion instead of pointing out an error, such as "The room was ugly" or "The products are overpriced," avoid non-apologies like this one: "I'm sorry you feel that way." Try the humbler alternative, "I'm sorry we did not live up to your expectations."

- Do not get defensive, make excuses, or argue. If you lose your cool, it will not reflect well on you for future readers. As Angie's List says, "Attack the issue, not the text."

- Your instinct might be to ask clarifying questions, or to try to open a dialogue about how the reviewer thinks things could be improved in the future. This may work well in a face-to-face conversation or private replies, but it is impractical on most review venues, which do not allow threaded discussions. You can absolutely encourage a reviewer to contact you to fix unresolved problems, but don't let questions dominate your response. If you do not receive answers, this could give the impression that you have a number of open issues hanging around.

- Correct any factual errors using simple language and without placing blame.

- If you are dealing with a false accusation, you will need to work up every ounce of diplomacy and Zen-like detachment you can muster before responding. Mike Blumenthal offers a great example of a dentist who takes the high road when responding to an accusation of improper conduct. The dentist describes the standards that he follows, and invites concerned readers to refer to his accolades and positive reviews. He does not call the reviewer a liar—and in fact does not address the reviewer directly at all. Rather, he says, "My staff and I felt forced to attempt to inquire into the identity of this reviewer and, unfortunately, had to conclude that this very hurtful review is the result of a personal conflict." Read more at:

http://blumenthals.com/blog/2011/03/25/responding-to-fake-reviews-return-of-the-dentist

- When a review contains a mix of positive and negative commentary, be sure to acknowledge the positive comments. You don't want your prospective customers to dwell on the negative, so you shouldn't either.

- Be real. Use your response as an opportunity to put a human face on your business.

- Describe specifically what you are doing to improve the situation. Although this may seem impossible if you don't think your business did anything wrong, you can always at least say you are keeping this feedback in mind for the future.

- Provide an email or phone contact where the reviewer can reach you. Sure, this information might be just a few inches above the review on your business listing page, but adding it to your response conveys a real willingness to connect.

- If you have already reached out to the reviewer privately, mention that in your public response. This communicates to anyone reading that you are taking steps to resolve the problem.

- If you can do so subtly and appropriately, describe the great aspects of your business in your response, for example, "We're sorry your experience prior to the massage was so unpleasant, but we hope our expert massage therapist was able to help you wash away some of the stress." Or gently point out reasons to give your business another try, for example, "We're proud to have 20 licensed massage therapists. Next time I'll be happy to personally help you pick the right one for you."

Keep your mantra top-of-mind while writing responses. Your primary audience here is your future potential customer who needs to see that you handled this exchange professionally.

Exercise: Rate Responses to Negative Reviews

The best way to get a feel for effective responses to negative reviews is to sift through your favorite review venue and read as many business responses as you can. Spending even an hour doing this will give you a solid feel for what sincerity looks like, what feels trite, and the difference between professionalism and pedantry. As you read, you'll likely run into several responses that come off as hotheaded because they were dashed off without that critical cooling-off period.

You can find review responses by clicking randomly through review sites, or you can try some advanced Google searches to get you there faster. To do this, you just need to know two little tricks:

- The Google `<site:>` search command causes Google to return pages from only the site that you specify. For example, start your Google search with `<site:www.yelp.com>` to tell Google to return only pages from Yelp. (Make sure there is no space between the colon and the name of the site.)

- Add the standard text that goes along with an owner response on the review site of your choice to your search query to see pages containing review responses. Here's the standard text from a few popular review sites:

Venue	Text (be sure to put it in quotes in your Google search)
Google+	"Response from the owner"
Yelp	"Comment from"
TripAdvisor	"This response is the subjective opinion of the management representative"

Here are a few example searches:

Use the following Google search to help you find owner responses from veterinary practices on Google+: `<site:https://plus.google.com "Response from the owner" veterinary>`

Use the following Google search to help you find management responses for a guest's terrible experience on TripAdvisor: `<site:www.tripadvisor.com "This response is the subjective opinion of the management representative" terrible experience>`

If you dare, use the following Google search to help you peruse pages on Yelp with owner responses or reviews that use the word "liar:" `<site:www.yelp.com "comment from" liar>`

Now, let's go through and grade a few responses to some particularly tricky negative reviews. For this exercise, you'll award points for the following good qualities:

- The response addresses the complaint directly.

- The response is professional and polite.

- The response states what is being done to address the problem.

- The response gives the reader a reason to like, trust, or try the business despite the negative review.

Continues

Exercise: Rate Responses to Negative Reviews *(Continued)*

Negative Review for a Car Rental Business

What makes it tricky: This review doesn't stick to describing just poor service; it contains specific details that raise questions about the ethics and trustworthiness of the business.

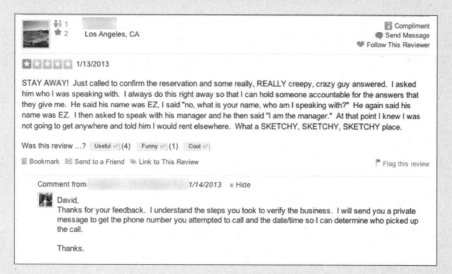

We give this response 2.5 out of 4. The response is polite and makes an attempt at addressing the complaint directly by offering to look into it further. However, the response leaves the ball in the reviewer's court. There is no reassurance that this type of behavior is against company policy or that steps will be taken to correct the issue if the reviewer does not respond. Thus it's missing important trust and likability signals for the prospective customers who read it.

Negative Review for a Tour Guide

What makes it tricky: This review has no constructive criticism to work with and seems to be more of an indication of a bad fit between customer and business rather than a flaw with the business.

Continues

We'll add to the zeroes by giving this response 0 out of 4. This response conveys the frustration that a business owner feels when a reviewer callously trashes the business. With the comment, "Out of well over 100,000 visitors you are the only one to say that," the response *almost* makes the case for why others should give the business a try, but falls short and instead becomes accusatory. Wouldn't a simple, "We have had over 100,000 visitors, and the feedback we get is overwhelmingly positive. I'm so sorry this wasn't your favorite experience!" have been better?

Because the review has so little information, it lacks credibility and might have been brushed off by readers if it weren't for the owner's petulant display. It's better to leave no response than to leave an angry or sarcastic one.

Negative Review for a Hotel

What makes it tricky: The reviewer delivers a serious accusation that must be addressed, but it is the management's word versus the guest's word.

"Thieves and liars"

◉○○○○ Reviewed July 11, 2013   📱 via mobile

We were told are belonging would be safe and that it was all there and put in there safe when we received it they had taken all the money out of it... The general manager said it was not his responsibility for are loss sorry about your luck

Stayed June 2013

◉○○○○ Cleanliness

Was this review helpful? Yes   Problem with this review?

Ask ▮▮▮▮▮ about ▮▮▮▮▮▮▮▮

This review is the subjective opinion of a TripAdvisor member and not of TripAdvisor LLC.

▮▮▮▮▮, **General Manager at** ▮▮▮▮▮▮▮▮, **responded to this review**
July 18, 2013
This guest is claiming to have left cash in a note book which he forgot in the room as he checked out. Called us asked to mail it to him which we did via UPS. Once he recieved the notebook, he called and told us that he had a few hundred dollars missing from it. Management obviously asked the H.keeper and front desk clerk who handled the book. No one had seen any money inside the note book. How is it that a person leaves hundred dollar bills, does not inform us of money being in the book . The guest waited until he received it back then accuses the hotel of our employees being theifs. He got his book back Did he not ? You, the readers of this post be the judge. His language and accustions are absurd. Our hotel is absolutely not responsible for his mistake. We regret his loss (if that actually happened) and suggest that he not leave money in inappropriate things like books.

By our count, this response gets 3 out of 4, but the score is less important here, because this is no ordinary situation. It's important to apologize for a lapse in service, but no one should feel pressured to apologize for a crime that they do not believe was committed. The response maintains a measure of professionalism while providing the hotel's side of the story and defending its integrity. We like that the general manager addresses the reader and not the reviewer in this response, and we think the directness of "You, the readers of this post be the judge" is appropriate and effective.

Negative Review for a Restaurant

What makes it tricky: The review uses inflammatory language and contains no glimmer of positivity.

"Island abatoir"

◎◎○○○ Reviewed July 6, 2013

limited menu to deal with coach parties, mass produced food which does not represent the good quality fresh produce that is available on the island. Sadly most of the interior decoration is done with stuffed animals, not sure if the owners are trainee taxidermists, but not the most suitable when one of your party are veggie

Visited July 2013

Was this review helpful? Yes   Problem with this review?

Ask   about

This review is the subjective opinion of a TripAdvisor member and not of TripAdvisor LLC.

, **General Manager at**   , **responded to this review**
July 14, 2013
I am sorry you feel the way you do. I completely disagree with every single point you make and quite happily say you are wrong. For your information we no longer accept coaches and have not since January. It is a shame that you are unable to read our menus properly and see that most of our produce is from the Isle of Wight and homemade, not mass produced bought in rubbish. I am also sorry you don't like the country feel of our establishment, or the traditional element and hope that you find a suitable place to dine that isn't so offensive.

So close! This response has the basic ingredients necessary for a 4 out of 4, but the general manager's tone ruins it. Would a cooling-off period of just a few hours have changed this snippy response into something that paints a better picture of the business? Here's our proposed rewrite that keeps all of the information while removing the hostile tone.

"I am sorry we didn't live up to your expectations. You may be pleased to learn that we no longer accept coaches, so our menu is not a concern in that regard. Like you, we dislike mass-produced food, and we're proud to say that most of our produce is from the Isle of Wight and homemade. Many of our diners say they love the country feel of our establishment or the traditional element. I'm sorry the ambience disappointed you."

Your readers are human too, and they know how easy it is to let loose with your unfiltered opinions. Like you, they may even think the reviewer deserves to be put in his place! But smart readers—the people you want as customers—know how much effort it takes to respond to rude remarks with restraint and professionalism, and your hard work to craft even-handed responses will make a favorable impression.

Negative Review for a Plumber

What makes it tricky: The reviewer gives specific, believable details about an experience that reflects poorly on the business.

★★☆☆☆   reviewed 4 months ago

I call ⬛⬛⬛⬛⬛, leave a message, they do not return my call, but I call them again since I had success in the past. I immediately speak to someone and they say they are 45-60 minutes out from being at my house. After 2 hours I call the plumber back, he goes on to tell me he is at the shop picking up a part and is only 15 minutes away. 3.5 hours later (total duration), I call them and cancel the service call. Just horrible communication.

Response from the owner - a month ago

Mr. ⬛⬛⬛, I sincerely apologize about the inconveniences. I have hired more staff to handle in-coming calls and scheduling. Please don't let this last incident deter you from calling us again. We guarantee an on time appearance and a ⬛⬛⬛⬛⬛ Discount.

This one gets a solid 4 out of 4! With professionalism, politeness, and not a hint of defensiveness, the owner apologizes and describes steps taken to make sure the problem won't happen again. He even closes out the comment by mentioning some good reasons to give this business a try: a guarantee and a discount. All of these factors add up to create the possibility that a reader may call this plumber despite the bad review.

Responding in Social Media

Your protocol for responding to social media comments can be slightly different from responses on review sites like Yelp and Google+ Local. On one hand, there may be less pressure, because social media commentary does not have the permanence of online reviews. On the other hand, the situation can escalate quickly if a social media comment gains a lot of visibility by shares, retweets, or upvotes. Responding to criticism in social media requires some thinking on your feet, so consider these questions before you respond:

How visible is the comment? Did the comment come from someone with a lot of followers or influence among your target customers? Has it been reposted, retweeted, or upvoted into the spotlight? There's a bit of added complexity when a particularly visible negative comment comes your way: Your response should be published quickly, and it should probably also receive additional scrutiny from inside your organization before it's published.

To save time when you're in damage control mode, it's best to have a response plan ready in advance. Creating a social media response plan can be as simple as sitting down and brainstorming as many complaints as you can think of about your company, scripting possible responses, and mapping out which types of issues should be moved to offline conversations and which types require a team effort for composing and approving responses. Additionally, make a plan with your team on how the appropriate team members will be alerted if you need to escalate a comment for a quicker response.

How can I make this better? Just like online reviews, negative social media commentary can take the form of constructive criticism, helpful suggestions, unhelpful vents, or hateful screeds. Your job is to respond politely to anything that seems genuine, help those who need help correcting an issue, and ignore or delete comments that cross the line into hate speech or profanity. Just as with online reviews, you must craft your responses with both the general public and the individual commenter in mind. You may have to do it a little more quickly, and with fewer characters at your disposal, than you would on a review site. Transparency and honesty are always key. If the issue is complex, an initial soft response like, "We're sorry you're having this problem! We're looking into it" or "I'm so sorry you had a bad experience. Please contact me at [email address or phone] to discuss" may be effective in communicating to both the commenter and the public that you listen and care about your customers. See Figure 7.4 for an example of a comment on Twitter that was handled nicely by Fitbit's social media team. Figure 7.5 shows an example from the Domino's Pizza Facebook page. Although Domino's responses lean toward the formulaic, they do a good job of ensuring that no comment is ignored or forgotten.

Figure 7.4 Fitbit responds to a customer's problem on Twitter.

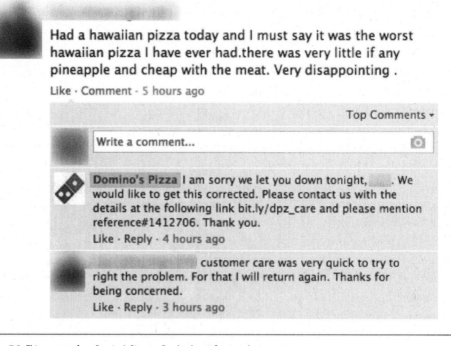

Figure 7.5 This response from Domino's Pizza on Facebook satisfies an unhappy customer.

Is a response necessary? Maybe you've heard the phrase "Don't feed the trolls." Sometimes social media comments are posted with the sole objective of provoking, annoying, or stirring up controversy, and these can often be left alone, especially if the comment has not achieved a significant level of visibility and is blatantly inflammatory, puerile, or obnoxious. Another scenario that might not require a response would be two people interacting with no expectation of a response from your business. If you're not sure whether a response is appropriate, take a minute to view the commenter's profile and get an understanding of their past interactions and their follower or friend count. This may provide some insight into whether they are worth your precious response time—or whether they are a real person.

Staying positive and keeping a cool head are imperative, and honesty and transparency are always key in social media communications.

Most Online Reviews are Positive

If there's one piece of advice you take away from this book, we hope it's this: You can't avoid getting reviews online, so pay attention to them and get involved in the conversation. If you've been avoiding cultivating online reviews because you're afraid that you'll be flooded with negative ones, Matt McGee, Editor-in-Chief of Marketingland.com, has some news that you should find heartening: The majority of online reviews are positive. Here are the statistics as reported by major review venues:

- Yelp reports that 79% of reviews on its site are 3-star or higher.

- A manager at TripAdvisor was quoted in 2012 as stating that three-quarters of all TripAdvisor reviews have ratings of "very good" or "excellent."

- According to Bazaarvoice's Conversation Index from June 2012, "Overall, 82 percent of all consumer opinions are positive."

Perhaps you've been thinking that only angry people write reviews. That just isn't the case—in fact, as you learned in Chapter 3, both a very good and a very bad experience can trigger a review. So why do so many businesses think that only customers with an axe to grind write reviews? It may be partly because of hype coming from reputation management companies. As Matt says: "Some of the voices that are emphasizing the negative reviews have a stake in getting business owners to be aware of the services they offer." Also, negative reviews tend to get more attention, both from business owners and from customers. "Negative reviews are the ones that sting."

For most businesses, the majority of customers are happy. If you engage your customers in an open dialogue about your business and cultivate reviews from a representative sample of your clientele, we're confident you'll find good things happening in your online reviews.

Crisis Management

We'll start by letting you know that a single negative review does not a reputation crisis make. Even a few negative reviews don't constitute a crisis, as long as there are positive reviews to counterbalance them. A true reputation crisis—one in which a business's future is genuinely threatened by negative reviews that receive a great deal of attention—is rare indeed.

Here are some factors defining a reputation crisis that demands your rapid attention:

- A negative comment has grown legs in social media, getting amplified by retweeting, reposting, or upvotes.

- Someone with a great deal of influence on the opinions of your prospective customers has said something negative about your business in a popular public forum.

- A complaint pointing out major or dangerous concerns is published in one of your top-priority review venues, or is visible in top search engine results for your company or product name.

- Multiple negative reviews are voicing the same grievance in rapid succession.

If you are experiencing an online reputation crisis, we have another mantra to add to the one we gave you previously in this chapter: *Don't make things worse.* You do not want to get in an exchange that turns a single negative comment into a full-fledged embarrassment. Well-known examples include a chef reacting to a mildly negative review with harsh tweets that escalated to this doozy of a comment: "I think your [sic] a c*** and this its [sic] personal...." That will do bit more reputation damage than the original 3-star review, dontcha think? In another example, a construction company reacted to a scathing Yelp review by threatening to sue the reviewer. The reviewer updated his review to reflect this, and the whole ugly exchange made it to the front page of the hugely popular site reddit.com.

Your response will make all the difference: A 2011 study by the Altimeter Group concluded that more than three quarters of social media crises could have been diminished or averted with proper handling; in some cases, the primary catalyst was a slow or inappropriate response by the business to a negative online remark.

Most of the advice in this chapter applies to any crisis, especially the need for calm and professionalism in your responses. However, especially in high-visibility social media situations, your reaction will also need to be rapid. Focus on these qualities in your response:

- De-escalation
- Transparency
- Humility
- Contrition, if the complaint is valid
- Moving the conversation offline

You may not have time to get all the facts before you respond. It's okay to start by just stating that you are looking into the problem.

Continues

Redress and Removal

What's the best way to get a review site to take action if you've been the victim of a false or defamatory negative review? Even if you are clearly and demonstrably in the right, you may be surprised to learn how limited your options are. Read on for some important background on why review sites are protected and for some options for review removal that might apply to you.

Why It's Not Easy to Sue Review Sites

When a damaging or false review is published on a review venue, some business owners want to take legal action. This is a scenario that comes up frequently enough that Yelp has "I'm considering legal action—what are my rights?" on its Common Questions page. We're not lawyers, but even us common folk can figure this one out:

If you decide to sue a review site over the content of its reviews, it's not likely to be a good use of your time or money.

Review sites get their legal armor from Section 230 of the Communications Decency Act (CDA), which provides extensive immunities for sites that post user-generated content. We had a conversation with Katherine Fibiger, who has an advanced degree in IP law as well as an MS in MIS, to get her explanation. She told us, "Section 230 is a powerful tool for protecting free speech. What someone would be liable for in the non-online world, they are immunized from in the online world."

Section 230 protects websites from liability for information that is created by others and presented on the website. Katherine offers up some helpful interpretation here: "Section 230 added protection for internet service providers and users from actions against them based on content posted by third parties. The Act defines 'interactive computer service providers' very broadly and includes any online website or service that publishes any third-party content." The Act has been interpreted to include search engines, moderators of discussion groups, owners of chat rooms, and review sites, among others.

Under Section 230 protections, bloggers aren't liable for comments left by readers, search engines aren't liable for the content of websites they display, and review sites aren't liable for the content of reviews they show. "The Act immunizes anyone who runs a website or who acts as an intermediary."

We wondered if there were any scenarios in which the protections of Section 230 of the CDA do not apply. Here's what we learned:

When the Site Authors Its Own Statements Although a site can't be held responsible for the defamatory statements of its users, the site is not protected if it writes defamatory content or edits someone else's nondefamatory content to make it defamatory. Moderating reviews, or even making editorial judgments about what reviews to display, is not considered authorship.

When a Site Agrees to Remove Content The act of flagging or notifying a site does not make the site liable for defamatory statements, but if a website agrees to remove content and then does not comply, the site may lose its protection under Section 230. According to Katherine, "If you see a report about your business that is clearly factually incorrect, you can contact the site and ask that it be removed, and if they agree to remove it, they are responsible for removing that content."

Certain Types of Content Katherine says, "Most speech is protected by the First Amendment in the United States, but there are exceptions to the broad coverage it affords someone posting an online review." Here are some quotes from Katherine that we hope will provide some insight:

- On hate speech: "Hate speech is not protected speech and is never acceptable under the First Amendment, but the ISP will not be liable for posting it."

- On copyrighted works: "If you have taken some photographs and an online reviewer claims ownership of the photos, that use is not protected—it is a copyright violation."

- On the use of a person's image and likeness: "If someone posts a picture of you (and you are not newsworthy or famous) then that use is prohibited by privacy laws. Similarly, private information cannot be posted by anyone."

That's a big legalese sandwich for you to chew on! Our intention is neither to encourage or discourage anyone's litigious aspirations but rather to provide a little background information that will help you get a feeling for reasonable expectations.

When Can a Review Be Removed?

Uh-oh. A bad review's got you down, and you're hoping to get it removed from public view. If you believe what you hear from some reputation management companies, or what you see when you run your eyes over the Google search ads for "remove negative reviews" (shown in Figure 7.6), you might have the impression that getting reviews taken down is just a matter of greasing the right palms.

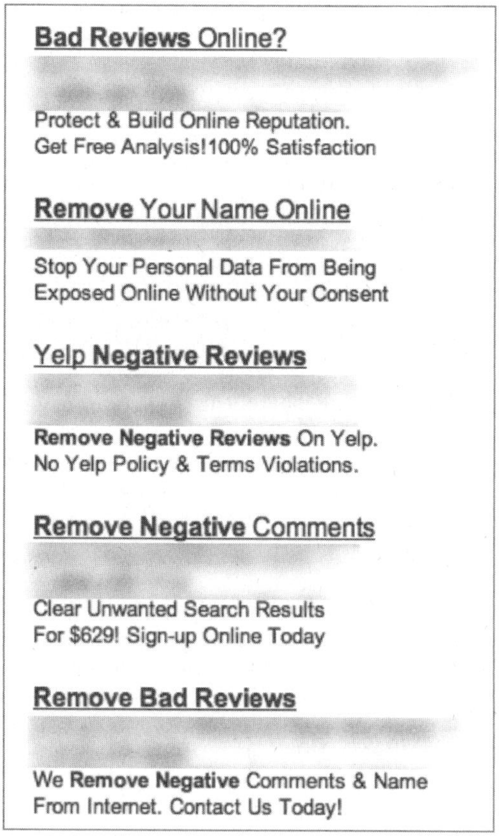

Bad Reviews Online?

Protect & Build Online Reputation.
Get Free Analysis!100% Satisfaction

Remove Your Name Online

Stop Your Personal Data From Being
Exposed Online Without Your Consent

Yelp Negative Reviews

Remove Negative Reviews On Yelp.
No Yelp Policy & Terms Violations.

Remove Negative Comments

Clear Unwanted Search Results
For $629! Sign-up Online Today

Remove Bad Reviews

We **Remove Negative** Comments & Name
From Internet. Contact Us Today!

Figure 7.6 These ads imply that you can pay a service to get reviews removed.

The reality is there's no reputation management firm with strong enough super-powers to clear away all your negative reviews. And this is a good thing: Remember, even though you're probably sick of reading it by now, bad reviews can have some benefits for your business, and any sort of pay-to-remove process would deeply damage both your credibility and that of the review site. While you're resisting the kneejerk reaction to kill your bad reviews, read on to learn some scenarios when one can legitimately be snuffed out:

Removal by the Original Reviewer Most review venues give a reviewer the opportunity to remove or edit his or her review to reflect a change of heart. We've already described how you should respond to your negative reviews and attempt to resolve the problem. Getting a negative review taken down may be a nice side effect of your response, but you should not apply any pressure or directly ask customers to change or remove their review. Besides being uncool and potentially embarrassing to you if exposed, this is discouraged by review sites and may even violate their rules.

Violations of Review Site Rules or Guidelines You already know that review venues prohibit threats, bigotry, and profanity in reviews. Did you also know that TripAdvisor does not accept reviews of hotels if someone didn't actually visit the property? And Yelp's Content Guidelines suggest that reviews should include firsthand experiences, "not what you heard from your co-worker or significant other." If you are suffering from a negative review that violates any of these guidelines, removal may be an option. Figures 7.7 and 7.8 are two examples of negative reviews that we believe could be candidates for removal.

Don't expect a review site to take down a review just because you think it's a pack of lies; that's not going to happen.

But if you think a review violates site guidelines, flag that sucker! And when you flag, be sure to write a detailed explanation of how you believe the guidelines were violated.

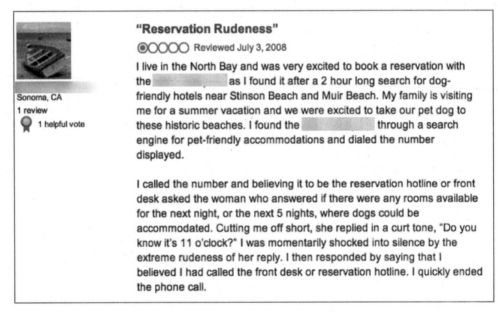

"Reservation Rudeness"

⊙○○○○ Reviewed July 3, 2008

Sonoma, CA
1 review
1 helpful vote

I live in the North Bay and was very excited to book a reservation with the ▓▓▓▓▓ as I found it after a 2 hour long search for dog-friendly hotels near Stinson Beach and Muir Beach. My family is visiting me for a summer vacation and we were excited to take our pet dog to these historic beaches. I found the ▓▓▓▓▓ through a search engine for pet-friendly accommodations and dialed the number displayed.

I called the number and believing it to be the reservation hotline or front desk asked the woman who answered if there were any rooms available for the next night, or the next 5 nights, where dogs could be accommodated. Cutting me off short, she replied in a curt tone, "Do you know it's 11 o'clock?" I was momentarily shocked into silence by the extreme rudeness of her reply. I then responded by saying that I believed I had called the front desk or reservation hotline. I quickly ended the phone call.

Figure 7.7 This review on TripAdvisor is based on a reservation phone call and not firsthand experience of the property.

0
★ 5   Studio City, Los Angeles, CA

⊡ Compliment
● Send Message
♥ Follow This Reviewer

★☆☆☆☆ 4/16/2013   ✸ First to Review

This place gets 1 star cuz I have to put a rating but definitely no stars!! Worst place iv ever lived in! The fat ass dark short lady who works is the office is retarded! She harasses all the tenants for no reason! I dont even know what her damn title is exactly! Her fat daughter also works in the office as well so u can imagine how much of a pain in the ass they are!! Oh and they also live in the park too so u get harasses 24/7 even when the office is closed!!! they probably steal money from

Figure 7.8 This Yelp review contains several slurs, which could be grounds for removal.

On Your Facebook Page You have the ability to delete posts on your Facebook page, but think carefully before you use this option. If a complaint is posted on your Facebook page, do not remove it unless it contains profanity or is otherwise offensive to readers. Removing complaints sends a message that you have something to cover up, and it also provides ammunition to reputation bashers, who can then say "I complained about their product and they censored me!" Remove only the truly inappropriate comments, and for all others, stick to leaving the kinds of professional and transparent responses that we described earlier in this chapter.

On Your Website In general, website owners have a lot of control over reviews that are posted on their own sites. In Chapter 6, we mentioned that Bazaarvoice, the dominant provider of product review infrastructure for e-commerce sites, allows retailers to reject product reviews within the tool's dashboard. The WordPress review plug-ins we've seen also allow this, as do the customer review modules offered with e-commerce solutions such as Volusion. This capability should only be used to remove reviews that are clearly inappropriate, and not just those that are negative or unpleasant.

Some other review-gathering tools give business owners a great deal of control over which reviews are published to their website. For example, GetFiveStars at https:// getfivestars.com is a tool that helps businesses gather reviews and allows businesses to choose which reviews to publish. We think it's any business's prerogative what they want to post on their own site, but if you're only publishing positive feedback, those are testimonials, not reviews, and they should be labeled accordingly.

Review Site Arbitration If you and a reviewer have a factual disagreement, you generally can't look to the review site for assistance. Google's statement, "We do not arbitrate disputes and more often than not, we leave the review up," is echoed by Yelp: "We don't take sides when it comes to factual disputes." TripAdvisor also does not mediate or arbitrate reviews. And an Angie's List representative told us, "Generally speaking, if the member stands by the report, we tend to side with the member." Of all the major review sites we have researched, Angie's List is the only one that offers a formal arbitration process; however, their arbitration can be initiated only by the dissatisfied customer and not by the business.

It would be great if more review sites offered arbitration services for businesses, but it's clearly much simpler for them to maintain an objective distance, framing themselves as conduits for information and not as keepers of the truth.

Blackmail Deep in the darkest, sleaziest corner of the online reviews universe lurks the review blackmailer: a customer who either demands a payment to remove a negative review or threatens to write a negative review if payment is not received. Review sites are aware of these diabolical deeds. In January 2013, TripAdvisor released a blackmail reporting tool for businesses to use "when a guest threatens to write a negative review unless a demand for a refund, upgrade, or other request is met." To report an incident, log into your TripAdvisor management dashboard and select "Manage your Reviews > Dispute a Review", then select "Report blackmail." Prompt reporting of a threat may prevent the review from ever being published. On other review sites, you can post a public response and flag the review, and consider seeking a court order and Google removal as described in the following section.

Court Orders and Google Removal A nasty review will do much less damage if it doesn't show up in Google search results. Attorney Kenton Hutcherson spends much of his time working to get false reviews taken down—not from the review sites, but from Google search results. The process involves first filing a lawsuit against the original author of the review (not against Google or the review site), and getting a court order declaring the review to be false and defamatory. Submit the court order to Google at this URL:

```
https://support.google.com/legal/contact/lr_courtorder?product=websearch
```

Within a few weeks, the page should be removed from Google's search results.

In addition to removing pages due to a court order, Google may remove a page from search results if it contains highly sensitive personal information such as your social security number or an image of your handwritten signature. If this applies to you, start here:

```
https://support.google.com/websearch/troubleshooter/3111061#ts=2889054
```

Here's hoping you have more positive reviews to show off than negative ones to fret about! In Chapter 8, "Showing Off and Being Found," you'll learn how to make your reviews more visible.

Showing Off and Being Found

8

This chapter is all about visibility: how to improve visibility for your reviews and how reviews can benefit your business's visibility in search engines. You'll learn how to get even more mileage out of your positive customer sentiment by integrating it into marketing and communications channels you control. And we'll show you how online reviews can also boost your search engine results.

In this chapter:

Show off your reviews

Improve your search results

Show Off Your Reviews

When positive customer reviews come your way, you should do everything you can to broaden their visibility. After all, a good review can't influence people who don't see it. Here are some great ways to add your earned media (reviews) to your owned media, such as your website, social media accounts, and marketing communications.

Badges and Widgets

Some review venues provide badges or widgets that dress up your website and link to your business listing. We talked about these in Chapter 4, "Monitoring and Learning from Your Reviews," as tools for gathering more reviews, but they can also provide compelling social proof to visitors by showing off the quality and quantity of your reviews. Examples include TripAdvisor badges that show review excerpts and awards, Yelp badges that display aggregate star ratings, and Judy's Book KidScore badges that rate the kid-friendliness of a business. Many reputation management and ecommerce review collection services such as ShopperApproved, Trustpilot, Reevoo, and ResellerRatings offer badges as part of their service offerings.

Badges and widgets can bolster your credibility, broadcast your best qualities, dispel distrust, and even serve up a measurable sales lift. Ali Alami, interim CEO and general manager of Judy's Book, told us, "Our experiments with displaying KidScores have shown that they increase conversion from parent users to customers by an average of 18%." Figure 8.1 shows several options.

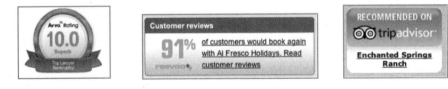

Figure 8.1 Badges and widgets from Avvo, Reevoo, Yelp, TripAdvisor, Trustpilot, and KidScore

If you have a claimed profile on a review site, the typical way to implement badges and widgets is to log into your profile, copy the widget code provided by the review site, and add it to your web page. Badges for reputation management services and e-commerce review collection services are available after signing up with the service.

Some businesses prefer to incorporate a link to a review site in their website design rather than add a prefabricated widget. Figure 8.2 shows an example of a link to reviews as a major design component of a home services website.

Figure 8.2 This service provider prominently links to its Customer Lobby reviews at the bottom of its home page.

Here are some tips for using badges and widgets:

Know where they take your visitors. Most review site badges are clickable and could draw your visitors off your site. To minimize the risk of losing a prospective customer, be sure that your business listing on the review site links back to your site, has accurate contact information and an up-to-date business description, and contains enough information to help a visitor make the decision to become your customer.

Show good data or none at all. It's great to use badges and widgets that display up-to-date ratings information. But if your business has few reviews or a shabby star rating, you're not ready for the badge. You'll no doubt add a widget to your site when you are proud of the data it shows, but remember that most widgets display a live feed from the review venue. Keep an eye on your site and be sure to remove the widgets—or change to one that does not show ratings data—if your reviews take a turn for the worse.

Keep it classy. Don't sacrifice your website design for the sake of a badge. An overly cluttered or hodgepodge layout can detract from the credibility you are trying to build.

Table 8.1 shows links to badges and widgets for a partial list of review sites.

▶ **Table 8.1** Where to find badges and widgets

Site	Where to find the badge or widget
Yelp	Log into your business account at www.biz.yelp.com and click on "review badges"
Google+	https://developers.google.com/+/web/badge/ (does not currently show reviews)
TripAdvisor	www.tripadvisor.com/WidgetEmbed
Avvo	www.avvo.com/partner_with_us/syndication
Angie's List	http://reviews.angieslist.com/webbadges/sp.aspx
Zillow	Agents and lenders can show off their expertise with badges available at www.zillow.com/webtools/badges
Goodreads	Select a book title, then add review data to your site at www.goodreads.com/api/reviews_demo_widget_iframe
ResellerRating Elite Badge	www.resellerratings.com/elite
Judy's Book	Click on the badge button on the lower right of your profile, or replace the "38779477" in this URL with your business profile number: www.judysbook.com/badges/0/38779477
Kudzu	www.kudzubizsuccess.com/?p=599

As of this writing, the Google+ badge for websites does not display Google+ Local reviews; however, we hope to see Google add this capability to its badges in the future.

Review Excerpts

While you're in the mood to show off, you may be feeling the inclination to cut and paste reviews or excerpts of reviews onto your site. Proceed with caution here: Publishing someone else's content can violate copyright rules, even if that content is written about your business.

To avoid complexity, you can always play it safe by sticking with widgets that the review venues provide. But if you are set on copying review text from another site, you will need to check with the review venue to understand their rules. Is using review text okay? What about using a reviewer's name or screen name—do you need their permission? And which elements of the review interface (stars, icons, naming conventions, and so on) are protected by copyright or trademark?

For answers to Yelp-specific questions, read the sidebar "Yelp Guidelines for Excerpting Ratings and Reviews."

Yelp Guidelines for Excerpting Ratings and Reviews

We asked Yelp for their guidelines on excerpting reviews and ratings in marketing materials, and here's what we learned:

- DO ask the reviewers themselves before using their reviews. You can contact them by sending them a "Private Message" on Yelp.

- DO stick to verbatim quotes, and don't quote out of context. If a review has colorful language that doesn't suit your needs, you should probably move on to the next review.

- DO attribute the reviews to Yelp (e.g., "Reviews from Yelp"), and do attribute the reviews to their authors and the date written (e.g., "- Mike S. on 4/5/09").

- DON'T alter star ratings. Average star ratings change over time, so you also need to include the date of your rating nearby (e.g., "**** as of 5/1/09").

Thanks to Katrina Hafford, PR Coordinator at Yelp for communicating these guidelines.

Maximize Your Social Proof

Social proof is the psychological phenomenon in which people in ambiguous situations look to the behaviors of others to help inform their actions. Some examples of social proof in the offline world include the "Billions and Billions Served" sign at McDonald's, lines outside of nightclubs, and laugh tracks on television comedy shows. *If a significant number of people eat Big Macs,* or *want to get into this club, or think this show is funny,* goes the consumer mindset, *maybe I should, too.* In the digital world, examples of social proof include the "popular on Netflix" label, the "most shared" label on a news site, and the Facebook Like box, which shows the people who like a page:

Continues

Maximize Your Social Proof *(Continued)*

Reviews are a particularly powerful form of social proof. You can harness that power by incorporating reviews strategically into the properties that you control, such as your website and social media channels, as described in this chapter.

Here are some ways to maximize the value of your social proof:

Display Social Proof at Your Visitors' Decision Points

The goal is to show your persuasive information at the point where your site visitors are open to being influenced. For example, if you place a TripAdvisor widget on your site showing how many people love your hotel, don't hide it away on your Reservations page. By the time visitors reach the Reservations page, they've already made a decision to connect with you. Also, not every visitor will enter your site on its home page, so add your social proof on other likely entry points, too. Many forms of social proof, such as badges, are easy to integrate on every page of your site.

Don't Prove a Negative

If you want to show that the wisdom of the crowd supports becoming your customer, be sure the crowd conveys the right message. A Yelp widget showing one review or a Facebook Like box with just a couple of lonely Likes may have the opposite effect of what you intend. Leave them off until you've built up enough positive data to benefit you.

Play Up the "People Like Me" Factor

People are influenced more strongly by people they know or feel similar to. Facebook plug-ins that list the names of friends who have connected with a brand add a nice touch of influence, as do product reviews that show photos or details about the reviewer. Case studies, review excerpts, and testimonials are more effective when they feature details that make the customer experience relatable to your target customer.

Feature Influencers and Experts

Everyone wants spontaneous celebrity endorsements, and if you receive one, you probably don't need us to tell you to show it off, assuming you have permission. But influencers don't have to be celebrities. Effective social proof can come from a list of your most impressive customers, or a positive mention from the kinds of people your prospective customers look up to. Positive mentions in the press are sometimes called expert social proof; here's an example of press mentions on the home page of tattly.com, a temporary tattoo store.

YAY! WE'RE FEATURED IN: *New York*   *Atlantic*   ©   ℭ   The New York Times   THE GLOBE AND MAIL*

Visibility on E-commerce Sites

At the risk of stating the obvious, if you want to show off your product reviews on your e-commerce site, the first step is to enable your site to collect and display product reviews, either by using your e-commerce platform's feature set or a product review tool such as Bazaarvoice. The next step is to allow reviews to be integrated into more than just the product page so they can influence the entire shopping experience. Here are some ways to increase the exposure of your product reviews:

Make reviews part of the browsing experience. Given how useful reviews are, it's a huge missed opportunity to keep them hidden until your customers have made their way to a product page. If your product review platform gives you the option to display reviews or review stars on category pages, search results pages, featured product pages, or related product links, take advantage of all of these visibility opportunities.

Identify top products. Adding social-proof-driven categories such as "top rated" and "best sellers" to your navigation can steer some undecided shoppers toward a purchase. You can even add visuals such as stars or "top rated," "best seller," or "staff favorite" labels to your product photos or search results. See Figure 8.3 for a search results page that is spiffed up with both review stars and labels.

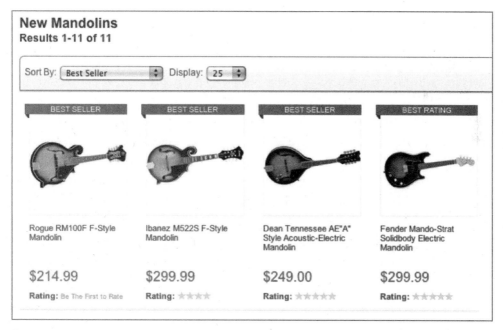

Figure 8.3 On guitarcenter.com, in-site search results display review stars along with Best Seller and Best Rating banners.

Show reviews prominently on product pages. On some e-commerce site product pages, a shopper must scroll below the fold to see customer reviews. You know that reviews increase sales, so why hide them away? If your product review tool allows it, we recommend including review stars front-and-center on your product pages, as seen in Figure 8.4.

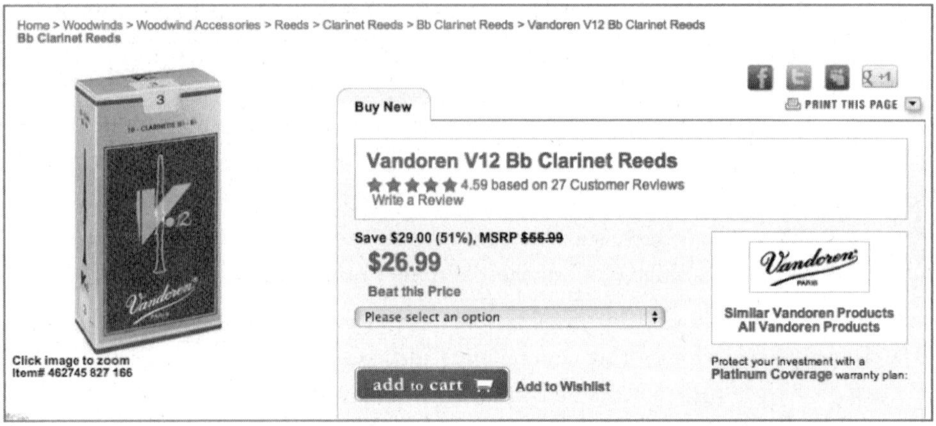

(Figure 8.4 product page is shown here)

Figure 8.4 Positive sentiment is easy to see on this page.

Amplification in Social Media

Social media sites long ago nailed the concept of social proof, and they make it easy to bring your site into the mix. As we've discussed previously in this book, Facebook, Twitter, Pinterest, and other social media channels are not primarily review venues, but they are repositories of a great deal of positive word-of-mouth. Here are ways to showcase your social media love:

Embed individual comments. Many businesses are in the habit of retweeting or sharing compliments to draw attention to them, but did you know you can embed individual tweets and public Facebook statuses on your website? With just a click, you can get the code you need to transform an advocate's passing comment into a permanent fixture on your site. See Figure 8.5 for an example.

Figure 8.5 Twitter's Embed Tweet feature

Embed your own feeds on your site. The primary purpose of embedding your own social media streams onto your site is to keep your website updated with fresh content and encourage more followers. But if you regularly take the time to find and share or retweet your most glowing compliments, you'll be adding some positive third-party influence to your site as well. See Figure 8.6 for an example.

Figure 8.6 Children's Fairyland embeds its Twitter stream on its website, which provides home page visibility for any retweeted compliments.

Share reviews on social media. Some companies seem to retweet or share every single nice thing that's said about them, which may come off as overly self-congratulatory and may be a turnoff to social followers. But if you use a light touch, we encourage you to share the reviews that are particularly glorious. For reviews that customers post on your own site, or for public reviews on a site you don't own, you can tweet a link to the review or share in Facebook. Social sharing icons can sometimes be found next to reviews, or you may need to do some work to find the individual review URL to copy into your post, such as by clicking "Link to This Review" on Yelp:

Don't try this with Angie's List: Angie's List reviews are not public, so posting a link to an individual review will take most people to the Angie's List home page, and only logged-in members will see the review.

The legal site Avvo offers a particularly chatty social media integration for its lawyers. Those who opt in will automatically tweet every time a new 4- or 5-star review is posted to their Avvo listing. See Figure 8.7.

Scott J Corwin, APLC @SJCLaw
I just got a 5-star review from a Car Accident client on Avvo
rpx.me/1/4VTp

Figure 8.7 Avvo autotweeted this review on an attorney's Twitter stream.

On Pinterest, some companies create dedicated boards to showcase their favorite customer reviews and testimonials. Pinterest marketing is an evolving discipline, and we think Rich Pins may grow into a useful opportunity to show off reviews. Pinterest's Rich Pins are a type of enhanced Pin that pulls data such as price, brand, and availability from product pages and displays them on pins from your product page. To be seen, the data must be formatted with Schema.org markup (learn more about Schema markup in "Improve Your Search Results," later in this chapter) and sites must request validation from Pinterest. As of this writing, product reviews are not supported in Rich Pins, but keep an eye out for new developments at `http://developers.pinterest.com/rich_pins`.

Show off your following. Although they're not technically reviews and don't convey the same influence that reviews do, social media buttons that display Likes, followers, +1s, and shares of your content are solid displays of social proof and are typically easy to integrate onto your website. Add them by getting code from the social media venues or by embedding social sharing tools such as AddThis or AddToAny. Social media engagement is a vote of confidence, so show it off.

Testimonials and Case Studies

Testimonials and case studies are different from reviews in that they are always positive and always solicited, and you are in control of where they are seen. But like reviews, they illustrate how real people feel about your product or service. Some businesses solicit testimonials by reaching out directly to customers, initiating surveys, or running video or essay contests. Here are some ways to position testimonials and case studies for optimal influence:

Include details. Anonymous endorsements are less credible than ones with real people attached. Whenever possible, include identifying details such as the full names, photos, and cities of residence of featured customers, along with the product or service they received from you. A video testimonial is another way to add credibility. Remember, too, that people are most influenced by reviews from people who are similar to themselves. Aim to display testimonials featuring customers and scenarios that you think will resonate with your target audience.

Integrate them into the shopping experience. Many small-scale ecommerce sites don't have reviews but do collect and display customer testimonials. If this describes your situation, don't sequester all of your customer love onto a separate page that your users have to look for outside of the shopping experience. Add these testimonials, or relevant excerpts, to your product pages so your shoppers can get a dose of trust while they shop. See Figure 8.8 for an example of a home page design that features customer testimonials.

Figure 8.8 Customer testimonials on the home page of Okabashi.com

Make 'em pop! If you have long case studies, use pull quotes or summaries to let your readers take in the main points with a quick skim. Use attention-grabbing visual elements such as quotation marks, speech bubbles, and photos.

Never falsify Just because you control the content of testimonials does not mean that you can alter the meaning of a customer's comment or fabricate positive sentiment. If you want your customers to trust you, be trustworthy. End of story.

Marketing Communications

Think of any communication you have with your customers as an opportunity to show off your positive reviews. If you send email blasts, you can feature recent testimonials or reviews, or label your top-rated products. See Figure 8.9 for a great example of a product newsletter featuring hand-picked customer reviews.

Figure 8.9 Customer testimonials featured in a newsletter from Orion Telescopes & Binoculars

Advertisements—both online and in print—can also feature reviews, as seen in Figure 8.10.

At Your Physical Location

When a person is visiting your brick-and-mortar establishment, reviews can help with a purchase decision or encourage a window-shopper to venture inside. Local businesses can translate online reviews into in-person positivity with displays such as these:

Window Decals You can remind your customers of your much-loved status with window clings from review sites like Yelp, TripAdvisor, and Angie's List (we showed you how to find some of these in Chapter 6, "Review Venues: Need-to-Know Tips for Your Action Plan"). Often, these window decorations are only distributed to businesses that have reached a designated level of acclaim on the review site. The "People Love Us on Yelp" is a well-known example of a decal that can't be requested but must instead be earned. Figure 8.11 shows a Judy's Book window decal for Featured Places.

Figure 8.10 This display ad features an excerpt from an online review.

Figure 8.11 Judy's Book distributes this window decal to select businesses.

Should you clog up your windows with every imaginable window decal? We haven't seen any studies that determine whether or not window decals have a positive effect on customer acquisition, so it's probably best to choose a middle ground and slap up decals only for the review sites that are important to you.

In-store Signs and Displays Table tents and printouts can be used to show off online reviews. Some review sites distribute suitable-for-framing certificates that can be displayed on the wall or even in an entrance, like the TripAdvisor certificate of excellence shown in Figure 8.12.

Figure 8.12 A restaurant proudly displays a TripAdvisor certificate of excellence near its front door.

Product Reviews As consumers become accustomed to reading product reviews before making a purchase decision, brick-and-mortar shops can find themselves at a disadvantage to e-commerce sites. Some brick-and-mortar businesses are fighting back by offering product information accessible via smartphones or printing out product review excerpts and displaying them alongside products on their shelves. The Sephora to Go app appeals to showrooming customers by letting them scan items in the store to read reviews and other product information on sephora.com from their smartphones. See Figure 8.13.

Figure 8.13 Using the Sephora to Go app, customers can scan a product barcode and access reviews.

Improve Your Search Results

There's a good chance you're reading this book because something you don't love is showing up in search engine results. Maybe you have a bad review poised unsettlingly in Google's top ranks for your brand, or a competitor of yours is sporting shiny stars on its listings and you want some, too. Read on to learn how to make the best of the relationship between your reviews and your search results.

Branded Search Results

In Chapter 4, we introduced you to the concept of checking Google's results for branded terms. These terms include the name of your business as well as spelling variations, major product names, your personal name if applicable, and all of these plus the word "reviews." We probably don't need to tell you the importance of these search results: Prospective clients and customers who are researching your business will be fascinated to see all the kudos or condemnation found here. If you completed the exercise in Chapter 4, you already know which review sites are showing up in your branded search results, but here's one undeniable fact we haven't mentioned yet: Your own website should be highly ranked in those search results as well.

Google, Bing, and Yahoo! usually do a good job of finding the official site of a business and displaying it in top ranks for its own name, as seen in Figure 8.14.

Figure 8.14 Bing displays an official business site in search results for <mountain secure systems>.

Sometimes businesses or brands struggle to nail the top position in these results. We've seen this happen when a business does not have a website of its own (this often applies to professionals whose personal name is their brand), or when a site has structural problems that prevent the search engines from finding its pages, or when a site lacks search engine–readable keywords (in other words, when the site is poorly *optimized*). Another scenario that can interfere with branded search results is when a business shares its name with other businesses or organizations, or with a common word in the English language.

Online Reviews and Google's Local Search Rankings

If your business has a physical presence or serves clients in person at their locations, you probably have a strong interest in gaining search engine ranks for local-intent search terms like <cat sitter> or <foundation contractor anaheim> that describe your business. We talked about local results and the keywords that trigger them in Chapter 6; here's a visual reminder:

Local Listings

Numerous factors are weighed when Google decides which businesses will receive a coveted spot among top local search results, including basics like these:

- The business has a Google+ Local listing.

- The business is located where the searcher is looking.

- Online business listings, called citations, mirror the name, address, and phone number on the Google+ Local listing.

- The business has a website.

In addition to these factors and many others, there is general agreement among experts that online reviews for your business can have a positive effect on your local ranks.

Online Reviews and Google's Local Search Rankings *(Continued)*

Each year, local search expert David Mihm, director of local search strategy at Moz, compiles local ranking factors based on opinions from leaders in the industry. We have distilled these expert opinions into a few pointers about the impact of reviews on your Google+ Local ranks:

- Reviews written on a diverse assortment of review sites can help ranks, but the biggest impact is probably from reviews written directly on Google+ Local (called *native reviews*).

- Keywords such as locations and product names in reviews may factor into ranks.

- Native reviews that cause stars to show up in your search engine listings can indirectly help your ranks by increasing click-through rates, which are another likely positive ranking factor.

- Once you have more reviews than your competitors, there is probably no additional ranking advantage to gaining an even larger number of reviews.

Like all things involving Google algorithms, these factors are educated guesses and not confirmed by Google. To learn more about local ranking factors and keep up with new findings, visit the Moz local ranking factors page here:

```
http://moz.com/local-search-ranking-factors
```

Following the steps to claiming and optimizing your Google+ Local listing described in Chapter 6 will give your local optimization a solid start, and gaining reviews may just be the shot in the arm your listing needs to make it into the top results.

Search engine optimization (SEO) is a form of online marketing in which efforts are made to improve your website's visibility in organic (unpaid) search engine results and to identify and attract the most valuable search traffic to your site. It's a multifaceted effort deserving of its own book, so we won't go into a great deal of detail here. But gaining top ranks for your own brand name can sometimes be relatively simple. If you don't currently dominate these ranks, here are a few simple pointers to help get you there:

- Create a website on your own domain, for example, www.mybusinessname.com rather than mybusinessname.wordpress.com.

- Include your business name in the home page <title> tag and within visible text on the home page.

- If you include reviews on your own site, use the word "reviews" in text on your site to describe them. For example, instead of "Read what our customers have to say," use the text "Read our customer reviews." This may improve your chances of being found for search queries that include your branded terms and the word "review."

- If you're a local business, take the steps described in the sidebar "Online Reviews and Google's Local Search Rankings."

- Differentiate yourself. If your business or product is referred to by an acronym or a common word, get in the habit of adding a unique descriptor a few times in your website's text. For example, even if all your customers know your product as TCCS, expand the acronym to "TCCS—Total Car Cleaning System." If your company has a generic name like "The Scene," describe it more clearly: "The Scene, a Koreatown Dance Club." If you have a common personal name, consider using a middle initial.

These are just baby steps on the long journey that is SEO, but for many businesses they're all you need to gain a good position for your branded terms. And if your website is already ranking well for your branded keywords, make it a habit to keep an eye on these search results so you'll know if something goes awry with them.

Rich Snippets

In search engine results, the text you see below the clickable title of each listing is called a snippet. A basic snippet includes a text description of the site, which is pulled from either a meta description tag or visible text on the page. Rich snippets show more than just a description; they are enhanced with additional details collected from specially formatted code on the site. Rich snippets can showcase things like author photos, dates and times of events listed on the web page, and review stars. Naturally, if you display reviews on your own site, you're interested in getting those review stars into your search engine results. Figure 8.15 shows a rich snippet example in Google results for a site built with the Volusion platform.

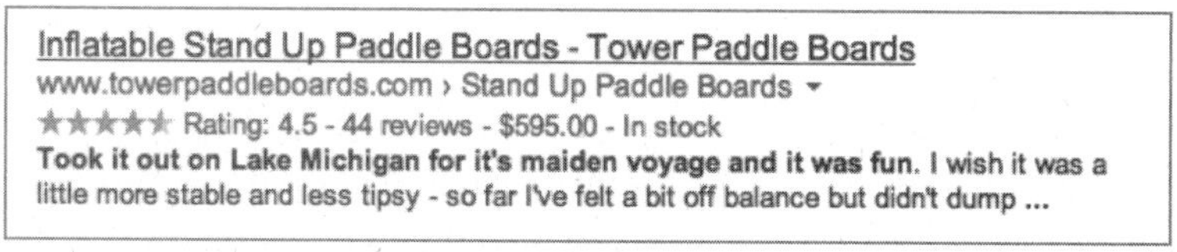

> **Inflatable Stand Up Paddle Boards - Tower Paddle Boards**
> www.towerpaddleboards.com › Stand Up Paddle Boards ▾
> ★★★★★ Rating: 4.5 - 44 reviews - $595.00 - In stock
> **Took it out on Lake Michigan for it's maiden voyage and it was fun.** I wish it was a little more stable and less tipsy - so far I've felt a bit off balance but didn't dump ...

Figure 8.15 This Google listing shows appealing review stars.

Many businesses obsess about search engine ranks but forget to think about search engine *real estate*: How much of a search result page is your business controlling, and how attractive is your presence there? Rich snippets can increase your search results' real estate and maximize the appeal of your search engine listings. How much more appealing will your listing be? Google is noncommittal, saying that rich snippets "may result in more clicks to your page," but case studies indicate that some rich snippets can increase the proportion of searchers who click on the listings by up to 30%.

It's important to understand that the review stars in rich snippets are generated by a different method than the stars you see in AdWords ads. We'll discuss AdWords stars in the next section.

Google generates rich snippets by reading text identified with a special type of code, called semantic markup, and any website that displays reviews has the opportunity to use this code. In fact, the rich snippet code can be used for several different types of reviews, such as the following:

- Product reviews on a retailer site
- Business reviews on a review site such as Yelp
- Business reviews on the business's own site
- Reviews by a single expert (such as a movie reviewer)

Google's description and limitations can be found here:

https://support.google.com/webmasters/answer/146645

If anyone tries to make you think they're extra smart because they use the words "semantic markup," we encourage you to sniff at them derisively. The concept is simple. Semantic markup just means wrapping content on your page with meaningful explanations that search engines can understand. Here's an example that's meant to illustrate the concept, but it's not real markup:

```
<this next thing is the average star rating>4.0
</and that's the end of the average star rating>

<this next thing is the number of reviews>6
</and that's the end of the number of reviews>

<this next thing is a review title>Best blender ever!
</and that's the end of the review title>
```

Simple, right? Figure 8.16 shows an example of how semantic markup can look within the code of a web page. This markup, which was generated by the Volusion e-commerce platform, resulted in the Google snippet that you saw in Figure 8.15.

Several different formats are available for this markup. Fortunately, in 2011 Google, Bing, and Yahoo! all agreed to honor a single format called Schema.org. We're sure there must be some perfectly good reasons a website would use a different format, but we haven't found them yet.

If you display customer reviews on your website, we encourage you to look into adding rich snippet markup, preferably in the Schema.org format. Some solutions, such as Bazaarvoice and GetFiveStars, already have semantic markup baked into their code. If you use a WordPress plug-in or an e-commerce platform to display reviews, check with the provider to see if Schema.org markup is an option. If your website is homemade, you can add the code yourself.

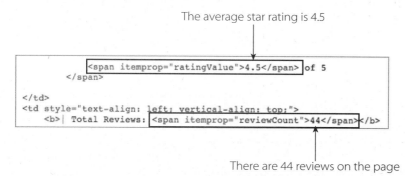

The average star rating is 4.5

```
              <span itemprop="ratingValue">4.5</span> of 5
         </span>

</td>
<td style="text-align: left; vertical-align: top;">
    <b>| Total Reviews: <span itemprop="reviewCount">44</span></b>
```

There are 44 reviews on the page

Figure 8.16 This semantic markup caused a review star snippet to display in Google search results.

A guide to rich snippet implementation can be found here:

`http://blog.search-mojo.com/2013/07/23/new-download-the-definitive-guide-to-rich-snippets-for-google-and-bing`

As an alternative to putting semantic markup on your site for rich snippets, Google offers the ability for website owners to identify the meaning of information on their pages using Google Webmaster Tools data highlighting, which is described here:

`https://support.google.com/webmasters/answer/2692911?hl=en`

As of this writing, this method does not allow highlighting for products other than books, but its capabilities are likely to improve in the future.

AdWords Seller Rating Stars

Businesses that sponsor Google AdWords have a few kinds of review-related ad enhancements available:

- Seller rating stars in Google AdWords
- Third-party expert review highlighting in Google AdWords
- Google+ Local review stars in Google AdWords Express ads for local merchants

Of these, seller rating stars in Google AdWords seem to generate the most confusion and curiosity from businesses and consumers alike. Here's everything you need to know about these adorable critters.

E-commerce merchants can benefit from a seller ratings extension in Google AdWords. Figure 8.17 shows an example of ads featuring seller rating stars.

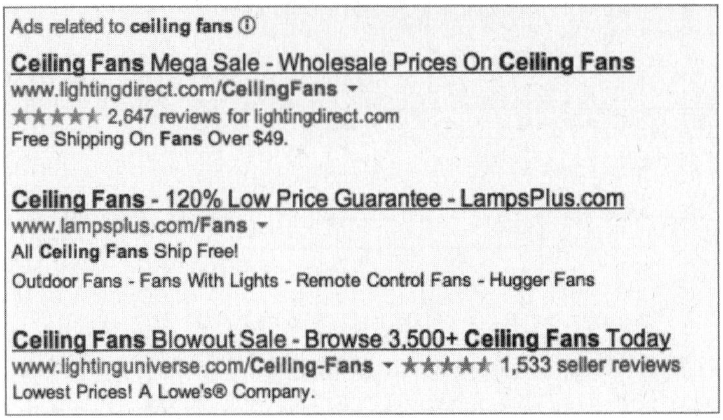

Figure 8.17 Two of these Google AdWords listings have nice-looking seller rating stars.

Google claims what you already intuitively know: Seller rating stars make people more likely to click on your ad. According to Google, the increase in click-through rate that results from seller rating stars is 17%.

Seller rating stars are based on company reviews that Google Shopping aggregates from a variety of sources, including many of the e-commerce merchant review collection services and shopping comparison sites we described in Chapter 2, "The Online Reviews Landscape," along with others. Here is a short list of examples:

- ResellerRatings
- Shopper Approved
- Trustpilot
- RateItAll
- Google Wallet
- Shopping.com
- NexTag
- Bizrate

As you learned in previous chapters, in order to gain reviews on one of these sources, your business must establish a relationship with it. This is usually a paid relationship, involving either a monthly fee for review collection services or a per-click fee to be listed on shopping comparison sites. Once this third-party source is accumulating reviews of your business, they will begin to feed into Google shopping, as seen in Figure 8.18.

Not every ad is eligible to display stars; here are some of Google's restrictions:

- The business must have at least 30 customer reviews within the last 12 months.
- The average star rating must be 3.5 stars or higher.
- Stars are not available in all countries. See Google's help page for a current list:

```
https://support.google.com/adwords/answer/2375474?hl=en
```

LightingDirect.com

Seller rating: 4.6 / 5 - Based on 2,672 reviews from the past 12 months

What people are saying

price	▌▌▌▌	"Good price, good item"
shipping	▌▌	"Good quick delivery."
customer service	▌▌▌▌	"Great super fast service."
selection	▌▌▌▌▌	"Great selection, great service"
ordering process	▌▌▌▌	"Overall, very pleased with purchase process."
packaging	▌▌▌	"Fast delivery , safe packing, good quality."
return policy	▌▌▌▌	"Your return policy is good."

★★★★★
5 / 5

We love LightingDirect. They have the best selection, prices, and the delivery is always fast. They tell you exactly when it ships; start looking for your packages soon! If you happen to have a question, their customer service is VERY responsive.
By ▓▓▓▓ - Aug 12, 2013 - Bizrate

Was this review helpful? Yes - No

★★★★☆
4 / 5

I had trouble with IE10 working with your website. Then I used Chrome and it worked fine.
By ▓▓▓▓ - Aug 5, 2013 - Bizrate

Was this review helpful? Yes - No

★★★★★
5 / 5

Great experience
By ▓▓ - Aug 9, 2013 - Bizrate

Was this review helpful? Yes - No

★★★★★
5 / 5

This was my first order with LightingDirect and was very leased with their selection of products and availability. Shipping was fast and they emailed the status of the order.I am waiting for my next order which is on its way now.
By ▓▓ - Aug 13, 2013 - Bizrate

Show reviews by rating

1 star (114)
2 stars (106)
3 stars (309)
4 stars (969)
5 stars (3,508)

Sort reviews

Sort by relevance
Sort by date

Show reviews by source

Bizrate (4809)
Epinions (62)
PriceGrabber.com (105)
ResellerRatings.com (25)
TRUSTPILOT (2)
Yahoo! (3)

Figure 8.18 Seller ratings from several sources are displayed in this Google Shopping listing.

A Google Merchant Center account is not required for seller rating stars to display in your ads.

Troubleshooting Google's seller ratings can be frustrating because the reviews are gathered through an automated process. Here are some troubleshooting tips you should know:

Give the reviews some time to feed into Google. We've heard of reviews taking several weeks to show up in Google after being posted on third-party review sites, so if you don't see them right away, that doesn't necessarily mean there's a problem.

Be sure that your URLs and business name are consistent everywhere. To ensure that Google can correctly pair up your third-party reviews with your AdWords listings, make sure that the URL and business name are exactly the same in all potential review sources as they are in AdWords and in your Merchant Center account if you have one.

Google may change its mind about what sources to use. If you choose to enter a relationship with a review venue based solely on its role as a provider of Google Shopping reviews, try to avoid a binding long-term contract. Google's sources can change at any time.

Product Reviews and SEO

What online retailer would not want to rank well in search results for product keywords like <carrera sunglasses>, <catnip toys>, and <dryland grass seeds>? In the eternal quest for high rankings, many e-commerce businesses choose to include product reviews on their websites because they believe that higher search engine rankings will follow.

We want to temper the hype around the SEO value of product reviews: We are not aware of any studies or even strong anecdotal examples of dramatic increases in rankings or search traffic that have occurred as a result of product reviews on a site, and we have not observed this with our clients, either.

HARD TRUTH There are no magic bullets to gaining high ranks in search engines. Product reviews on your site are just one of many website components that can result in a modest benefit.

This section is specifically addressing the SEO impacts of product reviews on e-commerce sites. See the sidebar "Online Reviews and Google's Local Search Rankings" to learn about the impact of online reviews on local business rankings within local results on Google.

With disclaimers out of the way, here are several ways that customer reviews can help a site's presence in search engines:

Fresh Content Customer reviews result in the continual addition of fresh, meaningful content to a site, with little or no effort on the part of the website owner. SEO pros agree that abundant, fresh content is a positive factor for search engine ranks.

Text That Customers Naturally Use Search engines generally give better ranks to pages that contain words that match the words being searched. Reviews can increase the text content on the site dramatically and are inherently flush with words that customers naturally use. For example, here's a top result for the search query <aquarium with nice glowing light>:

> **Marineland LED Double Bright Aquarium** Lighting System Reviews
> reviews.petco.com › ... › Fish Reviews › Hoods & Lighting Reviews ▾
> ★★★★☆ Rating: 3.9 - 28 votes
> It makes my **tank** look 10x than is did with the flouresent **light**. ..... pop and is very
> **nice** to have the black **light** switch too, it makes my **glowing** axolotls **glow**!

The presence of the words *nice*, *glowing*, and *light* in a customer review is probably helping this page to rank well.

Another SEO bonus of having online reviews on your site is that they can help optimize your site for words that your business cannot or will not use. For example, a business may have editorial restrictions that prevent it from using the phrase "Christmas gift" or a competitor name in a product description, but customers can freely use those words in their reviews.

Differentiation Online retailers often sell products that are offered by many other retailers and use standard manufacturer-supplied descriptions on product pages. This means that there isn't much to differentiate one retailer's product page from another. Customer reviews provide unique content on product pages that can show up in search results, giving your page a more appealing listing than its online twins. Rich review star snippets, discussed previously, can help search engine listings stand out.

In order to gain these SEO benefits, there are several requirements you should look for in any product review solution:

Search Engine–Indexable Reviews If you're going to get any kind of boost from customer reviews on your site, *search engines need to be able to see the review text.* This is not currently the case for every product review solution, so it deserves your attention as you're researching options.

Here's a simple technique for determining whether customer review text is indexable by Google.

Step 1: Navigate to a product page that displays customer reviews and select a line of text from within the body of a review. Try to choose text that appears reasonably unique, such as the example seen here:

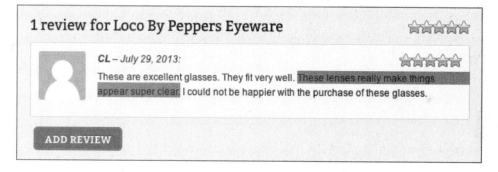

Step 2: Using cut-and-paste, copy the exact text from the review into Google's search bar. Put quotes around it, and perform your search:

Did Google find the text you lifted from the review? If so, you should see it bolded in Google's snippet, as seen in this example.

Rich Snippet Code As described previously, pages that contain reviews should have semantic markup, formatted to encourage rich snippets in search results.

Reviews on Your Own Domain Some product review solutions display reviews on your site but host the reviews on their own domain. In this setup, there is no SEO advantage for your website because the search engines can see that the reviews do not reside on your pages. Another way that reviews are sometimes shown, by Bazaarvoice in particular, is on a subdomain of your own website, for example: `reviews.yourdomain.com`. Displaying your reviews on a subdomain has both advantages and disadvantages: These pages may get better ranks for search terms containing the word "reviews," but they can also compete with your product pages. We think it's usually best to have reviews indexable on your product pages, but individual strategies may vary.

A roundup of the SEO friendliness of several product review solutions can be found here:

`www.seoverflow.com/ecommerce-product-reviews`

Now that you're nearing the end of this book, we hope your head is overflowing with useful knowledge about the world of online reviews. You may be wondering what your next steps will be. In Chapter 9, "Maintaining Your Momentum," you'll learn how you can apply this knowledge to a sustainable plan of action for your business.

Maintaining Your Momentum

It's time to take the valuable knowledge you've gained about your reviewscape and translate it into action. In this chapter, you'll set your course for a sustainable ongoing effort of managing and leveraging your business's online reviews. Don't get distracted by thoughts about the amount of work ahead or the size of the gap you're trying to close; just take it one step at a time. The key to a successful review management plan, like any successful business improvement effort, is to set practical goals and build on them as you move forward.

In this chapter:
Developing your plan
Power moves for a time-strapped small business
Reaching for the stars

Developing Your Plan

Dealing with your online reviews is a fluid process, one that requires agility and reactivity on your part. But that doesn't mean you can't have a plan going into it. As consultants, we've learned that it's often a good idea to plan ahead with a linear framework, even if you know that you'll need to change course at times to follow a shifting landscape. Here, we'll help you march forward with a roadmap in hand that best meets your business's needs and capabilities.

This book covers a lot of ground and a wide range of recommended activities. Let's break it down. Here are the basic elements of a review management program:

- Completing and optimizing the business's profiles
- Monitoring reviews
- Learning from reviews and making changes for the better
- Seeking reviews
- Responding to reviews
- Advertising
- Measuring results

With the exception of advertising, each of these elements is a must-have component of your ongoing online reviews project. Some can be skimped on; others can't. Some of them can be aided along the way with paid tools, but most will require a degree of labor on your part. How this plays out pragmatically for your business depends on the resources you have available and the priority you place on online reviews, online reputation, and online acquisition as a whole.

In the following sections, you'll find a sample set of activities that covers the key components we think any review management plan should include. Every business is different, so this plan may fit you like a glove or need a little tailoring. Read for insights, then adapt to your reality.

Local Businesses: Find and Update Your Presence on Review Venues

Basic profile housekeeping is a great first step for businesses that are reviewed on third-party sites, including local businesses, service providers, hotels and destinations, nonprofits, and professionals. Create or claim your business profiles and clean up and optimize the elements that you have control over to ensure that your business is represented accurately and all the pieces are in place for you to accumulate reviews.

The following steps should be performed as kick-start activities and revisited on a regular basis when your time allows:

- ❑ Identify the review venues that are most important to your business. See the sidebar "Exercise: Know Which Review Venues Deserve Your Attention" in Chapter 4, "Monitoring and Learning from Your Reviews."

❑ Claim or create and optimize your business's review site profiles, starting with your top-priority venues. If the venues you want to approach are Yelp, Google+ Local, TripAdvisor, Angie's List, or ResellerRatings, you've got detailed instructions in Chapter 6, "Review Venues: Need-to-Know Tips for Your Action Plan." The following graphic shows the first step in creating a new local listing on Google. Most likely, there will be some sites on your list for which this book has not provided detailed instructions. If that's the case, you'll need to improvise, following the patterns and philosophy described in Chapter 6.

❑ Eliminate any duplicate listings you find, correct inaccuracies, and fill out your listings completely. Don't skimp on compelling details about your business, and be sure to add up-to-date photos. Optimize your text with keywords to the best of your ability. See the sidebar "Optimize Your Listings with Keywords" in Chapter 6.

❑ Claim your business listings in feeder directories such as Acxiom, Express Update, and Localeze; these can feed into review sites and provide citations that may improve your search engine visibility. The following graphic shows an example. Update, de-duplicate, and edit your business directory listings to ensure that they are accurate and consistent. See the sidebar "Online Reviews and Google's Local Search Rankings" in Chapter 8, "Showing Off and Being Found."

Your search has resulted in 2 possible matches

Our directory contains millions of business listings. If we have your listing, you will be able to modify, close, or enhance it.

If your business isn't found, you may add it to our directory.

Add Your Business Listing

Search to **get started!**   ● By Business Name & Zip   ○ Business Phone

| california dental group | | 90041 | Search |
| Business Name | | Zip Code | |

❏   Documentation is crucial: As part of your commitment to being found and represented accurately online, be sure to document logins for all venues on which your business has a listing.

If you have a marketing department, they are likely to be the right team to take charge of the above tasks. In a smaller business, this work can be handled by the owner. If you hire an outside vendor to complete this work, be sure that your business is in control of the logins; you do not want to lose access when a paid relationship ends.

E-commerce Sites and Brands: Make the Most of Product Reviews

E-commerce businesses, manufacturers, and brands should take maximum advantage of the benefits of product reviews. Here are some important activities for you to include in your plan:

❏   If you sell products on your site but you don't have the capability to gather and display customer reviews, get the technology in place to make that happen, either with your e-commerce platform or a social commerce tool such as Bazaarvoice or Reevoo. See "Social Commerce/Product Review Platforms" in Chapter 2, "The Online Reviews Landscape," and "Product Reviews and SEO" in Chapter 8 for products and capabilities to think about.

❏   Identify ways to increase the prominence or effectiveness of reviews on product pages and throughout your site, as described in the section "Visibility on E-commerce Sites" in Chapter 8. If you're able to customize review features and functionality, such as displaying reviewer names, photos, and reviewing history, read the section "Influencing Factors in Reviews" in Chapter 3, "Understanding Reviewers and Reviews," so that you can be sure to include all the information your potential customers want to see.

❏ Get stars in your organic search engine listings if you can. Learn how these enhancements are achieved in the section "Rich Snippets" in Chapter 8.

Your product review effort is likely to require an up-front investment of time and money in setting up and configuring a review tool, but the real return comes over time. With product reviews on your site, you have a chance to reap the rewards of a documented sales lift, and you'll be able to continually improve your products or services based on the feedback you receive.

All Businesses: Monitor Your Reviews

Sure, you've had an eye on your reviews all along, but the goal here is to arrive at a sustainable, repeatable monitoring process that allows you to gather information wisely and not get bogged down in details or the occasional slam. This task does not need to fall on the business owner. A brand manager, marketing director, or any smart staffer can take on regular monitoring duty—and there are tools to help. Here are some recommended activities for monitoring reviews of your business:

❏ Commit to having a business representative read your reviews on a regular basis—the frequency depends on the volume of reviews you receive. See Table 4.1, "Review Monitoring Tools," in Chapter 4 for tools that can make this easier for you. If you have more reviews or social media mentions than you can realistically absorb, focus on a sample of recent reviews, or just on your most popular products or top venues for now. If you need inspiration, here's an example of a happy ending that never could have happened without monitoring:

> *1 Previous Review: Hide »*
>
> ⭐⭐⭐⭐⭐ *1/12/2012*
> UPDATE: I nearly fell off my chair when Bella called this morning, they noticed my review on Yelp and reminded me I have a lifetime warranty. The fact they look at their Yelp reviews, and were willing to research who I was, my purchase, and actually call me to rectify the problem changes them a 5 star in my book. WOW!

❏ Configure and use alert tools from review venues that you've identified as important to your business. See the "Review Monitoring Tools" section in Chapter 4, and learn details about dashboard capabilities for Yelp, Angie's List, and TripAdvisor in Chapter 6.

❏ Determine a process for communicating takeaways, review sentiment summaries, and red-flag alerts to the people who can address the customer's problem or craft a response. See the sidebar "Creating a Boss-Friendly Weekly Reviews Digest" in Chapter 4 for inspiration, as well as the sidebar "Crisis Management" in Chapter 7, "Navigating Negative Reviews," for perspective.

Monitoring your online reviews is a task that will never end. Plan to periodically adjust the venues that you're watching to be sure you're keeping an eye on the ones with the best chance of landing in front of a prospective customer.

All Businesses: Use Feedback to Improve

In our opinion, businesses that think of reviews as first and foremost an opportunity to learn are the most likely to achieve success in the online review space. You don't want to just fix bad reviews—you want to fix the problems that cause them. We know there are plenty of yo-yos out there with an axe to grind, but there are also many reviewers who are communicating something that your business needs to hear. Here are some ways to use review feedback effectively:

- Absorbing your reviews and using them to change for the better is likely to be a meandering process, but we encourage you to make it routine by folding it into an activity that's already on your calendar, such as staff meetings, performance reviews, or product development brainstorming. Communicate actionable take-aways to your team, and ask them to share insights they have gleaned from direct customer interaction. Deliver compliments to the folks who have earned them and education and guidance to those who need it to improve. Hand off your customers' great suggestions to those who can run with them.

- Document the sentiment in your reviews to help you transform raw feedback into workable directives following the approach described in the section "Learn from Your Reviews" in Chapter 4.

- Prioritize and take action on correcting issues, for example, by attacking easy fixes first, then moving on to better manage customer expectations and to address more pervasive issues that require a shift in your company's culture or a step outside your comfort zone. See the section "Create a Process for Learning from Negative Feedback" in Chapter 7 and the sidebar "Brands Learn from Big Data with Bazaarvoice" in Chapter 4 for a few real-world examples.

- There are many ways to check in with customers aside from online reviews; meet with your staff to brainstorm ways to introduce more opportunities for customers to provide feedback. See the section "Check In With Customers" in Chapter 7, for some nonreview communication channels that you can use. This activity serves double duty by giving you just-in-time information you need to keep your customers happy and by discouraging negative reviews.

Making changes to your business based on online reviews may require an attitude adjustment; however, take this on and we think you'll reap generous rewards in the form of happier customers and better reviews.

All Businesses: Respond to Reviews

No business should leave negative reviews hanging in the wind, and responding to reviews does not require a huge amount of time, though it does require a generous supply of humility. Here are some review response activities to consider for your business:

❏ There are lots of reasons to respond to reviews, but here's one simple rule of thumb: If it's visible, credible, and negative, it deserves a response. Set aside some time each week to carefully compose your responses to negative reviews. For guidance, see the section "Responding to Negative Reviews" in Chapter 7 and the sidebar "Exercise: Rate Responses to Negative Reviews," also in Chapter 7, for real-world examples.

❏ Beyond negative reviews, try to determine which positive or neutral reviews you should respond to by putting yourself in your prospective customers' shoes and deciding whether acknowledgment, thanks, correction, or reassurance would convey that you are a trustworthy and appealing business. See Chapter 6 for logistics and guidelines for communicating with customers in Yelp, Google+ Local, TripAdvisor, Angie's List, and ResellerRatings. The sidebar "Hotel Commonwealth: Online Review Management Done Right," later in this chapter, provides some review response ideas worth emulating.

❏ As part of your commitment to improving your online appeal to prospective customers, formalize your process for responding to future reviews (positive and negative). Determine which staffer or staffers will publish responses, and whether an approval cycle or internal review is required before posting. Develop templates, written policies, or style guides to streamline your future responses.

All Businesses: Encourage New Reviews and Leverage the Ones You Have

After the desire to seek-and-destroy bad reviews, the next line item on many businesses' wish lists is to accumulate a healthy pile of positive reviews. Here are some activities we recommend:

❏ Formalize a review request process with a combination of outreach techniques such as post-transaction emails, incorporating links on your website, reminders in your brick-and-mortar business, or requests in your customer communications. See Chapter 5, "How to Get More Reviews," for effective ways to cultivate reviews, as well as Chapter 6 for specific opportunities to gather more reviews on several major venues.

❏ Take opportunities to direct your customers to your review profiles. See the section "Badges and Widgets" in Chapter 8 for ideas on linking to review venues from your site.

❏ If Yelp is a priority for your business, remember that Yelp has a policy against requesting reviews from customers. Pursue alternative approaches such as asking customers for check-ins. See the sidebar "Don't Ask, Don't Yelp" in Chapter 5 and the Yelp section in Chapter 6 for details.

❏ If you have the budget for it, consider advertising opportunities on review sites. See Chapter 6 for ad options on Yelp, Google+ Local, TripAdvisor, and Angie's List.

❏ Google your branded keywords—your company name, principals' names, or products—to identify reputation concerns or problems with search engine ranks. Take steps to boost your brand and polish your online reputation in search engine results as described in the section "Improve Your Search Results" in Chapter 8. If you're ready for a deeper dive into SEO, follow up with the sidebar "Opportunities for Further Learning," later in this chapter.

❏ If you've got a good-looking collection of reviews, do what you can to place them in front of as many prospective customers as possible—for example, by featuring reviews on your website or in printouts at your brick-and-mortar location. See Chapter 8 for ideas on maximizing the benefit of your positive reviews, and see Chapter 6 for suggestions to increase your visibility on Yelp, Google+, TripAdvisor, and Angie's List.

❏ You know all about the pitfalls of writing fake reviews or paying for positive ones, but does your team? Now might be a good time to create and distribute some guidelines to your in-house staff and outsourced team about staying within strict ethical boundaries when pursuing new reviews. Read the section "Authenticity and Ethics" in Chapter 5, the section "Fake Reviews" in Chapter 2, the sidebar "Yelp's Controversial Filter," in Chapter 5, and the sections focusing on review filters for several venues in Chapter 6.

Your review cultivation effort is likely to require persistence and flexibility. Document what works, and leave behind ineffective methods.

Power Moves for a Time-Strapped Small Business

Small business owners, we know how hard it is for you: If there's one thing in scarcer supply than your cash, it's your time. As one small business owner told us, "When it comes to marketing, I feel like I have to do everything! It's exhausting. I need to know what's really necessary." We have a special place in our hearts for very small businesses, so we've put together some hit-the-ground-running steps for organizations with bare-bones resources.

Start with a couple of quick setup activities:

❏ Claim your profiles and fill them out as completely as you can. This will be the smartest 30 minutes you spend this week.

❏ Set up Google Alerts. A few simple Google alerts will keep you well informed about any new dings or points of light in your business's online reputation. Go to www.google.com/alerts.

Now, follow up by integrating manageable ongoing tasks into your normal routine. Here are some tasks that we want you to practice until they become as natural to you as pouring your morning cuppa:

Ask for reviews the low-effort way. It may not fit with your business personality to send email follow-ups or post signs encouraging check-ins at your brick-and-mortar location, and you may not have the budget at present to pay for advertisements on review sites. But every business has some interactions with customers, and we are confident that some of these interactions allow you to personally request a review. So just ask. (And remember, it is against Yelp's rules to ask for reviews, but it's fine to ask for check-ins.)

Until you're ready for an integrated email review solicitation method, you can simply add a link to your review profile in your email signature or place a badge or widget on your website's home page.

Respond to negative reviews. Companies that respond to all of their reviews will spend some time figuring out which reviews would benefit from responses and what types of response are most effective. You don't have that kind of time, so stick to responding to negative reviews, following the guidelines in Chapter 7. Lucky for you, there's no need to respond the minute a bad review comes in, since your primary audience is not the reviewer but future readers. If you're a one-person shop, be sure you get some outside opinions on the content and tone of your responses before you click the submit button—this is one task where a business owner's gut instincts may be at odds with best practices.

Absorb feedback. The biggest barrier we've seen to effective use of online review feedback is avoidance, and the second biggest is denial. But pleasing your customers is key to maintaining a healthy business, isn't it? So even the most harried business stakeholders must not skimp on listening to reviewers. If your business has received negative reviews that share similar complaints, open yourself up to the possibility that those reviews are legitimate and important, and determine what you can do to address those issues.

Finally, a word of warning: As you approach your online reviews, use an abundance of caution about shortcuts and quick fixes like the ones promised in Figure 9.1. We've seen multiple examples of small businesses getting into hot water, or at the very least wasting money, because they believed over-the-top promises from shady reputation management outlets. Apply the highest level of skepticism to any unsolicited communications you receive from reputation management companies. If you do nothing else, avoiding ethically questionable practices is a good minimum. If a review management promise sounds too good to be true, it probably is.

Figure 9.1 Some advertisements require an extra dose of skepticism.

Hotel Commonwealth: Online Review Management Done Right

Of all the businesses we've spoken with about their review management processes, we've been the most impressed by Boston's Hotel Commonwealth. In a chat with General Manager Adam Sperling and Director of Operations Shane McWeeny, we learned what makes their review management effort run like a well-oiled machine. Here are some highlights:

They regard online reviews as an important feedback channel. Rather than approaching their online reviews primarily as a marketing tool, Hotel Commonwealth sees reviews as a key channel for customer feedback: "TripAdvisor is the main tool we use to gauge the guest experience."

They make it a habit to encourage online reviews. The hotel does not use old-fashioned guest comment cards but instead directs visitors to post their feedback on TripAdvisor. Most of their review cultivation arises organically during conversations, like this: "How was everything? We'd love to get your feedback; we use TripAdvisor." The hotel also sends a follow-up email that includes a request to post a review and a link to TripAdvisor.

They discuss customer feedback daily. In the daily operations meeting, hotel staff discusses the reviews that were posted the previous day. Reviews are used both for motivation and learning: "If they're great and they mention an employee, we clap our hands and say 'job well done!' Conversely, if someone has offered criticism, we have to look inside ourselves and say 'Okay, what happened here?'" Adam emphasizes that they do not discipline internally based on reviews: "I don't want anyone to fear what will be written, I want it to be a constructive learning tool."

They respond to every review. Shane personally responds to each review, mostly to express appreciation for them: "Usually we're just saying thank you." Their policy prohibits getting defensive or challenging a negative comment. When a review includes complaints or concerns, he offers his email address and invites the reviewer to contact him directly. When a reviewer expresses a preference—for example, by saying they'd hoped for a coffee maker or extra towels in the room—Shane offers to update the hotel records for the guest accordingly: "It's a matter of a couple minutes to put that scenario in and exceed their expectations next time!" By responding to every review, they send a strong message that they are listening: "This is an independent hotel; we read every review and we care."

Continues

Hotel Commonwealth: Online Review Management Done Right *(Continued)*

They use tools to ease the process. The hotel uses Revinate and Market Metrix to help monitor reviews not only on TripAdvisor but also on Twitter and Facebook. Shane tells us, "I will get an alert for every single review. That's really key." They also use these tools to benchmark against other luxury hotels.

They use paid services from their review site of choice. The hotel has upgraded its TripAdvisor listing to a Business Listing, which shows contact information and links on their profile, and it selectively publishes special offers on TripAdvisor.

The investment Hotel Commonwealth makes in its review management process is not small. In addition to the cost of tools and TripAdvisor advertising, they estimate that they spend an average of two person-hours per day on review management. But the return has been remarkable: Hotel Commonwealth is currently the #1 Boston hotel on TripAdvisor, and TripAdvisor is one of their biggest site referrers.

Hotel Commonwealth ★★★★☆

🏆 Travelers' Choice® 2013 Winner Top Hotels

Ranked #1 of 77 hotels in Boston
◉◉◉◉◉ 2,048 reviews

"5 star treatment" 09/25/2013
"Great hotel in an excellent location." 09/25/2013

Professional photos | Traveler photos (232) | Map

📷 Slideshow

Measuring the success of a review management process is always difficult, but Hotel Commonwealth's attention to reviews, conscientious customer service, and excellent TripAdvisor visibility come together to form an enviable virtuous cycle. Here's Adam's take on it: "Success for us is to really embrace [reviews], celebrate the good, use the constructive criticism, never get defensive, never take it personally, take all of it to heart, and make a good faith effort to be better. And it seems to be working!"

Opportunities for Further Learning

Online review management is cross-disciplinary and includes elements of marketing, PR, business operations, and more. So, your further explorations into this area will probably require you to read up on a range of topics. Here are some trusted sources for learning materials:

Online Word of Mouth and Social Media

- http://wordofmouth.org, the sister site to www.socialmedia.org, is a great resource for tips, examples, and inspiration to help you achieve positive word-of-mouth.

- The Word of Mouth Marketing Association is a nonprofit trade organization that offers education in word-of-mouth and social media marketing. See www.womma.org.

- There are numerous social media marketing conferences, including Social Media Marketing World (www.socialmediaexaminer.com/smmworld) and the SMX Social Media Marketing conference (http://searchmarketingexpo.com/socialmediamarketing).

Local SEO

- Search Engine Land is a news and information site covering all things SEO. Look to their local channel for locally oriented information: http://searchengineland.com/library/channel/local.

- Local U at http://localu.org offers seminars for businesses to learn about local search marketing in depth.

Reputation Management

- The International Association of Business Communicators offers reputation management training programs; read more here: www.iabc.com/education/ria/.

- The Public Relations Society of America offers many training opportunities, some of which touch on reputation management: www.prsa.org/Learning.

Reaching for the Stars

Most of the activities we've recommended in this book aren't technically demanding or expensive. But we have asked you to embark on a mindset shift. If you started out with the idea that your customer reviews are mysterious and vaguely upsetting, you have now arrived at a better understanding of who and where they come from, what triggers them, and how to respond to them. If you started out believing that you could find a quick way to bury bad reviews or pump up your star rating, you now grasp that bolstering your online reputation is a good deal more complex than that. If you once held the notion that reviews have nothing to do with the workings of your business, you now realize that reviews represent not just opinions, but also opportunities for improving your offerings and attracting new customers.

Along with the shift in mindset, we have encouraged a shift in resources. You need time, dedication, and patience to read and absorb your customer feedback and to let actionable insights filter through your organization. You'll need a bit of marketing skill to represent your offerings fully and attractively in review venues, and you'll need a significant amount of humility and restraint to respond to negative reviews in a way that will resonate favorably with the customers you are trying to win over.

There is no "done" in online reviews management. Just like running a business, you'll keep evolving into higher levels of confidence and skill as you reach for the stars. We wish you every success!

Index

overview of, 185–186
Review Express tool, 120
review site dashboard, 85
rules for review responses, 223
status holders, 65
support, 193
visitor engagement as key to, 29
TripAdvisor for Mobile, 185–186
troubleshooting
Angie's List, 199–200
Google+ Local, 180–181
Google's seller ratings, 265
Yelp, 153–155
trust. *See also* fake reviews
badges and widgets bolstering credibility, 244
credibility of OTA customer reviews, 43
culling reputation management service reviews and, 48–49
developing credible review sites, 28–29
perceived motivation for review and, 74
TrustYou, 86
Twitter
influence of social media reviews, 38
manufacturer, brand, and software reviews in, 9
reputation management reviews, 48
social media listening tools, 86–89

U

Unlock This Business Page link, Yelp, 147
Urbanspoon, 30
URL filtering, Google+ Local, 177

V

venues. *See* review venues
videos, professionally produced Yelp, 161
Viewpoints.com, 9
visibility, of reviews
Angie's List, 197–199
badges and widgets, 244–246
e-commerce merchant review collection services, 39
on e-commerce sites, 249–250
Google Shopping/Google Ad Words, 37
Google+ Local, 182–184
improving search results. *See* search engine optimization (SEO)
local search venues, 51–54
marketing communications, 253–254
maximizing your social proof, 247–248
negative reviews in social media, 233
reputation management services, 48–50
review excerpts, 246–248
review sites, 29–30

shopping comparison sites/online travel agencies, 43–45
social commerce/product review sites, 53–54
in social media, 250–252
testimonials and case studies, 252–253
TripAdvisor, 189–192
Yelp, 147–149, 152
at your location, 254–257
volume of reviews, influencing consumers, 72–73
volume of transactions, brick-and-mortar business advantages, 7

W

web analytics, measuring site visitors, 167
websites
Bazaarvoice posting reviews on your, 206
driving visitors to, 191–192
removing negative reviews, 241
showing Yelp reviews on, 165
why it's not easy to sue review sites, 237–238
widgets
Angie's List reviews, 198
implementing Bazaarvoice reviews, 207
initiating calls to action on your site, 116–117
showing off your reviews with, 244–246
TripAdvisor link, 191
Yelp API to build, 165
window decals, showing off online reviews at business location, 254–256
word-of-mouth
enabling team of advocates, 128–129
gaining online reviews, 121
giving free wifi, 125–128
resources for learning materials, 280
review and feedback apps, 124–125
social media conversations, 121–124
social profiles, 124
WordPress plug-ins, 165

Y

Yahoo! Answers, 24
Yahoo! Local, 51
Yelp
claiming listings on, 146–149
communicating with reviewers, 155–156
community event giveaways, 117
destinations and activities, 12
directing personal request for review to, 107
discouraging businesses from asking for reviews, 119
Elite Squad, 63, 66
encouraging reviews and, 275–276
evaluating effectiveness of, 168
fake review management, 58, 60

Z